Logistics, Transport and the COVID-19 Crisis

Under and post COVID-19 conditions, companies are adapting to smart ways of operating and managing logistics processes to counteract the negative implications of the pandemic. This book offers an analysis and guidance on how to manage these processes, including transport, inventory, operations and waste management, to meet the complex need of enterprises.

This edited collection presents selected and key aspects of the implementation of logistics processes in the conditions of the COVID-19 pandemic, enriched with empirical analyses and international examples. The book is a contribution to the considerations on the role and importance of logistics processes in the management of organisations in the conditions of the COVID-19 pandemic, as well as reducing its negative socio-economic and technological effects. With contributions from global scholars, the book demonstrates the direction in which logistics processes should change so that they can take the form of "smart".

Logistics, Transport and the COVID-19 Crisis will be directly relevant for researchers and academics across logistics, supply chain management and transport management as well as risk management and related fields.

Jacek Woźniak, Ph.D. – Doctor of Social Sciences in the discipline of Management and Quality. He is employed at the Institute of Organization and Management of the Military University of Technology in Warsaw, where for 10 years he has been conducting research and teaching in the fields of risk management, safety and efficiency in organisations; innovation management and process-based approach to management, among others. He is also the author and co-author of several scientific monographs and textbooks in the field of safety and risk management in organisations, and project and innovation management, as well as several dozen scientific articles.

Wioletta Sylwia Wereda, Ph.D. – Doctor of Economics in the sciences of Management; associate professor in Faculty of Security, Logistics and Management, Military University of Technology in Warsaw, Poland. She is the author of a variety of studies and business. She has also written and co-written three monographs and over 100 scientific articles in the field of management, published both in Poland and abroad. The scientific interests of Wioletta focus on the issues of modern and smart organisations, efficient stakeholder relationship management, sales management methods and new approaches to the designing of relational sales. She is also a member of Scientific Boards of International Journals (inter alia Management Dynamics in the Knowledge Economy, Hyperion International Journal of Econophysics and New Economy), and she is the scientific reviewer in different entities (USA, Italy, Romania, Lithuania) and in Scientific Boards of National Journals.

Bogdan Nogalski – Professor of Economic Sciences in the field of Organisation and Management. Currently, he is a full professor at the Gdańsk School of Banking. In the years 1973–2018 he was a research and didactic employee of the University of Gdańsk and later a Doctor honoris causa of the Biotter University in Bucharest (2004) and the Silesian University of Technology in Gliwice (2016). He deals with problems of organisation management and improvement of various forms of organisation and management systems. His scientific specialty is issues related to various aspects of strategic management. He is the author of many original scientific researches, applications and expert opinions. He has been holding responsible functions in the scientific community for many years. He is the Honorary Chairman of the Committee of Organisation and Management Sciences of the Polish Academy of Sciences. In the years 2003–2020 he was its chairman. In the years 2007–2016 he was a member of the Economic Sciences Section of the Central Commission for Degrees and Titles, and in the years 2013–2016 he was its chairman and a member of the presidium of this commission.

Routledge Studies in Transport Analysis

Advances in Shipping Data Analysis and Modeling
Tracking and Mapping Maritime Flows in the Age of Big Data
Edited by César Ducruet

Maritime Mobilities
Edited by Jason Monios and Gordon Wilmsmeier

U.S. Freight Rail Economics and Policy
Are We on the Right Track?
Edited by Jeffrey T. Macher and John W. Mayo

Arctic Shipping
Climate Change, Commercial Traffic and Port Development
Edited by Frédéric Lasserre and Olivier Faury

Parking Regulation and Management
The Emerging Tool for a Sustainable City
Edited by Daniel Albalate and Albert Gragera

Human Resource Management in Shipping
Issues, Challenges and Solutions
Lijun Tang and Pengfei Zhang

Container Logistics and Maritime Transport
Dong-Ping Song

Logistics, Transport and the COVID-19 Crisis
Managing and Operating Logistics Processes
Edited by Jacek Woźniak, Wioletta Sylwia Wereda and Bogdan Nogalski

For more information about this series, please visit: www.routledge.com/Routledge-Studies-in-Transport-Analysis/book-series/RSTA

Logistics, Transport and the COVID-19 Crisis

Managing and Operating Logistics Processes

Edited by
Jacek Woźniak, Wioletta Sylwia Wereda and Bogdan Nogalski

Routledge
Taylor & Francis Group
LONDON AND NEW YORK

First published 2022
by Routledge
4 Park Square, Milton Park, Abingdon, Oxon OX14 4RN

and by Routledge
605 Third Avenue, New York, NY 10158

Routledge is an imprint of the Taylor & Francis Group, an informa business

British Library Cataloguing-in-Publication Data
A catalogue record for this book is available from the British Library

ISBN: 978-1-032-25583-5 (hbk)
ISBN: 978-1-032-25935-2 (pbk)
ISBN: 978-1-003-28573-1 (ebk)

DOI: 10.4324/9781003285731

Typeset in Times New Roman
by Apex CoVantage, LLC

Contents

Figures

Charts

Tables

Preface

The modern world has been changing dynamically. It is a statement that has been quoted for many years by both representatives of the world of science and practitioners of management processes. Nevertheless, until March 2020, this phrase was understood mainly in the context of the processes of globalisation and glocalisation, as well as the digitisation of life. Currently, dynamic changes in the world are associated with the situation of the COVID-19 pandemic and its specificity and forces governing the evolution of this pandemic, both on a global and local scale. The COVID-19 pandemic is developing on two main levels: forces and processes taking place in specific regions (countries, cities, etc.) and global phenomena. On the one hand, such a state of affairs facilitates the management of economic processes (e.g. it is easier to adjust the economy of a given country, health service, media messages, etc. to the local dynamics of the COVID-19 pandemic), and on the other hand, it makes it difficult (it is often difficult to combine local changes with global changes, which have their own specificity and divergent trends, requirements and limitations).

That is why today it is such a big challenge to find the "golden mean" in the management of organisations of various types (social groups, enterprises, public administration entities, etc.) in the conditions of the constantly growing COVID-19 pandemic. Currently, individual countries and regions of the world are either struggling or are just preparing for the advent of the so-called third (or fourth) wave of the pandemic. Nevertheless, more than a year after the outbreak of a pandemic on a global scale and the accumulated experience to date, there is still a lack of a recipe for the socio-economic and technological consequences of the pandemic in many countries. Most of the actions taken are either temporary "firefighting" or "trial and error" in conditions of uncertainty (according to the "maybe you can do it" principle). The whole world is fighting and looking for the aforementioned golden mean and at the same time a panacea for the effects of the COVID-19 pandemic. Taking action – in view of the nature of the pandemic and its consequences – must even be holistic. Therefore, people must refer to cultural, legal, economic, technical and technological, demographic, environmental and social conditions. Moreover, in the modern world there are no boundaries, and production factors can easily move around and create value for different groups of recipients (stakeholders). That is why it is so important to take actions aimed at identifying the bottlenecks that will be able to influence the state and potential of preventive and recovery actions in relation to the effects (and the dynamics of evolution in general) of the COVID-19 pandemic.

One such bottleneck is logistics processes. They combine production, migration and social processes, and they are determined by the state of technology development, the level of infrastructure development (technical, transport, etc.) and the economic potential of a given region. Agile ("smart") management of logistics processes becomes a kind of "catalyst" of activities aimed at eliminating the negative effects of the COVID-19 pandemic and efficient and effective implementation of processes in the conditions of this pandemic. Examples include the processes of distribution of food products, transport and storage of medical supplies (especially vaccines), creating stocks of cleaning/disinfecting agents and equipment for hospitals and medical devices, as well as supporting the transport of people by means of mass transport (urban, national and global – rail, airplanes, etc.), organising waste disposal (municipal and medical) and streamlining purchasing processes carried out on the basis of e-commerce. Logistics processes are an integral component of virtually all phenomena occurring in the modern world and, in a way, determine their effectiveness and efficiency.

Therefore, in this monograph, a bold thesis is put forward that claims logistic processes are the core of activities aimed at combating the effects of the COVID-19 pandemic and may be the basis for eliminating its negative effects, as well as the starting point for restoring "normality" (if it is at all possible – in the sense of normality before the COVID-19 era). Nevertheless, logistic processes should also change and adapt to the conditions dictated by the state of the pandemic. Therefore, in the opinion of the authors of individual chapters of this monograph, these processes should take the form of "smart", i.e. they should become flexible, fully scalable, supported by extensive analytics, largely automated and holistic. Moreover, logistic processes should be fully aware of the activities and purposeful on the part of their implementers. These processes even must move from the position of auxiliary processes and at the same time complementary to the management system of various organisations and management processes to the position of key (and even critical) processes that stimulate changes in organisations. It is the logistics processes that should "stand at the front of the fight" against the changes caused by the evolution of the COVID-19 pandemic. Without properly instrumented logistics, preventive and reconstruction activities will not have the appropriate power and potential, and thus most likely will not bring the intended results.

Therefore, this monograph presents selected, but at the same time key, aspects of the implementation of logistics processes in the conditions of the COVID-19 pandemic, enriched with empirical analyses relating to various countries of the world. The monograph is a contribution to the considerations on the role and importance of logistics processes in the management of organisations of various types in the conditions of the COVID-19 pandemic, as well as reducing its negative socio-economic and technological effects.

The main goal of this book is to show the direction in which logistics processes should change so that they can take the form of "smart", as well as to highlight the role and importance of logistics processes in the so-called COVID-19 era. Generally, it can be assumed that the book exposes the processes of smart logistics against the background of the processes of solving security problems in the contemporary world.

The book consists of 11 chapters that explore the following problem areas:

- the role and significance, as well as conditions for the implementation, of logistics processes in modern organisations (in particular in logistics companies);
- supply chain, inventory and waste management;
- shaping transport processes (with a special exhibition motor vehicle and air transport);
- implementation of procurement processes (with particular emphasis on digital risk and the widespread use of Information and Communication Technologies (ICTs)).

Chapter 1 comprises a series of conducted studies, the subject of which was an attempt to assess managerial maturity as a derivative of competencies, which, in the face of the COVID-19 pandemic, should be acquired by contemporary managers (also in logistic units and processes). The fundamental aim of the research is an attempt to answer the question about the anticipated level of acquisition of selected competencies that on the one hand determine the continuity of the functioning and on the other determine managerial maturity.

The aim of Chapter 2 is to present the real problems and challenges faced by companies operating in the logistics industry in the context of the implementation of their operational activities under the threat of COVID-19. Functioning in the new reality results in the creation of special models of tactics and the development of procedures aimed at enabling companies to work safely. This chapter serves as a guide or an inspiration for other enterprises in the field of transport logistics in a similar situation. Developed sets of procedure algorithms can be modified and implemented in company structures. What's more, this chapter classifies risks and problems related to the implementation of ongoing operational activity in logistic companies operating in the event of the COVID-19 epidemic threat and presents their service abilities. It is a database of ready-made prescriptions to be used when specific risks occur. Chapter 2, thanks to the shared experience of logistic companies, can serve in the future as a source of valuable information, good practices or tried and tested prescriptions for companies in the logistic industry.

The aim of Chapter 3 is developing a universal procedure for analysing and evaluating management of logistic centres to ensure that inspections under conditions of COVID-19 threats are carried out successfully. This study's structure comprises identification, analysis and evaluation of the efficiency of management of a logistics centre under conditions of COVID-19 threats, as well as the results of conducted analysis and evaluations.

The aim of Chapter 4 is to show the possibility of using fuzzy logic to forecast the behaviour of the supply chain under the conditions of specific epidemic nature of threats. The methodology adopted by the researchers was based on the identification of potential factors affecting chain stability with respect to epidemiological disturbances. In the next step, the brainstormed threats were categorised to obtain input data for the fuzzy logic model of the supply chain behaviour, which appears to be the major novelty. Authors try to conduct preliminary tests of the developed model. The result of the research is both the model itself and its verification, which provide the basis for the forecast of chain vulnerability to disruptions caused by the epidemic kinds of threats. Studies of the subject matter sources indicate that until recently no such approach has been applied. Given the unprecedented nature of the disturbance caused by COVID-19 outbreak, along with many measurable and immeasurable data, fuzzy logic seems to be a perfect engine for analysing and forecasting a given supply chain vulnerability to the disruptions resulting from the epidemic nature of threats.

Chapter 5 describes the process of material inventory management during the COVID-19 pandemic. Based on the example of the market leader in e-commerce, Amazon UK, the basic problems of ordering goods in a crisis in the global supply chain are presented. In the second part of this chapter, a model of material inventory management in the supply chain is proposed. The model was developed in compliance with the BPMN notation and concerned the analysis and assessment of risks and attempts to eliminate them in the supply chain, as well as activities related to determining the optimal size of inventory of essential and medical supplies.

The aim of Chapter 6 is an analysis and evaluation of the way the sustainable waste management functions under the COVID-19 conditions, as well as proposals for solutions in the waste management system aiming for the prevention or mitigation of crisis situations in the context of an adverse impact on the environment. The research has been based on a combination of both quantitative and qualitative data on sustainable waste management in the conditions of a crisis. It relates to the collection of empirical material based on exemplary entities operating in the waste chain, from waste producer, through recyclers, to the consumers of end products. Following the aim of the research, a research hypothesis has been formed relating directly to the research issues in the following wording: the effective functioning of sustainable waste management under the conditions of an epidemic threat is hindered due to an increased amount of waste infected with the SARS-CoV-2 virus. Only the use of universal system-based and standardised solutions for the monitoring of processes of sustainable waste management and dedicated facilities for final recycling can guarantee effective protection without harm to health and the environment. Solutions presented in this chapter will allow for the construction of a universal system-based approach to waste management, based on – among others – system-based procedures and standardisation documents and an extended responsibility of all participants of waste supply chain, on all management levels. What's more, solutions included in Chapter 6 may have a practical application for all participants of waste supply chain in the conditions of the COVID-19 epidemic and after its end, as preventive actions. This chapter presents solutions for companies operating in the field of waste management, organisations collecting and transporting waste, companies specialising in waste treatment and recyclers, representatives of municipal engineering bodies and municipal facilities. It proposes a change in the way of waste treatment during the epidemic and after its end.

Chapter 7 contains deliberations in the framework of sustainable transport in the 21st century, which has been and is a stimulus for economic development in the European Union. This branch of the economy supports the construction of modern infrastructure facilities ensuring security and trade in goods at every organisational/structural level. Thanks to the developed transport system, European integration and free movement of people, goods and services is being improved. Transport sectors such as road, rail and air transport are key branches of the economy, whose contribution to gross value added for the entire European Union is over 9% and employs about 11 million people. This situation, due to the COVID-19 pandemic, became unstable, and in some areas even collapsed. The aim of Chapter 7 is to present how transport tasks are carried out in the conditions of closing borders and mandatory quarantine, and what actions should be taken to be resistant to this type of interference in the future.

In Chapter 8 a multivariate comparative analysis of the data on passenger air transport in terms of economic security considering the outbreak of the COVID-19 pandemic for 124 countries is conducted (from 2000 to 2018). The raw data on the number of air passengers was classified into seven regions of the world, ranked and subsequently analysed and assessed. The results were presented on grouped bar and line charts. For reference purposes, the charts were extended with additional scales of the Y or X axis to clearly present the observed regularities and trends. A multivariate comparative analysis, in the form of Chernoff's face, was used to compare the seven regions in question in terms of the number of transported passengers in each year between 2000 and 2018.

Chapter 9 presents a multivariate comparative analysis of the number of passengers departing from the Great Britain before the pandemic and during the COVID-19 pandemic in terms of economic security. The UK is the leader in terms of the number of passengers carried by air in Europe. The study began by examining existing trends in the form of an upward trend between 2010 and 2019 in terms of the number of passengers carried by air in the UK. A further part of the study is a multivariate comparative analysis of passengers departing from the UK (in two groups: total number of passengers and British) in the homonymous time frames between January and July 2019–2020.

Chapter 10 carries out a multivariate comparative analysis of the number of passengers landing at one of the leaders of this industry in Europe, which is Germany, by five continents of destination between 2000 and 2019 and of the changes caused by the COVID-19 pandemic in terms of economic security. The analysed primary data was grouped, untangled and ranked in dynamic terms. The obtained research results are plotted on categorised line charts and bar charts. Additionally, for illustrative purposes, the charts include measures in the form of medians or the raw data under consideration. Chernoff's faces were also used in the study, which made it possible to observe the similarities and differences of four objects – continents described by explanatory variables in the form of the number of passengers landing in Germany by destination in the years 2000–2019.

Chapter 11 is aimed to identify and assess the correlation between the complexity and importance of digital risk in the opinion of Polish customers and the complexity of the use of ICTs in purchasing processes. In the study, three composite indexes were constructed – i.e. the Digital Risk Complexity Index (DRCI), the Digital Risk Importance Index (DRII) and the Consumers' Use of ICTs Complexity Index (CUICI). In particular, the study showed that there is a moderate positive correlation between the digital risk complexity, the digital risk importance, and the consumers' use of ICTs complexity. It should be noted here that the phenomenon of digital risk accompanies today's consumers every day, when executing purchase transactions. Today's customers ("the Customers 4.0"), who use ICTs on a large scale and are very prone to exploiting the potential of ICTs in purchasing processes, are usually aware of the digital risk but do not appoint it a high priority – which can significantly influence logistics processes in the era of the COVID-19 pandemic.

* * *

At this point, the editors would like to thank the authors of the chapters and the entire community of the Faculty of Security, Logistics and Management of the Military University of Technology in Warsaw for their substantive support and constructive criticism of the monograph project at various stages of the research and analytical process.

Probably many issues from the presented area of considerations were not sufficiently illustrated in the book – but it results from certain methodological and formal limitations. Nevertheless, all not fully explored detailed problems will certainly be the subject of further research and publications by the authors of this volume.

We wish all readers a pleasant and useful reading!
– Editors:
Jacek Woźniak, Wioletta Sylwia Wereda
and Bogdan Nogalski

1 The SARS-CoV-2 epidemic as the impetus for a discussion of managerial maturity

The significance of cognitive competencies

Bogdan Nogalski, Przemysław Niewiadomski and Agnieszka Szpitter

Introduction

The dynamically changing situation, which is the result of the SARS-CoV-2 epidemic, emphasises the need to have managers who enable companies to cope effectively in times of constant uncertainty. In the face of this situation, the managers of companies of different sizes, which operate in various sectors of the economy, must be more open than ever to the new conditions and principles of functioning, which primarily result from limitations in the supply chain, network work or the demand for new knowledge. The aftermath of the pandemic is therefore the fundamental re-evaluation of management orientation in terms of operational objectives and functioning processes. The process of these changes takes place on several levels, i.e. structure (online organisation), work systems (remote work), technology (agile manufacturing systems), organisational procedures and values (emphasis on social responsibility) and competencies (creating new knowledge).

Taking into account the empirical evidence which confirms the existence of the strong relationship between the market success of businesses and competent managers (Niewiadomski, Stachowiak, Pawlak, 2019, pp. 574–582), the following research direction makes competencies the attribute of a "mature" manager.[1] On the one hand, it means that competencies are recognised as a critical factor which is decisive for the survival of a company, and on the other hand, it implies the maturity of a manager appropriately to his or her behaviour in complex situations.

In the wide discussion that has recently been taking place in the community of scientists, politicians, local government officials and management practitioners (cf: Gorynia, 2020; Paprocki et al., 2020; Hausner et al., 2020), the question about the level of managerial competencies arises once again, giving them legitimacy to manage in times of deepening philosophical and existential, medical, sanitary and biological, economic and material and financial crisis, where the decline in demand and investment is so great that it will probably end in a deeper recession, as the coronavirus will affect not only the economy but also other spheres of life, science, etc. (Yue et al., 2020, pp. 2–6; Wang et al., 2020, pp. 2–6).

DOI: 10.4324/9781003285731-1

Although the analysis of the relevant literature shows that so far research has been conducted into the direction of adaptation measures in the context of crisis situations (Michaels, Handfield-Jones, Axelrod, 2001; Nogalski, Macinkiewicz, 2004; Simon, 2009; Dźwigoł-Barosz, 2017), the inference was mainly based on the literature review or empirical research conducted in companies from various sectors of the economy. For several reasons, no comprehensive research based on result analysis has been undertaken in the face of the pandemic threat.[2] In order to fill the existing knowledge gap, a series of research was conducted, the subject of which was an attempt to assess managerial maturity perceived through the prism of competencies, which modern managers should possess in the face of the COVID-19 pandemic. In-depth research in this area and the authors' own observations of the economic practice led to the formulation of specific questions, the solution to which determined an answer to the main question:

- What competencies are crucial from the perspective of managers who manage in non-linear conditions?
- Will research by means of inventive methods allow for the development of a research model which will reflect the areas of competencies that should be applied by modern managers in the face of the COVID-19 pandemic (research coincidence)?
- Do managers demonstrate such a level of competencies that predisposes them to being described as "mature"?

The study undertook research whose main goal was to identify the level of acquisition of specific competences, which on the one hand determine the continuity in conditions of uncertainty, and on the other hand, managerial maturity. The aim was pursued by three specific objectives, which cover the following issues:

- indicating the areas of competencies, on the one hand significant in terms of management in conditions of uncertainty (crisis), and on the other hand, likely to represent managerial maturity in the domain of adopted desiderata (the review and interpretation of literature);
- compiling a research model in the form of an evaluation sheet, which is the outcome of the literature review and the discussion among deliberately selected field experts (inventive methods);
- recognising the desired level of competencies – vivisection among selected managers.

The formulated research questions and the belief that there is an economic need for applicable results were, on the one hand, the main inspiration for undertaking research, and on the other hand, they became the starting point for the formulation of the following presumptions[3]:

P_1: The research model developed as a result of brainstorming that reflects competencies characteristic of managers who manage in non-linear conditions.

P_2: Research by means of brainstorming allows for the development of a research model that reflects the areas of competencies that modern managers should acquire in the context of the current COVID-19 pandemic.

P_3: Managers should demonstrate a relatively high level of cognitive skills acquisition, which predisposes them to being described as "mature" in terms of desiderata conducive to management in non-linear conditions.

To pursue the goal outlined in this way, the scientific literature (secondary sources) was analysed and statistical analyses were conducted based on the data obtained during the research. To complete individual research stages, virtual brainstorming and individual interviews were conducted among selected managers. Research results made it possible to indicate constructive conclusions and recommendations within individual threads.

The starting point

Along with the progressive complication of living conditions and in connection with the SARS-CoV-2 virus epidemic, the way in which enterprises operate is changing (Trocki, Grucza, Ogonek, 2009, p. 11). Unique activities – called complex undertakings or projects – which require a different approach to management are crucial (Szpitter, 2018). Currently, managers cannot rely on solutions proven so far, but they must make decisions and be guided by the flow of information in a completely new, previously untested situation. The complexity and unpredictability of the environment caused by the COVID-19 disease results in the emergence of numerous threats that should be immediately identified by managers. Observation and drawing the right conclusions as well as taking appropriate remedial action can determine the survival of the company. In general, the thesis is that due to the rapid pace of changes in the conditions of the company's operation, all activities should be anticipatory, i.e. they should be undertaken with the focus on future, anticipated conditions of the environment (Krupski, 2003, p. 11; Krzakiewicz, 2014, p. 99). The difficulty is that with such variable conditions of the environment (the non-linear conditions of operations), as in the case of the pandemic, predictions can be unreliable. Therefore, it is important, from this point of view, to create adaptive organisations capable of agile responding to the non-linearly changing conditions of the environment (Koźmiński, 2016, p. 18).

The efficient management of an organisation in a complex, dynamic and uncertain environment requires managers to limit the negative impact of the complexity and unpredictability (uncertainty) of the environment. It is about the ability not to fall into crises or to deal with them when they arise. This means responding to the effects of impeding factors; however, it is not about the immunity to changes that may imply such an ability. Recapitulating, the functioning of the business and the effectiveness of actions taken depend on how managers can use the existing potential, but also on whether they are able to intelligently choose the best solutions tailored to the needs of the moment and the current requirements of the environment.

This shows that a significant feature of the "era" of the coronavirus is the recognition of competency as a critical factor which determines the survival of the organisation, and the probability of the survival of the organisation is determined both by processes which take place in the environment and resources at the disposal of the organisation, which determine the possibilities of its further survival and development (Cyfert, 2012, p. 19).

In the literature on management and quality sciences, much attention is paid to competency modelling (Whiddett, Hollyforde, 2003; Czapla, 2012; Załoga, 2013). It has an external dimension and means adapting competencies to the needs and current requirements of the environment. Competency modelling theory is important for management practice because it allows for the identification of the essence, significance and influence of managerial competencies on the organisation performance (it indicates why it is necessary to match competencies and enables their identification) and is the basis for their improvement (Jabłoński, 2006, pp. 71–85).

Although it is not the task of the authors of this study to develop a universally accepted definition of managerial competencies, it should be emphasised that management theory and practice shows that it is far from adopting a single, universally accepted definition. Despite numerous attempts by researchers to agree on a common position, there is no clear agreement as to the meaning of this concept. However, it is emphasised that the only proper way to pursue management and quality sciences, at least at the current stage of their development, is the multiplicity of ways of perceiving, interpreting and shaping the studied fragment of reality (Krzyżanowski, 1992). It seems that this is not a defect or limitation in the practical application of this concept. This is rather due to a pragmatic approach where efficiency is more important than theoretical construction. Moreover, the search for a single, common or universal definition, if at all possible, would not enrich the knowledge or practice of management, and at the same time it could narrow the research field. Therefore, in the context of the research, the authors propose a definition that makes sense in terms of the conditions in which modern managers have to operate, and they assume that as such it can be used consistently in the discourse on managerial "maturity" – defined as the manager's ability to systematically deliver increasingly better results of activity, regardless of the conditions in which he or she will operate.

With reference to the literature review[4], it was assumed that managerial competences are a system of related knowledge, abilities, skills, personality traits, values and attitudes as well as experiences, motivations and behaviors aimed at efficient and effective management; on the one hand, they imply the functioning of the organization in a dynamic and uncertain non-linear structure of the environment, on the other hand, they contribute to its development.

To recapitulate, for the purposes of the study, it is assumed that a mature manager is a person whose knowledge, skills, personal qualities, experience, attitudes, motivation and behaviour imply the efficient and effective performance of tasks in an ever-changing, unpredictable environment determined by the COVID-19 pandemic (the high-level competencies proposed later in the study).

The challenge for managerial activity is to ensure safe working conditions during the COVID-19 pandemic. A manager must be able to adjust the scope of employees' duties to the requirements of remote work. Technological adaptation in this respect is also important in terms of the functioning of the organisation. Moreover, managers face the need to ensure work safety in completely new conditions and institutional constraints, and offices must manage remote work and provide new technologies.

Most managers now face many challenges related to the introduction of new procedures and ensuring appropriate working conditions for their employees. Due to earlier standards, companies provided their employees with appropriate working conditions almost immediately. For many organisations, however, additional security measures, hygienic materials, fewer people in shifts, a greater number of changeovers on production lines, as well as a change in the organisation of transport are new challenges that they must cope with.

As a result, it can be assumed that the level of maturity depends on the acquired knowledge, which includes experience, current information and its context, as well as personal abilities and the ability to use them, and finally, attitude, motivation, behaviour, values and beliefs. A manager is mature when his or her competencies can be considered complete from a qualitative point of view. For a manager to be mature, he or she must be efficient, predictable and deliver high-quality results. He or she must demonstrate the ability to perform tasks effectively and efficiently and to systematically deliver increasingly better business results.

Material and method

The development of each discipline of science requires the use of reliable research methods that make it possible to obtain knowledge with a known degree of certainty (Czakon, Klimas, Kawa, 2019, p. 28). To recognise the level of managerial maturity implied by the acquisition of specific competencies, a series of research was conducted. At its first stage, which was preparatory research [B_A], the authors used the method of the literature review [B_{A1}] and creative problem solving with the use of experts [B_{A2}]. The preparatory research was a precondition for the main research [B_B]. The research scheme is presented in Figure 1.1.

When undertaking the assessment of managerial maturity in terms of competencies characteristic of managers who operate in non-linear conditions implied by the crisis, several methodological problems must be solved: How to design the evaluation system from the perspective of the "moment"? What assessment planes to consider when proposing a research model? How to analyse the obtained results? These are the most common questions that researchers and entrepreneurs are searching to answer. This problem is very important in terms of the goal of this research.

The methodological rigor of the research affects the quality of conclusions, and further the correctness of the hypotheses and the interpretation of empirical research. Therefore, the importance of the selection of the studied literature is emphasised (Czakon, 2011, pp. 57–61; Klimas, 2011, pp. 169–184). The literature

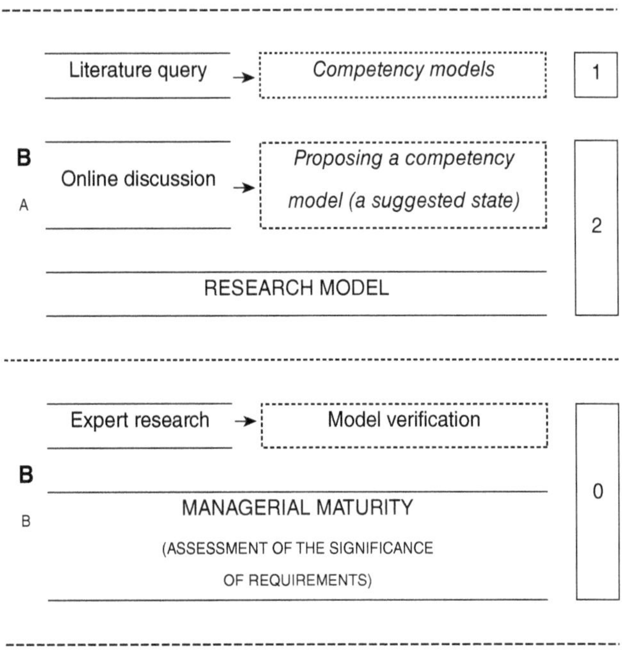

Figure 1.1 The scheme of research implementation

Source: Own study.

review (Green, 2005, pp. 270–273; Conn et al., 2003, pp. 256–261) proceeded in three stages, starting from creating a literature database, through the selection of works included for further analysis, and ending with a critical content analysis (Anello, Fleiss, 1995, pp. 109–116). The methodology of the literature review allowed not only for the formalised and objectified synthesis of the existing literature (Columb, Lalkhen, 2005, pp. 391–394), but above all, it allowed for the identification of areas important for further research (Gimenez, Tachizawa, 2012, p. 531–543).[5] The process of creating a literature database assumed the use of a blended approach, i.e. the scholarly literature indexed in scientific databases and the so-called grey literature. Extending the process of creating a literature database by the grey literature was considered important due to the possibility of including the latest scientific publications, publications of a less scientific nature and publications not necessarily peer reviewed but fulfilling the requirements of the methodological rigor (Czakon, 2011, pp. 57–61). The process of creating a literature database assumed the use of the literature indexed in EBSCO, Proquest, ResearchGate.net and Academia.edu. scientific databases.

As it was impossible to organise a face-to-face meeting, virtual brainstorming made it possible to solve the problem by means of group creative thinking.[6] This solution, to select the best group of ideas, enabled each invited user to present his or her suggestions, and other members of the virtual community could debate on them. In addition to commenting on ideas, participants could also vote for them. Eleven experts related to the agricultural machinery sector were invited to participate in the research (Table 1.1).[7] The evaluation team consisted only of specialists in the problem being solved, which was verified based on the competency coefficient expressing the relationship between the informativeness coefficient and the argumentation coefficient. The informativeness coefficient (Ki) was determined based on an expert self-assessment. The argumentation coefficient (Ka) was determined based on an interview with a given expert. Competence expressing the level of qualifications of an expert in the field was determined based on the creative analysis of the expert's activity, knowledge of the field and understanding of the problems raised at work.

The general research mechanism was based on four planes and included: (1) a group of participants (experts) deliberately selected because of their specialist knowledge related to the research issue; (2) the process of "virtual" interaction, thanks to which the opinions of experts which implied the development of a research model were revealed (unanimity); (3) feedback given to participants, the purpose of which is mutual interaction and reflection; and (4) opinions expressed by experts that bring the problem nearer the solution (Plummer, Armitage, 2007, p. 3).

Table 1.1 List of experts (N=11)

Institution/Position	*Number*	*Specialisation*	*Share %*
Company owners	6	Organisation and management of a small (2), medium-sized (4) enterprise	54.55
President of the Management Board in the limited liability company, limited partnership	1	Development and supervision of the strategy implementation	18.18
Board member for strategy in the limited liability company, limited partnership	1	Participation in the development and implementation of the strategy	
Management strategy consultant	1	Design and improvement of management systems with the use of lean management instruments	18.18
University professor, postdoctoral degree in engineering	1	Strategic management, business models	
Deputy Director of the Department of Regional Policy of the Marshal's Office of the Wielkopolska Province	1	Development strategies and modelling of draft regional programs; active participation in their implementation	9.09
Total			**100%**

Source: Own study.

The use of the method was very useful in terms of research in the conditions of high uncertainty, when studying unknown problems which were a relatively new research field and which were not covered by empirical research, or research which allowed for the determination of certain trends. The research allowed for a hypothetical mental construction, i.e. a system of assumptions, concepts and relationships between them, which enabled an approximate modelling of the verified aspect of reality (Gospodarek, 2009, p. 61 et seq.). The authors' intention is that the proposed research model is closely related to the theory (cf: Boyatzis, 1982; Caruso, Salovey, 2009; Antti, Greenhalgh, 2012, pp. 421–428; Cappellen, Janssens, 2008, pp. 514–537; Cheetham, Chivers, 2005) and complements it (Sztoff, 1971).[8] The developed research model played a very important role, because on the one hand it provided a specific picture of reality, and on the other hand, it enabled empirical research (Zakrzewska-Bielawska, 2018, p. 22).

Making conducted research practical expresses their subordination to the problems of managers.[9] This determines the usefulness of obtained results to improve management efficiency; it was necessary because the recipients of research results were a selected group of managers. The main stage of the research was conducted from March to April 2020. Due to the situation and the related difficulty in obtaining data, the key criterion was that the authors knew the respondents.[10] On the one hand, it allowed the authors to determine whether a given person would be interested in expressing his or her views, and on the other hand, to determine whether he or she had sufficient knowledge and experience in the issue under consideration. The respondents were the representatives (49 people) of micro (16.33%), small (30.61%), medium-sized (48.98%) and large (4.08%) manufacturing enterprises which operate in the agricultural machinery sector. The group of people between 31 and 40 years of age dominated (42.86%); 4.08% were respondents aged up to 30 years old; 28.57% of the respondents were between 41 and 50 years old; 16.33% of the respondents were between 51 and 60 years old; and 8.16% of the respondents were over 60 years old. The group of people who completed higher education prevailed among the respondents (71.43%); 22.45% completed secondary education and 6.12%, vocational. The respondents were asked to indicate to what degree a mature manager should acquire indicated competencies in the face of the crisis. For this purpose, a five-level scale was used, where 1 meant a low level of competencies, and 5 meant very high. The survey questionnaire was, among others, an annex to the commercial offer, and it was sent by traditional mail or via e-mail. Depending on the research technique used, completed questionnaires were returned directly to the authors, sent in specially prepared envelopes or sent by e-mail using a specially prepared application that made it possible to answer the questions. During the research, the results were interpreted based on the respondents' declarations.

Results and discussion

Managerial maturity viewed in terms of competency is perceived as a set of certain traits. These traits are regarded as evaluation criteria. Competencies identified in the literature and project research were subjected to detailed verification at a later stage of the research procedure. To be able to discuss the key ones (which are the strongest determinants of maturity), it was necessary to reduce them by the method of hierarchical organisation (Table 1.2).

In the context of the assessment, 26 competencies were analysed.[11] They were identified by the mean value calculated based on the indications of the respondents, which is a practice commonly used in the preparation of survey results. Instability, the continuity of change and at the same time numerous opportunities are the reality which business is struggling with in the face of the current pandemic. Such an environment creates many more challenges and puts companies to more serious tests than before. Unique resources as well as efficient and effective management are no longer a guarantee of a stable market position. Operating in such a complex, rapidly changing macroeconomic environment, managers recognise the importance of leadership skills. By engaging other team members to cooperate, using the knowledge, capabilities and experience of subordinates or partners, they increase the possibilities of developing innovative solutions. Thus, the ability to shape a development strategy and focus the attention of the organisation and employees on the most important issues becomes the trait of a mature manager. It is supplemented with the ability to cooperate with people and the appropriate choice of ways to motivate employees to achieve the company goals, which is the fundamental factor of the company's existence. Meeting today's challenges requires a certain number of permanent skills, and at the same time high stress resistance, self-control and willingness to take risks.

The coronavirus creates a global community, which changes the point of view on many issues after the universal experience of the threat. In times of crisis, the choices that must be made using digital technologies are highlighted. The use of the internet as the technology of collaboration and open exchange is an alternative to acting in a way that, until recently, would have been inconceivable for most companies. At this point, it is worth emphasising that the current crisis is an opportunity to popularise these positive experiences (Gorynia, 2020). Virtual networks of cooperation and mutual support will be essential to survive this crisis. This will allow technologies to be designed to serve companies once the crisis is over. This forces managers to take the problem seriously, which translates into their ability to work online and thus design virtual organisational structures.

Another important aspect is the ability to learn quickly, also in the context of computerisation, new technologies or work automation. The ability and willingness to rapidly develop and adapt new skills are crucial. The authors believe that the ability to accept that the knowledge acquired so far is already outdated or irrelevant to the present reality is equally important.

Regardless of many other consequences, the problem of self-confidence and faith in a team arises in the current situation. It turns out that one of the biggest barriers may be noticing strengths in oneself and in the team. It is therefore crucial to realise how much you can do, how much has already been achieved, and how much you already know. Self-esteem and faith in a team of colleagues, which have always been an extremely important psychological need, have become an

Table 1.2 Research results – model verification

	Competencies	*Trait intensity*			*% Responses*		*Points*
		1	*2*	*3*	*4*	*5*	
(1)	Perception	–	–	2.0	12.0	35.0	4.67
(1)		–	–	4.1	24.5	71.4	
(2)	Beliefs	–	–	3.0	14.0	32.0	4.59
(1)		–	–	6.1	28.6	65.3	
(3)	Self-awareness	–	1.0	3.0	15.0	30.0	4.51
(1)		–	2.0	6.1	30.6	61.2	
(4)	Impressions; the	–	2.0	4.0	15.0	28.0	4.41
(1)	ability to perceive reality	–	4.1	8.2	30.6	57.1	
(5)	Processability	–	2.0	3.0	13.0	31.0	4.49
(1)		–	4.1	6.1	26.5	63.3	
(6)	Emissivity	–	–	3.0	13.0	33.0	4.61
(1)		–	–	6.1	26.5	67.3	
(7)	Sensitivity	–	2.0	4.0	16.0	27.0	4.39
(1)		–	4.1	8.2	32.7	55.1	
(8)	Emotions	–	–	5.0	16.0	28.0	4.47
(1)		–	–	10.2	32.7	57.1	
(9)	Imagination	–	–	4.0	15.0	30.0	4.53
(1)		–	–	8.2	30.6	61.2	
(10)	Professional experience in the sector;	–	2.0	2.0	15.0	30.0	4.49
(1)	knowledge of conditions	–	4.1	4.1	30.6	61.2	
(11)	Intelligence	–	–	2.0	16.0	31.0	4.59
(1)		–	–	4.1	32.7	63.3	
(12)	Managerial intuition	–	–	2.0	13.0	34.0	4.65
(1)		–	–	4.1	26.5	69.4	
(13)	Identification; diagnosis	–	2.0	3.0	14.0	30.0	4.47
(1)		–	4.1	6.1	28.6	61.2	
(14)	Leadership	–	–	1.0	8.0	40.0	4.80
(1)		–	–	2.0	16.3	81.6	
(15)	Cooperation skills	–	–	1.0	10.0	38.0	4.76
(1)		–	–	2.0	20.4	77.6	
(16)	Motivating others	–	–	2.0	11.0	36.0	4.69
(1)		–	–	4.1	22.4	73.5	
(17)	Risk orientation	–	1.0	1.0	17.0	30.0	4.55
(1)		–	2.0	2.0	34.7	61.2	
(18)	Composure	–	–	3.0	19.0	27.0	4.49
(1)		–	–	6.1	38.8	55.1	
(19)	Stress resistance	–	–	2.0	20.0	27.0	4.51
(1)		–	–	4.1	40.8	55.1	
(20)	Reconciliation skills; the ability to	–	–	2.0	22.0	25.0	4.47
(1)	resolve conflicts	–	–	4.1	44.9	51.0	
(21)	Ability to work online	–	2.0	3.0	15.0	29.0	4.45
(1)		–	4.1	6.1	30.6	59.2	
(22)	Fast learning skills	–	1.0	2.0	16.0	30.0	4.53
(1)		–	2.0	4.1	32.7	61.2	
(23)	Self-confidence and belief in the team	–	–	4.0	16.0	29.0	4.51
(1)		–	–	8.2	32.7	59.2	

	Competencies	Trait intensity 1	2	3	% Responses 4	5	Points
(24)	Responsibility	–	–	3.0	20.0	26.0	4.47
(1)		–	–	6.1	40.8	53.1	
(25)	Ethics and morality	–	1.0	2.0	22.0	24.0	4.41
(1)		–	2.0	4.1	44.9	49.0	
(26)	Ability to design "virtual"	–	2.0	3.0	13.0	31.0	4.49
(1)	organisational structures	–	4.1	6.1	26.5	63.3	

Source: Own study.

urgent economic need – an indispensable trait to be able to adapt in a complex, defiant and disorganised environment.[12]

In the wake of the pandemic, there was a heated debate about the responsibility and punishment of managers. This is an important theoretical as well as practical problem. Therefore, an inherent feature of managerial functions is moral and ethical responsibility.[13] In the praxeological cycle (act [decision] – effect – moral and ethical responsibility), there are several theoretical and practical problems concerning, in particular, the third component, i.e. responsibility. From the point of view of management and quality sciences, it is important to discuss the responsibility of managers not only in the praxeological context, but also in relation to ethics and morality that determine their maturity. In practice, an ethical problem arises related to the system of responsibility for decisions, including liability under the employment relationship and civil, administrative and legal liability. These areas are related to moral responsibility (Masiukiewicz, 2014, pp. 181–195).

Perception which enables a manager to be able to translate the external environment into the internal organisation is significant in terms of managerial maturity. The functions of perception include selection, organisation and interpretation of information, and the final image obtained because of this process differentiates managers. Perception is selective, which means that managers may tend to ignore certain information and decode others in a way that allows the information to fit into conscious and unconscious assumptions. The delusions and distortions of perception, like cognitive schemas, allow managers to achieve and maintain mental coherence and balance by reducing the tension and discomfort caused by the crisis.[14] Attention is paid to the manager's "open mind", broad intellectual horizons, striving to acquire new information and the ability to process it. Due to the high value of processability, the manager shows high intellectual efficiency, easily processes a large amount of all kinds of information, effectively analyses and evaluates the facts that have occurred, has the ability to think conceptually and systemically, has the ability to synthesise, skilfully copes with new situations (unforeseen and complicated), knows how to approach problems comprehensively, and sees and takes into account all their aspects, which makes him or her mature in the context of the discussion.

On the one hand, management in the pandemic requires managers to be effective; therefore all decisions must be carefully considered in terms of achieving the goal effectively and avoiding all possible harmful side effects (negative emissivity). A manager is expected to have creative ideas and concepts, and spontaneity in creating his or her own ideas (positive emissivity) but first to anticipate numerous undesirable side effects of these decisions. Therefore, it is negative emissivity that should characterise a mature manager, especially in the current pandemic, due to the effectiveness of action, the ability to introduce innovations, the ability to plan activities, mobilisation in difficult situations, action dynamism, the ability to cope with continuous and sometimes even radical changes, initiating the process of change, striving to take useful activities, focus on tasks, results and the future, the ability to predict, a task-oriented attitude to the future and the ability to implement innovations.[15] Stimuli adapted to the constant individual personality traits of a manager most effectively stimulate him or her to see through the prism of beliefs, i.e. generalised judgments that a manager has on a specific topic. Beliefs affect the perception of oneself, behaviour and approach to colleagues or other people, which seems to be important in the face of a crisis. They determine the way a team is managed. Some beliefs are more difficult to verify and change so that they do not restrict, but support in action. The basis, then, is their awareness, i.e. self-awareness.

Creating the desired image of the company, especially in the face of a crisis, is usually associated with the so-called aggressive manipulation, the essence of which consists of the conscious application of such principles and methods so that the model economic situation of the company could be presented, depending on the needs and goals of the people who manage it. Although impression management is in contradiction with the commonly proclaimed postulate, i.e. the faithful and reliable presentation of information about the financial situation and performance of the company in a neutral and impartial manner, hence it proves managerial maturity. Given that the areas of impression management include building a reputation, creating an image (the dynamic perception of certain aspects of an organisation, such as a product image) and legitimisation (judging whether an individual is acting in accordance with the generally accepted restrictions in the face of a crisis), this approach seems to be justified.

The art of management requires a variety of tools, and managing people is one of the elements of this art (Golonka, 2014). A manager must be able to find himself in very different situations – pleasant when the company is developing, but also unpleasant in times of economic recession. Sensitivity to matters related to interpersonal relations should be present at every stage of the manager's conduct, especially in the face of a crisis. The source of energy for effective operation is the skilful use of soft skills, perceived through the prism of managerial maturity. The usefulness of listening to feelings carries a lot of valuable information, and emotions are not against logic, but should be its natural support. A manager who can recognise and control his and his subordinates' emotions has a huge impact on the productivity and quality of the team's work. One of the most important and crisis-specific features of managerial maturity is imagination. It enables the creation of visions of the future both in the form of comprehensive, wide images and their individual parts (Dworzecki, Leśniak-Łebkowska, 2018, p. 116). Factors which significantly affect the differentiation of the scope and manner of visualising the future include individual traits and professional experience. Experience, usually growing with age and maturity, influences the correction of previous expectations and visions in terms of the level of optimism or pessimism pertaining to the assessment of the observed trends of changes, their continuation and the strength of influence, and as such determines managerial maturity. Competencies which, on the one hand, are necessary for managers to manage in times of a crisis, and on the other hand, determine managerial maturity, are determined by the efficiency of the intellect. Interpersonal intelligence manifests itself in the so-called life wisdom of the manager and a strong will to work on himself or herself. Managers with this intelligence feel comfortable on the team. They read the intentions, motives and feelings of colleagues without much difficulty. As they are communicative and have mediation skills, they are predisposed to managerial work.

In the opinion of the respondents, managerial abilities referred to as "managerial intuition" are the determinant of managerial maturity in an increasingly complex, dynamic and difficult-to-predict environment, in a situation where the modern world economy ceases to function according to rational and logical market principles. An innovative approach to solving business problems is the concept of an intuitive understanding of strategy, the fundamental assumption of which is to treat an organisational problem as unique and to use knowledge from various areas to solve it. The sought solution should then be innovative. The ability to intuitively understand strategies is the result of the cognitive competencies of the human mind and the way the brain absorbs and stores various data and information. While making a programmed decision is an easy and routine task based on experience, the fulfilment of a specific procedure, custom or rules in unusual and rare situations it is necessary to make non-programmed decisions. Time pressure and a high degree of problem complexity may limit the work on finding optimal solutions, and discouraged managers may limit themselves to the first – in their opinion, the only and best – solution. However, mature managers cannot make important decisions without first preparing a few potential scenarios. Attention is paid to the need to respond early to signals that are a preview of upcoming problems and threats in the organisation, as their early detection results in responding in advance and applying remedial actions.

Conclusions

Collecting information by means of various research techniques helps to improve the reliability of research, the accuracy of inference and verification of information already collected (Mazurek-Łopacińska, Sobocińska, 2014, pp. 14–23), which was used in this study. By obtaining information collected in various ways, the issue was considered from the perspective of expert knowledge. The literature review, brainstorming and interviews were used to minimise the subjectivity of experts' perceptions and compare the results in the study. This is justified by a complex, multi-faceted and rich reality, which included present and past behaviour and statements, and products and ideas. By obtaining information collected in various ways, a given phenomenon can be observed from different points of view, which was completely justified in the context of the issue studied.

The material collected in the research procedure was confirmed in the theoretical and empirical study. The research model developed because of brainstorming reflects competencies characteristic of managers working in non-linear conditions. The study showed that research by means of brainstorming enables the preparation of a list of competencies which modern managers should acquire in the current COVID-19 pandemic. It was agreed that they should demonstrate a relatively high level of the acquisition of cognitive competencies, which predisposes them to being described as mature from the perspective of desiderata conducive to management in non-linear conditions.

To sum up, a defence mechanism in the times of the COVID-19 pandemic should be a conscious strategy in the form of simple rules (principles) developed as a result of the operationalisation of the process of building and implementing the strategy and the dominant logic of managers (Obłój, 2002, pp. 61–74). Therefore, building and implementing a strategy within which a company will be able to function in the face of a crisis requires the acquisition of the desired managerial competencies.

Notes

1 Especially as with the growing requirements, the concept of "managerial maturity" is becoming increasingly popular in strategic management, which implies the key role of competencies in the functioning of the organisation, where maturity expresses "the state of being complete, perfect or ready".

2 Here it is necessary to indicate the research project undertaken in the face of the pandemic by Prof. Szymon Cyfert (UE Poznań), Prof. Wojciech Dyduch (UE Katowice), Prof. Maciej Zastempowski (UMK Toruń) and Paweł Chudziński, PhD (UE Poznań). The aim of the research is to identify the factors of the survival of a company in the conditions of the crisis caused by the COVID-19 disease.

3 As the empirical decidability of hypotheses is limited to testing them (Hajduk, 2011, p. 116), the authors refrain from formulating them, due to the relatively small research sample. However, based on the identified cognitive gap in the precise identification of the constitutive factors of managerial maturity, the existence of an undetermined fact was articulated based on other established facts related to it, i.e. presumptions, especially that there is currently no full consensus among scientists concerning the correct ways to verify hypotheses.

4 The comprehensive research was presented, for example, in the works (Nogalski, Niewiadomski, Szpitter, 2018, pp. 17–36; Nogalski, Niewiadomski, 2018, pp. 305–323).

5 However, the literature review is not only a prelude to the main research, but a separate research method.

6 As the basic areas of using creative discussion in management and quality sciences include the identification and analysis of the factors of the overall development of the company, with particular emphasis on forecasting market trends and discussion in the individual sub-disciplines of management, including risk management and human

resources (Linstone, Turoff, 2002, p. 3), in this study the indicated technique of the structured process of group communication was used.

7 Including six owners (54.55%) of small (2) and medium-sized (4) manufacturing enterprises as well as five representatives (45.45%) of other organisations; 45.45% were experts ranging in age from 31 to 40 years, 27.27% ranging in age from 41 to 50 years, 9.09% ranging in age from 51 to 60, 18.18% of experts were over 60); 81.81% of experts had higher education, 9.09% – secondary and 9.09% – vocational education.

8 Due to limited publishing possibilities, the subsequent part of the study presents competencies which are crucial from the point of view of the conducted research (which were subject to verification).

9 Although the econometric formalisation of the research, the attempt to give the most elegant mathematical form to the recognised models or even reporting on reliability tests do not find astute recipients among management practitioners (Czakon, 2016, p. 46), the authors maintain appropriate proportions between the methodological rigor and the significance of research findings for managers (Vermeulen, 2005).

10 The main problem was not so much the selection of enterprises as the retention of all interested managers throughout the entire research procedure. As a result, selected individuals were subjected to the study, not the entire population (Stańczyk-Hugiet, 2014, p. 53).

11 The competencies are not unique in terms of COVID-19. Although during the expert discussion it was noted that specialist competencies such as the ability to organise work in conditions of increased epidemiological standards are important in terms of the functioning of the organisation, they were classified as general competencies, such as risk orientation because a model with a limited number of variables was presented.

12 The authors point out that a manager must be able to develop ways of organising work for creative, learning individuals. He or she should create space and support, assess performance rather than dominate and interfere in every moment of work; it proves his or her maturity.

13 Although morality is a set of specific rules of conduct and ethics is a branch of philosophy which deals with the study of morality, in this work they are treated as a joint competency that proves managerial maturity.

14 The influence of distortions in perception on human behaviour has been studied and confirmed in the sciences of organisation and management (Sharma, Borna, Stearns, 2009, pp. 251–260; Cho, Kessler, 2008, pp. 131–137).

15 Undoubtedly, these traits can be classified as advantages, but as regards managers who operate in dynamically changing situations, they can sometimes constitute a barrier to the implementation of innovations. In this respect, managerial maturity is reflected by other competencies, which are, in a sense, a "catalyst" for undesirable behaviour (more: Caruso, Salovey, 2009).

References

Anello, C. and Fleiss, J.L. (1995). Exploratory or analytic meta-analysis: should we distinguish between them? *Journal of Clinical Epidemiology*, 48(1), 109–116.

Antti, M. and Greenhalgh, N. (2012). Leadership competencies: a reference point for development and evaluation. *Library Management*, 33(6–7), 421–428.

Boyatzis, R.E. (1982). *The competent manager: the model for effective performance*. New York: John Wiley & Sons, Inc.

Cappellen, T. and Janssens, M. (2008). Global managers' career competencies. *Career Development International*, 13(6), 514–537.

Caruso, D.R. and Salovey, P. (2009). *Inteligentny emocjonalnie menedżer*. Poznań: Dom Wydawniczy REBIS.

Cheetham, G. and Chivers, G. (2005). *Professions, competence and informal learning*. Cheltenham: Edward Elgar Publishing.

Cho, J. and Kessler, S.R. (2008). Employees distributive justice perceptions and organizational citizenship behaviors: a social exchange perspective. *Review of Business Research*, 8(6), 131–137.

Columb, M.O. and Lalkhen, A.G. (2005). Systematic reviews & meta-analyses. *Current Anaesthesia & Critical Care*, 16(6), 391–394.

Conn, V.S., Valentine, J.C., Cooper, H.M. and Rantz, M.J. (2003). Grey literature in meta-analyses. *Nursing Research*, 52(4), 256–261.

Cyfert, S. (2012). *Granice organizacji*. Poznań: Wydawnictwo Uniwersytetu Ekonomicznego w Poznaniu.

Czakon, W. (2011). Metodyka systematycznego przeglądu literatury. *Przegląd Organizacji*, 3, 57–61.

Czakon, W. (2016). W kierunku rozwoju badań ilościowych w naukach o zarządzaniu. *Organizacja i Kierowanie*, 3(173), 41–52.

Czakon, W., Klimas, P. and Kawa, A. (2019). Krótkowzroczność strategiczna – metodyczne aspekty systematycznego przeglądu literatury. *Studia Oeconomica Posnaniensia*, 7(2), 27–37.

Czapla, T. (2012). *Modelowanie kompetencji pracowniczych w organizacji*. Łódź: Wydawnictwo UŁ.

Dworzecki, Z. and Leśniak-Łebkowska, G. (2018). Wyobraźnia strategiczna w biznesie. *Studia i Prace Kolegium Zarzadzania i Finansów*, 162, 115–142.

Dźwigoł-Barosz, M. (2017). Metody rozwoju kompetencji w warunkach kryzysu. *Studia Ekonomiczne: Zeszyty Naukowe Uniwersytetu Ekonomicznego w Katowicach*, 322, 19–31.

Gimenez, C. and Tachizawa, E. (2012). Extending sustainability to suppliers: a systematic literature review. *Supply Chain Management: International Journal*, 17(5), 531–543.

Golonka, M. (2014). *Zarzadzanie z przewaga sztuki*. Warszawa: Wolters Kluwer.

Gorynia, M. (2020). Jak poradzić sobie z koronawirusem. *Rzeczpospolita*, A27, 2 April.

Gospodarek, T. (2009). *Modelowanie w naukach o zarządzaniu oparte na metodzie programów badawczych i formalizmie reprezentatywnym*. Wrocław: Wydawnictwo Uniwersytetu Ekonomicznego we Wrocławiu.

Green, S. (2005). Systematic reviews and meta-analysis. *Singapore Medical Journal*, 46(6), 270–273.

Hajduk, Z. (2011). *Ogólna metodologia nauk*. Lublin: Wydawnictwo KUL.

Hausner, J. et al. (2020). *Międzynarodowy wymiar funkcjonowania polskiej gospodarki w warunkach pandemii*. Kraków: Open Eyes Economy Summit.

Jabłoński, M. (2006). Model rozwoju kompetencji menedżerskich. *Zeszyty Naukowe Akademii Ekonomicznej w Krakowie*, 713, 71–85.

Klimas, P. (2011). Bliskość organizacyjna – krytyczny przegląd literatury źródłem inspiracji badawczej. In Pyka, J. (Ed.), *Nowoczesność przemysłu i usług. Dynamika zmian w polskim przemyśle i usługach* (169–184). Katowice: TNOiK.

Koźmiński, A.K. (2016). Polskie zarządzanie: kontredans nauki i praktyki. *Kwartalnik Nauk o Przedsiębiorstwie*, 3, 9–20.

Krupski, R. (Ed.) (2003). *Zarządzanie strategiczne. Koncepcje – metody*. Wrocław: Wydawnictwo Akademii Ekonomicznej we Wrocławiu.

Krzakiewicz, K. (2014). Iluzje w procesie badania sukcesu organizacji. *Organizacja i Kierowanie*, 1A(159), 99–110.

Krzyżanowski, L. (1992). *Podstawy nauk organizacji i zarządzania*. Warszawa: PWN.

Linstone, H.A. and Turoff, M. (2002). Introduction. In Linstone, H.A. and Turoff, M. (Eds.), *The Delphi method: techniques and applications* (3–12). Reading, MA: Addison-Wesley.

Masiukiewicz, P. (2014). Finansowa odpowiedzialność top-menedżerów. *Zeszyty Naukowe Wyższej Szkoły Humanitas: Zarządzanie*, 2, 181–195.

Mazurek-Łopacińska, K. and Sobocińska, M. (2014). Triangulacja w badaniach marketingowych zachowań konsumentów na rynkach międzynarodowych. *Handel Wewnętrzny*, 1(2), 14–23.

Michaels, E., Handfield-Jones, H. and Axelrod, B. (2001). *The war for talent*. Boston: Harvard Business School Press.

Niewiadomski, P., Stachowiak, A. and Pawlak, N. (2019). Knowledge on IT tools based on AI maturity – industry 4.0 perspective. *Procedia Manufacturing*, 39, 574–582.

Nogalski, B. and Macinkiewicz, H. (2004). *Zarządzanie antykryzysowe przedsiębiorstwem. Pokonać kryzys i wygrać*. Warszawa: Difin.

Nogalski, B. and Niewiadomski, P. (2018). Competences dynamising the creation of business models: exploratory research. In Nalepka, A. and Ujwary-Gil, A. (Eds.), *Business and non-profit organizations facing increased competition and growing customers' demands* (305–323). Nowy Targ, Poland: Foundation for the Dissemination of Knowledge and Science "Cognitione".

Nogalski, B., Niewiadomski, P. and Szpitter, A. (2018). Dynamic competences in the opinion of the machine sector experts – from management theory to practice. *Management*, 22(1), 17–36.

Obłój, K. (2002). Dominująca logika działania jako strategia firmy: studium polskich przedsiębiorców. *Organizacja i Kierowanie*, 4(110), 61–74.

Paprocki, W. et al. (2020). *Diagnoza ostrzegawcza i wytyczne dalszych działań transportu drogowego rzeczy w warunkach kryzysu wywołanego pandemią COVID-19*. Kraków: Open Eyes Economy Summit.

Plummer, R. and Armitage, D.R. (2007). Charting the new territory of adaptive co-management: a Delphi study. *Ecology and Society*, 12(2), 1–13.

Sharma, D., Borna, S. and Stearns, J.M. (2009). An investigation of the effects of corporate ethical values on employee commitment and performance: examining the moderating role of perceived fairness. *Journal of Business Ethics*, 89, 251–260.

Simon, H. (2009). *33 sposoby na kryzys gospodarczy*. Warszawa: Difin.

Stańczyk-Hugiet, E. (2014). Badania longitudinalne w zarządzaniu, czyli jak dostrzec prawidłowości w dynamice. *Organizacja i Kierowanie*, 2(162), 45–56.

Szpitter, A. (2018). *Metodyki zarządzania projektami stosowane przez project managerów u operatorów systemu dystrybucyjnego w Polsce. Studium empiryczne*. Gdańsk: Wydawnictwo UG.

Sztoff, W. (1971). *Modelowanie i filozofia*. Warszawa: PWN.

Trocki, M., Grucza, B. and Ogonek K. (2009). *Zarządzanie projektami*. Warszawa: Polskie Wydawnictwo Ekonomiczne.

Vermeulen, F. (2005). On Rigor and Relevance: Fostering Dialectic Progress in Management Research. *Academy of Management Journal*, 48(6), 978–982.

Wang, C., Cheng, Z., Yue, X.-G. and McAleer, M. (2020). Risk management of COVID-19 by universities in China. *Journal of Risk Financial Management*, 13(36), 2–6.

Whiddett, S. and Hollyforde, S. (2003). *Modele kompetencyjne w zarządzaniu zasobami ludzkimi*. Kraków: Oficyna Ekonomiczna.

Yue, X.-G. et al. (2020). Risk management analysis for novel coronavirus in Wuhan, China. *Journal of Risk Financial Management*, 13(22), 2–6.

Zakrzewska-Bielawska, A. (2018). Modele badawcze w naukach o zarządzaniu. *Organizacja i Kierowanie*, 2(181), 11–25.

Załoga, W. (2013). Model kompetencji menedżera w nowoczesnej organizacji. *Zeszyty Naukowe Uniwersytetu Przyrodniczo-Humanistycznego w Siedlcach. Administracja i Zarządzanie*, 24(97), 449–468.

2 Logistics companies under COVID-19 threat

Selected tactics and procedures

Ewa Kalbarczyk-Guzek

Introduction

The COVID-19 pandemic, which began on November 17, 2019, in the Chinese town of Wuhan, Hubei Province, infected severely not only people but also the economy. The restrictions imposed by states have undoubtedly affected all its branches. In just a few moments, the way many industries operate has changed. Logistics companies turned out to be an example of one of them, particularly worried about the financial results. The logistics sector, which handles national and international trade in goods, including intercontinental trade, as well as the mobile sector, which handles mobility needs, form a strategic part of economic systems. The COVID-19 pandemic has had a huge impact on global supply chains. It made company employees comply with several restrictions and enforced constraints on the movement of people. The future and duration of the freeze is not predictable. Therefore, it is necessary to identify problems related to the ongoing operation of logistics companies and to present the possibilities of the support services addressed to them, which may improve the implementation of specific practices in the future.

The main purpose of the chapter is to present the real problems and challenges faced by companies operating in the logistics industry in the context of implementing their operational activities under the COVID-19 pandemic threat. Functioning in the new reality results in the creation of special models of tactics and the development of procedures to enable companies to work safely. Collected in one document, in the future they can serve as a kind of guide or a collection of good practices for logistics companies.

The partial aims of the paper are as follows:

- to describe the new reality in which logistics companies function after the outbreak of the pandemic;
- to specify selected tactical models and procedures to enable logistics companies to work safely under the COVID-19 threat.

DOI: 10.4324/9781003285731-2

The main research problem is focused on issues concerning the possibility of logistics companies to operate under the COVID-19 threat. Problems with answering the following questions come to the fore:

- Can they deal with emerging threats?
- Can they operate flexibly and implement new practices smoothly so as not to fall into financial disaster?
- Can they offer new services to the market in response to the ongoing crisis?

Detailed research problems require answers to the questions:

1 How has the situation of logistics companies operating under COVID-19 threat changed?
2 What challenges have they had to deal with?
3 What action scenarios have been prepared and implemented to respond effectively to the impact of these challenges?
4 Is it justified to invest in development and innovation during a crisis situation?

The following research methods and tools were used to achieve this objective: analysis of available literature and trade journals, as well as an expert opinion survey on the market experience of logistics companies operating under the COVID-19 threat. The expert opinion survey was conducted with six representatives of logistics companies in Poland. Three of them are Polish branches of international logistics concerns. These companies offer comprehensive services in the global market for contract logistics, road transport and e-commerce. They focus on the fashion, healthcare, industrial, consumer goods, tire, media and postal and multichannel retail sectors. Another two companies provide distribution logistics services, offering deliveries to retail and catering outlets, wholesalers, retail chains and manufacturers. The last of the companies participating in the interview provides e-commerce support, mainly distributing electronic equipment and household appliances.

A new reality for logistics companies operating under COVID-19 threat

Crisis situations can be defined as events or series of events that are devastating, occur suddenly and have significant consequences for both the organisation itself and its stakeholders (Smith, 2006). Among the negative consequences for the company, the most frequently mentioned are the threat to its reputation (Dardis, Haigh, 2009), or even ruining it, combined with the threat to the survival of the entire organisation (Pearson, Mitroff, 1993). The increased interest of the government and the media is considered to be another important feature of crisis situations (Fink, 1986). The negative impact of crisis situations is usually considered from a business perspective.

The main and primary objective of any logistics company providing services is to achieve an optimal level of customer service at minimum cost. On the one hand, customer requirements for speed of delivery, quality and flexibility are constantly increasing; on the other hand, there is a problem of price competitiveness (Černá, Buková, 2016, pp. 377–385). The coordination of supplies and material flow is now a globalised process. In the business sector, *logistics* is a term that describes the efficient flow and storage of goods from their origin to the point of consumption. The supply chain is an essential part of this process and may include transport, shipment, receipt, storage and management of all or one of these functions. Logistics can also concern information, transport, inventory, storage, material handling, packaging, disposal and safety in the business sector.

For logistics companies, the COVID-19 pandemic turned out to be an unforeseen event-changing reality, affecting people, societies and the economy. It has significantly affected supply chains and reduced stationary consumption. The disasters to date have affected supply, which has changed due to difficulties in production or delivery of goods (Cooper, Donnelly, Johnson, 2011, p. 3). It should be noted that COVID-19 caused changes in demand as it affected the volume and type of products consumed. The situation has had little impact on the supply.

Logistics companies had no previous experience of handling the risk of the COVID-19 pandemic. It was therefore not possible to immediately implement practices that would protect and allow them to continue their operations. In an effort to remain calm, the European authorities have taken the threats to the continent resulting from the pandemic very seriously. Since the beginning of the crisis, radical measures have been taken to halt the spread of the virus in Europe. Unfortunately, these measures have a direct impact on the road transport of goods, especially in places where more cases of disease have been registered. Examples of this are Northern Italy or borders with Asian countries. Following restrictive measures, the Italian government decided to isolate Milan, the country's economically strongest region. Entry to and exit from the entire region and the following Italian provinces listed was prohibited: Modena, Parma, Piacenza, Reggio-Emilia, Rimini, Pesaro and Urbino, Padua, Treviso, Asti, Alessandria, Verbano-Cusio-Ossola, Novara, Vercelli and Venice. The restrictions introduced affected directly 16 million inhabitants, while their effects were felt throughout the country and worldwide. In the case of transport, all forms of movement that required entry to and exit from the designated territory were prohibited. The only exceptions were urgent service requirements and emergencies.

It should be considered that the financial situation of companies providing services in supply chains depends largely on the structure of the portfolio of fixed contracts, the condition of their clients and the prospects for increased economic activity in the coming weeks. At the beginning of the pandemic, logistic companies noted a decrease in demand for their services, with a simultaneous need to meet financial liabilities and the appearance of payment bottlenecks. This clearly indicates the cause of the troublesome situation of companies. An important component of the collapse in demand for logistics services was the breaking of international supply chains.

The general situation of transport companies is much worse than that of forwarding or courier companies specialising in contract logistics, express or courier services. E-commerce companies declare that their situation is good. The forwarding companies are doing slightly better than transport companies. Although they have suffered from broken international supply chains, the fall in demand is considered moderate. There has been a change in geographical directions and the range of deliveries.

The reduction in the mobility of the population in individual European countries, as well as barriers to international movement, has led to changes in the level of economic activity in many countries.

Description of selected risks and tactics of action regarding human resources in logistics companies used in the fight against the COVID-19 pandemic

The new situation has forced countries around the world to radically reorganise their work. Decisions and regulations had to be made almost immediately, because transport and logistics never stop. Flexibility, the ability to react quickly to changes and to adapt to new market needs, is a feature that determines the survival of a company and allows it to minimise losses in the event of a crisis. Examples of such turbulence and consequences for logistics included people working remotely, closed restaurants, less frequent use of stationary store offers or larger single purchases. There was a need to deliver food to homes, and people started to prepare meals themselves.

In activities related to ensuring human resources security, one of the most important issues in logistics companies was the implementation of standards enabling employees responsible for securing continuity of supply to work in conditions that maximally reduce the risk of infection. This was a complicated issue as it was the first COVID-19 pandemic in history, and the Ministry of Health recommendations for hygiene standards were changing. The actions implemented by countries that had already experienced a pandemic were looked at. The level of awareness of protection against the risk of infection was raised, and the range of protective measures was extended, providing access to masks, visors and disposable gloves.

Additional measures were implemented to maintain the hygiene of the working areas where people are present, namely:

- disinfection was introduced at the entrance and exit of warehouses and in places where people were present;
- it was ordered to keep a safe distance between workers;
- zones for the safe movement of people were designated;
- to minimise the risk of cross-infection of employees, breaks of several minutes between shifts were ordered to prevent different shift workers from meeting, and thus to maintain the continuity of the processes;
- the ozonisation of premises was introduced;

- the frequency of washing of distribution vehicles was increased. In this respect, special attention was paid to the disinfection of refrigerated cars, as they have direct contact with food;
- the warehouses were isolated in such a way as to prevent access by people who are not directly involved in the workplace and the process to be performed.

Strong measures were taken to increase the security of office workers and adapt business solutions to the current situation. Some of the companies, especially those operating internationally, had a well-established experience in the implementation of tasks through remote work. This was influenced by frequent business trips and the need to communicate and implement business processes from different parts of the world. Such companies therefore had adequate web, hardware and architectural resources to enable employees to connect to the company's servers, hold teleconferences and carry out their duties. Figure 2.1 shows a sample architecture allowing remote working.

Unfortunately, such a reality was not a common practice. Companies allowing occasional work from home were forced to immediately redirect funds to equipment and architectural investments to enable employees to work remotely and thus ensure the continuity of the company's operations. This meant the purchase of appropriate programs for collision-free, mutual communication and purchase of computers, video cameras or other most necessary equipment. This allowed companies to implement business processes, manage operations and react to unforeseen situations.

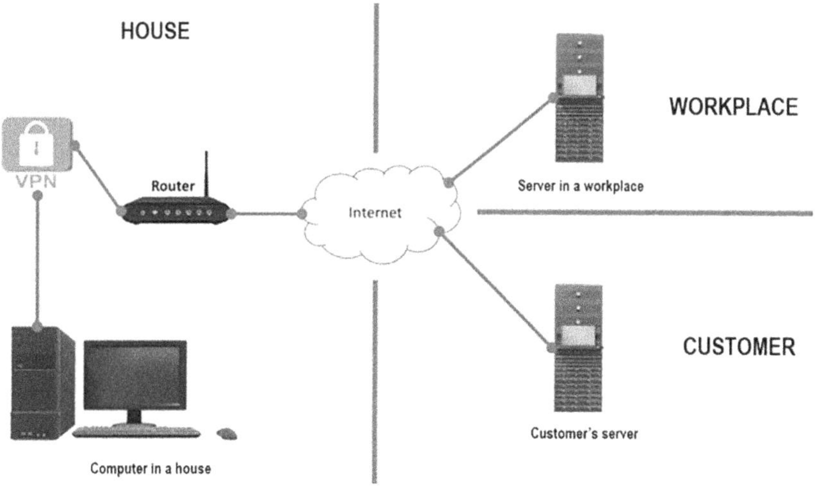

Figure 2.1 Sample architecture implemented in remote working

Source: Own study.

To ensure business continuity, a human resources management strategy covering the four basic areas described in Figure 2.2 has proven helpful.

The human factor is the key to increasing the effectiveness of an organisation. If, in the periods preceding the pandemic, companies had ongoing supervision of absenteeism rates and had recruitment processes in place, they were able to react quickly. When significant changes in staffing levels occurred due to sickness absenteeism, appropriate procedures and measures to regulate staffing levels were quickly put in place. The practices used at the time included hiring external temporary workers or seconding employees to other branches, which was an additional guarantee of security. Having knowledge of the processes being carried out, experienced employees quickly joined operational work in other branches without the need for induction training. Increasing absenteeism since March 2020 was caused by the use of a COVID-19 carer's benefit offered by the state and increased incidence of seasonal diseases such as colds and flu. Although the number of available workers decreased significantly in the first period of the pandemic, some of the logistics companies were able to compensate for this with the constant availability of temporary workers. This type of practice, focused on flexibility in cooperation with temporary work agencies, efficient recruitment processes, reporting and work safety, gives more opportunities to react in times of crisis. It turns out to be reasonable and worth recommending to other companies in the future.

Another group of employees in logistics companies directly exposed during the pandemic are drivers. Their daily work involves domestic and cross-border trips. Freight transport during the pandemic period was exempted from any restrictions on mandatory quarantine or border traffic suspension. Attention has been drawn to the need to ensure the continuity of economic activity to guarantee the flow of goods and the supply chain, especially for medical and food products. To ensure the safety of drivers, both the European Commission and individual community countries issued recommendations and guidelines, according to which the recommendations to protect the health and lives of drivers, shippers, logistics

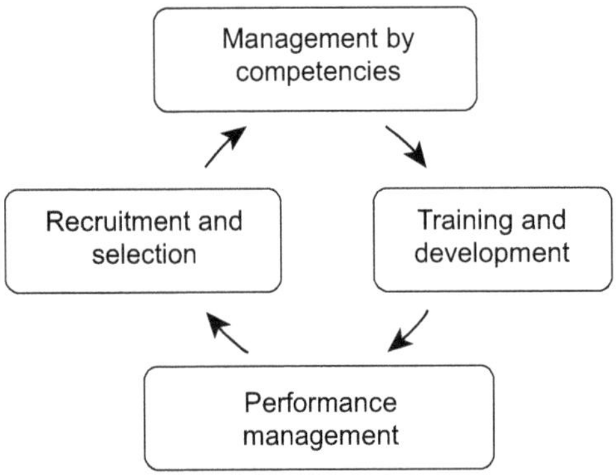

Figure 2.2 Areas of human resources management

Source: Own study.

providers and transport operators must be strictly observed. These recommendations include:

- the need of social distancing, which is understood differently in different Member States. In Poland, for example, it is a minimum distance of two meters, while in France the requirement is one meter between two people;
- limiting contact, including not leaving the cabin without a need, remote receipt and signature of transport documents, no contact with warehouse employees during loading or unloading of goods;
- transmission of documents by electronic means;
- allowing entrance to the logistics centres after measuring the temperature and checking whether one has a mask and gloves.

These restrictions undoubtedly lengthened the time of delivery of goods and initially disturbed the work of drivers and logistics companies, but their aim was to prevent paralysis of deliveries. In addition, the following safeguard measures were introduced:

- precautionary measures in the form of disinfection of hands and paper documentation and the wearing of protective gloves have been imposed;
- a supply of water and soap, as well as disposable towels or water-alcohol gel must be provided in every vehicle;
- it is recommended that during a roadside check, the driver should not get out of the vehicle and should fill in or sign the documents in the cabin;
- any new use of a tractor, for example when drivers exchange trucks, should take place with special care. This means disinfecting the cabin upon arrival from the route, and before the next employee leaves for another trip;
- in some European Union countries, drivers are required to have additional documents proving that they carry out transport tasks. In France, for example, this is a business travel certificate;
- there must be no passengers in the cabin, and the only person authorised to use the vehicle is the driver, who under current law should cross the territory as quickly and effectively as possible without violating road traffic regulations.

The carriers, knowing the seriousness of the danger, unanimously declared the importance of taking care of sanitary safety of drivers, as illness or quarantine means a loss of employee for them. In their view, the greatest threat to the sanitary safety of drivers would be long stoppages at borders.

Change in the business processes of logistics companies due to the COVID-19 pandemic

A business process is any sequence of activities or procedures leading to the achievement of a larger business objective in an organisation. It is divided into a sequence of individual activities and operations that are performed in a specific order. It includes flow, use of information and resources (Object Management Group, 2011). Processes, their quality and effectiveness are the determinant of the proper functioning of the organisation in terms of the objectives set in the short and long term (Nesternak, Jabłoński, Kowalski, 2020).

Business processes allow organisations to match existing customer demand with the supply of resources needed to meet the demand. In the digital age, the ever-changing needs of customers and rapid technological progress cause great variability and uncertainty. Such constant changes in market conditions force organisations to continuously adjust their business processes (Poll et al., 2018). This undoubtedly involves both adjusting resources to changes in quantitative demand (e.g. number of incoming customer orders) and securing business processes in terms of qualitative changes in demand (e.g. customers looking for new digital channels to interact with organisations). The ability to quickly anticipate gradual or radical changes in business processes that will be required in the future is a key success factor for the organisation.

It is established practice that logistic processes are modelled and rebuilt based on historical data analysis. The situation caused by the outbreak of the COVID-19 pandemic has deprived companies of such a possibility. They were forced to keep a watchful eye on market needs, to change consumer behaviour and to react immediately and follow the emerging trend. The services offered had to be quickly adapted or modified to the new behaviour of consumers and other operators. To minimise the risk of the virus spreading and be able to continue business operations in the state of higher necessity, the implemented processes were analysed and reorganised. It has become essential to ensure continuity of operations. Sanitary restrictions to protect human life and health were introduced into the process. They are characterised in point 2 of this chapter – Description of selected risks and tactics of action regarding human resources in logistics companies used in the fight against COVID-19 pandemic. In addition, in a situation of decreasing demand for services, it was decided to introduce the following measures:

- withdraw parts of the car fleet from service;
- limit the use of third-party carriers;
- reorganise the teams: forced leaves or layoffs of some employees;
- reduce wage rates;
- give an additional bonus for readiness to return to work.

The operations of logistics companies were most affected by:

- decline in demand for services;
- change of geography of demand for services;
- payment bottlenecks;
- broken international and national supply chains;
- tax and financial liabilities;
- change in the structure of demand for services;

- restrictions due to border closure;
- transport disruptions (traffic restrictions, sanitary inspections);
- unavailability of suitable fleet;
- pressure to reduce rates.

For logistics companies, one of the basic processes is vehicle route-planning activities. In mid-March 2020, as many as 75% of carriers faced problems in planning routes in the international transport system. The restrictions imposed complicated the operations. The closure of borders introduced at the beginning of the pandemic caused organisational chaos in the market. Initially, it was not known whether and how one could pass through Poland, which is after all a transit country. This, as well as controls introduced at Poland's internal borders with the European Union, resulted in giant traffic jams at the crossings, which at critical moments exceeded 50 kilometres. In Jędrzychowice (border with Germany), Kudowa Słone (border with the Czech Republic) and Budzisk (border with Lithuania) drivers had to wait 16 hours to enter Poland, while truck drivers had to wait even more than 30 hours. A similar situation occurred at the border with Germany, for example. Heavy traffic at the borders was partially cleared by the newly created points. At the time, companies could use a tool publicly available on https://covid-19.sixfold.com/ to track traffic at borders and determine the approximate duration of the route, including border stops, as shown in Figure 2.3.

Another challenge in the daily operations of logistics companies were restrictions on the carriage of goods that individual member states were introducing almost every day. In the process of route planning, an additional measure had to be considered, which was to keep track of newly emerging restrictions and

Figure 2.3 Review of border queues

Source: https://covid-19.sixfold.com.

to correct the routes according to the requirements of the transport plans. An example of such an impediment was the need to plan routes for transport arriving from Italian territory through the border points made available for this purpose in Hungary, Croatia, Slovenia and Austria. In such a case, the transport, which had to pass through 15 specifically designated humanitarian corridors, was not cost-optimal and the route was dictated by necessity. Stopovers on routes were only allowed at rest areas and gas stations specifically designated by the authorities of these countries, which meant that planners had to obtain information about such places on an ongoing basis and pass it on to drivers. This made the planning process even longer.

Logistics follows the changes taking place in the economy, and its slowdown translates into a decrease in handled volumes. One of the first indications of the upcoming new, previously unprecedented challenges was the emergence of obstacles to supplying warehouses with goods produced in China. Due to bans and closed borders, exporting became more difficult for both sides. In addition, a significant number of containers packed with Chinese manufactured goods were halted due to the COVID-19 virus epidemic, and thus supplies were stopped. This forced China-oriented logistics companies to look for other, alternative markets and sources of income, while the storage areas originally intended for goods from China were transformed by placing new assortments in them. It was reasonable at that time for many countries to introduce strategies to promote their domestic operators and products, thus increasing the chance for their development. It should be mentioned that the outbreak of the COVID-19 pandemic also resulted in changes in the stock strategy management, where the volumes of goods produced were increased without considering forecasts. Thus, a move away from the current business model of stock depletion has become noticeable. This measure was aimed at securing companies from having to limit production and reduce stocks in the future, caused by understaffing. Overproduction resulted in a lack of available storage space. The quickest way to counteract this risk was to erect additional tents for storing goods on pallets. Periodic quarantine measures were adopted for returned goods. In practice, this meant that the returned goods were put aside for a few days in special isolated storage areas dedicated to this process.

Processes related to the delivery of goods to retail outlets, e.g. the delivery of food to grocery stores, turned out to be problematic. To protect the health of workers (both drivers and those working in sales points), the driver had to wait for delivery to be completed when there were no customers and keep a safe distance between people. In addition, the forced use of sanitary measures (masks, gloves) made the process of delivery cumbersome. All these circumstances resulted in an increase in delivery time and a reduction in the number of points to be served by the driver during the day. The introduction of digital document circulation and new procedures related to speeding up delivery in secure conditions has slightly improved the whole process.

An important discovery brought about by the COVID-19 pandemic is the impact of company investments on further operations. The pandemic did not cause any reduction in spending on innovation, but rather mobilised businesses, including logistics, to undergo a digital transformation. Business perceives spending on innovation as an investment in searching for new sources of revenue generation or building new channels of communication with customers, which is particularly necessary in crisis situations. According to Twiss, innovation is a process that links science, technology, economics and management as it aims to achieve novelty and extends from the creation of an idea to its commercialisation in the form of production, exchange, consumption (Twiss, Goodridge, 1989). Innovation consists of generating a new idea and implementing it into a new product, process or service, leading to the dynamic development of the national economy and employment growth, as well as creating pure profit for an innovative company. Innovation is never a one-off phenomenon, but a long and cumulative process, from the phase of generating a new idea to its implementation. It is created as part of a cumulative process of gathering information, combined with a constantly ambitious vision of entrepreneurship (Kogabayev, Maziliauskas, 2017). In general, however, it can be concluded, following the Oslo Manual (2008), that there are four main types of innovation, also presented in Figure 2.4:

1 product innovation is the introduction of a product or service that is new or substantially improved in terms of its characteristics or applications. This includes significant improvements in terms of technical specifications, components and materials, embedded software, ease of use or other functional features;
2 process innovation, i.e. an innovation within a process, is the implementation of a new or significantly improved production or delivery method. This category includes significant changes in technology, equipment and/or software;
3 marketing innovation is the implementation of a new marketing method involving significant changes in product design/construction or packaging, distribution, promotion or pricing strategy;

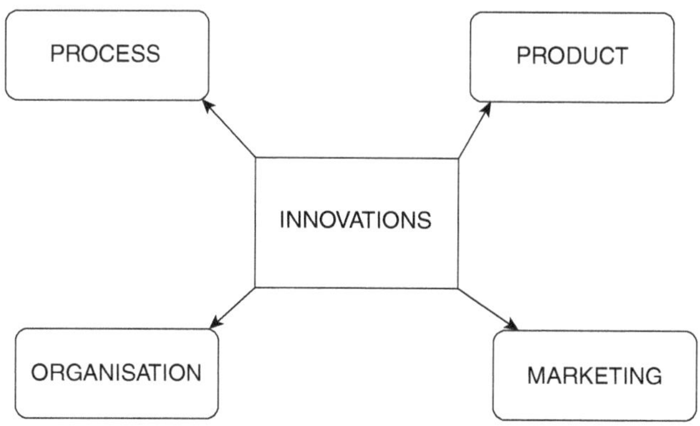

Figure 2.4 Types of innovation

Source: Own study.

4 organisational innovation is the implementation of a new organisational method in the operating principles adopted by the company, in the organisation of the workplace or in relations with the environment.

Uncertain times forced a change in the way we operate and a very fast, not always planned digitisation. This is a change that affects many areas of a company's operations, from distributed and asynchronous teamwork, through remote and digital collaboration with counterparties, electronic document circulation, to communication and delivering value to customers in a whole new way. Digitalisation enables logistics companies to operate flexibly even in difficult conditions, and the COVID-19 pandemic has clearly demonstrated the advantage of technological solutions over traditional business models. That is why logistics companies now see the need to invest in technology as a sustainable source of competitive advantage. One example of investment in innovation in the logistics market is the implementation of mechanisms for automatic planning and optimisation of vehicle routes, based on artificial intelligence algorithms. Through optimisation, it is possible to determine the best solution in terms of the adopted criterion (e.g. cost, profit, travel time, percentage of fleets used) from among the acceptable solutions to a given problem, assuming that an action is rational when the effect is maximised at a given outlay or when the outlay is minimised at an assumed effect (Jóźwiak, Kalbarczyk-Guzek, 2018, p. 114). A measure that can express the objective from the programming side is the objective function, which is the sum of many variables. Its minimisation means that the transport plan under construction complies with the restrictions, and no penalties are incurred for non-compliance. A growing objective function means that the transport plan will not be optimally implemented within the constraints imposed. There can be many reasons for this, e.g. lack of a sufficient number of vehicles, excessively restrictive delivery times (delivery time windows), lack of vehicles meeting additional requirements from customers, exceeding drivers' working time. Therefore, the system performs many mathematical calculations in a very short period and proposes the best solution to the planner, considering the cost of existing constraints, such as delivery time windows, driver's working time, vehicle load capacity, maximum number of stops along the route or the possibility of driving on a particular road (Figure 2.5).

This gives logistics companies a perspective on the reduction of operating costs, seen in the reduction of fuel consumption, better and faster route planning, efficient use of drivers' working time, automatic settlements with customers and subcontractors. Technological innovations are also a way to improve operational activity and communication within the company and to eliminate inefficient elements of the process and reduce costs, which is particularly important in times of an uncertain economic situation. Technologies such as artificial intelligence (AI) can be attractive not only to large players, as they also make it possible to improve the functioning of smaller companies, which are becoming more competitive on the European market.

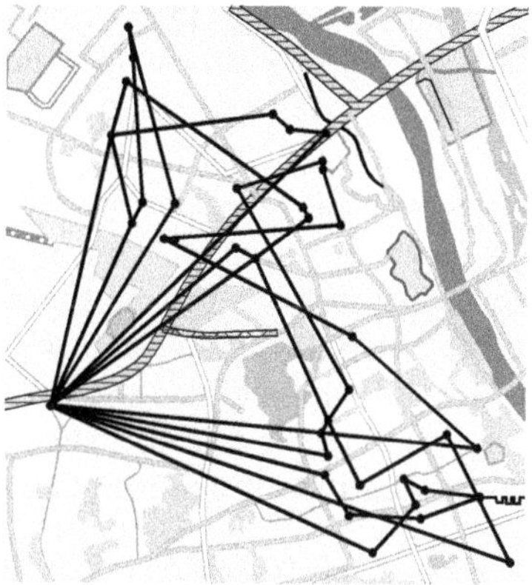

Figure 2.5 Sample route plan composed using the optimisation system

Source: Own study utilising the TMS system.

The outbreak of the pandemic corrected the investment plans of logistics companies, which had to give in to the need to carry out the works resulting from the consequences of the COVID-19 pandemic. Innovative, selected ideas for improving the implementation of processes during the pandemic included such areas as:

1 development of mobile applications. In this aspect, contactless goods delivery confirmation was made possible. Customers received an SMS code that had to be given to the driver during delivery. This eliminated the need for manual signature of the delivery and thus protected the health of drivers. Today, mobile and web applications play an important role in the e-commerce scene, as they are optimised to require as few steps as possible from login to finalisation of the order, which enhances user experience;
2 implementation of digital signatures, supporting electronic document circulation. Thanks to the ability to sign documents remotely, the time of their processing was reduced, errors were eliminated, administration costs were reduced and work automation was introduced. The drivers delivering the goods did not have to take the paper documents with them or make sure they were signed. This accelerated the executed process;
3 introduction of electronic non-cash billing, also known as cash on delivery (COD). Replacing cash with electronic billing is one way to ensure the safety of the driver delivering the goods;
4 introduction of automation of financial and accounting settlements – implementation of interfaces with financial and accounting systems supports logistics companies in financial management to control stability on an ongoing basis and to avoid payment bottlenecks. Making possible the automation

of the collection process at the stage of monitoring and amicable debt collection speeds up the receivables recovery time;

5 introduction of online work schedules to eliminate understaffing compared to workloads and loss of control over productivity and labour cost levels.

Logistics companies also noticed that the pandemic forced a change in the way deliveries were organised. There has been an increase in deliveries to individual customers in their places of residence, but not to the companies where they worked. Due to the possible absence of the customer at home during delivery, individual shipments are currently more difficult to deliver. Processes that have been implemented relate to informing the customer about the delivery in advance, the possibility of redirecting the delivery to another place or receiving the package at a designated point.

During the pandemic, there was a significant increase in the importance of e-commerce. It represents the business activity involving buying and selling products and services through internet platforms. E-commerce covers a wide range of business activities such as retail stores, online banking services, transport and hotel reservation services, money transfers, online payments, digital content, etc. (Pantelimon, Georgescu, Posedaru, 2020). The need to stay at home did not mean a radical abandonment of consumption by society. In times when it is difficult or impossible to access stationary shops, societies are much more likely to use e-commerce services and buy goods through the internet. Therefore, despite the restrictions and limitations introduced by governments, a strong stimulus for the development of the e-commerce sector has emerged. The employers in this sector, with an increase in turnover, even at a time of ubiquitous redundancies, are forecasting a continued high level of demand for workers, including the recruitment of new staff. Everything seems to indicate that the development of the e-commerce sector is a certain direction for the future for all sectors, as it is now not only an opportunity to purchase almost any goods without the need to leave home, but it is also becoming an increasingly important branch of the economy. The fact that the use of smartphones has increased dramatically has become more important. In January 2020, there were almost 4.54 billion internet users worldwide, which translates into 59% of the population and 4.18 billion unique mobile internet users (Statista, 2020a). This is important news for the e-commerce market.

When operating in the e-commerce industry, one of the key criteria for returning to an online store is efficient and fast delivery. An example of an offer that builds a positive purchasing experience can be a delivery on the order date. The technology plays an increasingly important role here, as the customer can track the entire route of the shipment from the moment it is sent by the online store. Efficient delivery adds to the satisfaction of shopping. This proposal will meet the expectations of customers and draw the consumer away from stationary stores in the future. The speed of the entire transaction is a challenge for the logistics operator. It requires the provision of an adequate number of means of transport, process personnel, IT system support and the organisation of logistics processes in such a way as to protect employees as much as possible and will make non-cash operations possible. Due to the reduction of human contact, the logistics companies are implementing non-contact delivery options and a novelty on the market – delivery by drone, straight to the customer's window.

Ensuring fast delivery will result in changes in the warehouse management processes. It will be necessary to have an extensive network of warehouses and an advanced logistic system, allowing for instant order picking. The most efficient delivery process is expected to be based on mini hubs and small facilities located on the outskirts of large cities, so that delivery can be made on the same day. This in turn will have impact on the maintenance of the current trend of consumer behaviour in the future, i.e. after the COVID-19 pandemic ends. Customers accustomed to fast delivery and convenience will remain with online shopping.

Due to the maintenance of social distance measures and employees starting to work from home, the behaviour related to the use of the internet has changed. The analysis of 1,400 websites carried out in April 2020, in comparison to January and February 2020, indicates that the situation caused by COVID-19 had a positive impact on market segments such as food and telecommunication as well as home and garden. The most affected segment was tourism, as most hotels, airlines and agencies suspended their operations (Statista, 2020b).

E-commerce has a huge potential, which is worth using now and in the coming months. To maintain sales and adapt to market transformation, many companies have been faced with the prospect of major changes in their business profile, distribution and logistics model, or the offer addressed to the market.

Conclusions

This chapter presents the real problems and challenges faced by companies operating in the logistics industry in the context of implementing their operational activities under the COVID-19 pandemic threat. The selected tactics and procedures introduced at that time can provide a hint and at the same time inspire companies operating in the field of logistics and transport in the event of changes in operating conditions. The described algorithms were developed in connection with the fight against the COVID-19 pandemic based on a literature review, trade magazines and analyses of market experience of logistics companies, collected mainly from surveys. Operating in a new, hitherto unknown and unrecognised reality does not give companies the most important thing – time to prepare for the situations they will face. The most important thing at such moments is to act efficiently and flexibly to ensure the fulfilment of one's operational tasks, not to allow the company to go bankrupt or significantly deteriorate its financial condition caused by the reduction of income. The classification of risks and problems associated with the implementation of current operations in logistics companies in a situation of various types of threats (including COVID-19) is an excellent starting point for creating prescriptions, evaluations and recommendations for one's own sector. In Table 2.1, selected tactics of proceedings mentioned in the chapter have been collected, which give the organisation a chance to survive, continue its activity and, to some extent, make up for the lost benefits.

Table 2.1 Selected tactics used by logistics companies during the pandemic

The breakdown of the selected tactics and procedures used into categories, concerning:	
PEOPLE	*PROCESSES*
Sanitary protection measures	Route planning
Social distance and security zones	Warehouse management
Collision-free exchange of shift workers and drivers	Confirmation of delivery
Ozonisation of premises and vehicles	Introduction of digitisation
Home offices	E-commerce
Human resources management strategy	Non-cash settlements

Source: Own study.

The importance of logistics in the economic ecosystem increased after the outbreak of the pandemic. Logistics companies have managed to cope with such a difficult time, compensating losses from activities in one area with activities in other areas to meet current customer needs. Everyone makes the greatest effort to ensure that logistics does not stop and that deliveries are made in the most secure manner possible. The companies that took care of their development before COVID-19 were much better prepared for the unpredictable and implemented without hesitation new algorithms of proceedings, thanks to which they managed to survive the most difficult moments.

References

Černá, L. and Buková, B. (2016). Supplier evaluation methodology in the logistics company. *Procedia Engineering*, 134, 377–385.

Cooper, W.H., Donnelly, J.M. and Johnson, R. (2011). *Japan's 2011 earthquake and tsunami: economic effects and implications for the United States*. Washington, DC: Congressional Research Service.

Dardis, F. and Haigh, M.M. (2009). Prescribing versus describing: testing image restoration strategies in a crisis situation. *Corporate Communications: An International Journal*, 14(1).

Fink, S. (1986). *Crisis management: planning for the inevitable*. New York: American Management Association, Amacom.

Jóźwiak, A. and Kalbarczyk-Guzek, E. (2018). Decyzje taktyczne firm w zakresie ustalania warunków dystrybucji towarów. *Systemy Logistyczne Wojsk*, 49, 114.

Kogabayev, T. and Maziliauskas, A. (2017). The definition and classification of innovation. *HOLISTICA*, 8(1), 59–72.

Nesterak, M., Jabłoński, M. and Kowalski, J. (2020). *Controlling procesów w praktyce przedsiębiorstw działających w Polsce*. Kraków: Wydawnictwo Uniwersytetu Ekonomicznego.

Object Management Group (2011). BPMN v. 2.0.

Oslo Manual (2008). *Zasady gromadzenia i interpretacji danych dotyczących innowacji*. Paris: OECD, Komisja Europejska.

Pantelimon, F., Georgescu, T. and Posedaru, B. (2020). The impact of mobile e-commerce on GDP: A comparative analysis between Romania and Germany and how Covid-19 influences the e-commerce activity worldwide. *Informatica Economică*, 24(2), 27.

Pearson, C.M. and Mitroff, I.I. (1993). From crisis proneto crisis prepared: a framework for crisis management. *The Academy of Management Executive*, 7(1).

Poll, R. et al. (2018). *Process forecasting: towards proactive business process management*. Sydney: Springer Nature.

Sixfold (2020). https://covid-19.sixfold.com.

Smith, D. (2006). Crisis management – practice in search of a paradigm. In Smith, D. and Elliott, D. (Eds.), *Key readings in crisis management: systems and structures for prevention and recovery*. London: Routledge.

Statista (2020a). *Worldwide digital populationas of April 2020*, www.statista.com/statistics/617136/digital-population-worldwide/.

Statista (2020b). *Coronavirus impact on online traffic of selected industries worldwide in week ending April 26*, www.statista.com/statistics/1105486/coronavirus-traffic-impact-industry/.

Twiss, B. and Goodridge, M. (1989). *Managing technology for competitive advantage: integrating technological and organisational development: from strategy to action*. Philadelphia, PA: Trans-Atlantic Publications.

3 The efficiency of management of a logistics centre under conditions of COVID-19 threats

Sławomir Bartosiewicz and Małgorzata Oziębło

Introduction

Due to the varied nature of operations carried out at logistics centres, their size and the novel threat of COVID-19, a universal procedure for conducting an analysis and evaluation of the level of efficiency of management that could be used at each such entity has not been developed so far.

Currently, tasks carried out at logistics centres and their operations are evaluated while they are under way, since their suspension would entail incurring additional costs and losing one's established position on the market. Therefore, the entire process is carried out by external consultants who are obliged to keep business secrets, or it is one of the duties of a dedicated functional unit at the organisation. Some of the tasks related to ongoing evaluation of operations are assigned to managers of individual departments, who are obliged to prepare reports summarising the operations of structures they are managing within the context of the entire entity's operations. Therefore, to ensure that the inspection of the level of security and evaluations at an organisation are properly carried out, it is necessary to distinguish their most frequently performed tasks. Considering this, the authors propose evaluation procedures that are adequate to the scale of the problem after considering the specific nature of operations, employed procedures and tools ensuring an organisation's management security under conditions of COVID-19 threats.

In March and April logistics centres had to face serious challenges, namely threats related to COVID-19, to ensure continuity of operations and supply chains. Moreover, they had to address the simultaneously occurring change of supply and demand for services.

The authors have developed a tool that enables capturing the most important changes in logistics centres' operations regarding the scale and trends in changes that occur in relation to their management under conditions of COVID-19 threats.

Methodology for carrying out the research process

The principal research question is focused on management efficiency issues, the most prominent of which are issues related to measuring tools showing the most important changes in their operations in relation to the ordinary state.

DOI: 10.4324/9781003285731-3

The chapter's main objective is to develop a methodology for the assessment of the efficiency of management of logistics centres to enable accurate measurement of the most important changes in their operations under conditions of COVID-19 threats in relation to the normal state.

The utilitarian objective is to implement a proprietary evaluation of the efficiency of management of logistics centres to enable carrying it out efficiently under conditions of COVID-19 threats.

Sub-objectives:

- characteristics of management of a logistics centre under conditions of COVID-19 threats;
- preventive measures for employees and clients of logistics centres to ensure continuation of operations under conditions of COVID-19 threats;
- development of a comprehensive method for evaluation of the most important changes in logistics centre management in relation to the ordinary state;
- performance of an evaluation of management of a selected logistics centre under conditions of COVID-19 threats.

Study hypothesis

The developed method for evaluation of management of logistics centres will ensure the efficiency of inspections conducted under conditions of COVID-19 threats.

The following test methods, techniques and study tools, and information sources were used during the study:

Test methods:

- an analysis of documentation from the National Court Register (KRS) and logistics centres;
- a flowchart;
- an analysis of statistical group's structure;
- an index analysis;
- a description and fact organisation method;
- a case study method;
- a synthesis method.

Techniques and study tools:

- Statistica software;
- descriptive statistics tools.

Information sources:

- primary: empirical data obtained at the analysed logistics centre; as well as financial statements from the National Court Register (KRS);

- secondary: international literature sources on logistics centres, enterprise assessment, statistical methods for multi-dimensional comparative analysis; materials obtained from international organisations dealing with analyses of supranational corporations; specialist magazines; papers published by research institutes; legal acts; as well as online sources.

Characteristics of management of a logistics centre under conditions of COVID-19 threats

Warehouse and transport management are the centrepiece of operating activities of logistics centres. Warehouse management concerns these activities of an entity that are aimed at storing goods (supplies) to secure the operations of a particular enterprise (Grzybowska, 2010, p. 13). 'The operations of a warehouse are required to change accordingly, due to the complex and high variety of customer orders as well as the demand for real-time information' (Lee et al., 2018, p. 2767). The essence of warehouse management is undertaking activities and selecting structures that will ensure appropriate cooperation between all warehouse components, whereas transport management's objective is transport of goods aimed to secure operations while using as few means of transport as possible and selecting the shortest routes. Because warehouse management constitutes a higher share in such entity's income, in the subsequent part of the chapter the authors will focus mainly on the functioning of warehouse management.

Warehouse logistics department employees are responsible for handling activities connected with appropriate and secure functioning of warehouses at the analysed logistics centre. Any goods received at logistics centre's warehouses are compliant with the scope of responsibilities and assigned tasks, in accordance with those listed in procedures and instructions. Warehouse processes are performed using the following means of internal transport:

- low-lifting trucks – horizontal transport (for transporting goods in front of them); load – in compliance with load table; performed operations – order completion, unloading, loading;
- reach trucks – vertical transport (for transporting foods up above them); load – in compliance with the load table; performed operations – transporting stock keeping units (SKUs) to pallet reserve areas, transport of SKUs from pallet reserve areas to KMD area or directly to an exit buffer; stock – taking, moving SKUs.

The verification of quantity of goods is performed using a mobile SMK control station and a platform scale. The warehouse management system (WMS) is used to manage the warehouse. It is a class system with modern tools for automatic identification and verification of the quantity of goods.

The contemporary WMS used by manufacturers is required to support the changes in production orders and to enhance the efficiency of the warehouse operation (Lee, Cao, Ng, 2017; Lee et al., 2018, pp. 2753–2768).

A wireless radio network through which mobile barcode reader terminals connect to the company's WMS system. Warehouses are equipped with temperature and humidity measurement and registration systems. Data transferred from sensors installed at the warehouse is processed in the Softrol CH 36 program, made available for viewing through an internal internet network and recorded at a server station. A materials technician is obliged to control temperature on an ongoing basis throughout his or her shift using an internal Softrol internet network to order corrective actions in case of any irregularities. The battery room is located at the end of the warehouse, behind shelving units. It is equipped with rectifiers, loading tables and a lift available 24/7.

Warehouses are equipped with:

- ventilation systems that perform a full exchange of air within 1.5 hours;
- emergency smoke vents that open automatically once the air temperature exceeds 140°C and fire sprinklers that turn on once the air temperature exceeds 74°C.

The technological warehousing system as a set of activities performed during a flow of charges in separate warehousing areas is presented here:

1 acceptance area – unloading goods off external means of transport, acceptance into warehouses;
2 pallet reserve area – storing involving placing (stacking) stock on a surface or within storage space in a systematic manner, corresponding with stock properties and current physical and chemical storage conditions;
3 picking area – picking/matching ranges of goods with internal orders drawn based on clients' orders;
4 release area – release and loading of goods onto external means of transport.

Moreover, there are separate areas at warehouses, such as:

- "BW-01" technical buffer – occupied solely during the time required to clarify any issues related to a particular product;
- "GENERAL CARGO" buffer – used for accepting small deliveries;
- "CROSS DOCKING" buffer.

A centre's warehouses are coordinated by the warehouse logistics department at which warehouse processes are carried out, including:

1 unloading external means of transport;
2 moving goods to the acceptance area;
3 unpacking transport freight units, sorting, forming uniform storage units;
4 qualitative and quantitative acceptance;
5 moving goods to pallet reserve area;
6 storage;

7 moving goods to the picking area;
8 temporary storage in the picking area and picking goods for release;
9 moving picked freight units to the release area;
10 moving freight units directly from the pallet reserve area to the release area;
11 quantitative and qualitative release;
12 loading goods onto external means of transport.

All operations – starting from unloading in the acceptance area, through moving goods to the pallet reserve area, up to loading the goods onto external means of transport – are performed in a manner ensuring that the goods owned by the client are not damaged, while paying particular attention to one's own and others' safety. Workers who move around the warehouse are obliged to abide by certain rules, including an absolute obligation to use personal protective equipment, such as:

- a helmet;
- a warning vest;
- safety steel-toe boots;
- protective glasses in case of work with ADR materials.

Binding Occupational Safety and Health regulations require that warehouse workers maintain order and cleanliness within the warehouse and adjacent areas. They are also obliged to control technical efficiency of mechanical warehouse equipment. People who are not employed at the logistics centre may move around the warehouses solely in the presence of an authorised worker who is obliged to ensure that appropriate personal protection equipment is used, i.e.:

- a warning vest;
- a helmet;
- a protective mask.

People from external companies who are working at the warehouse must undergo training in compliance with the 1/Z/P4.1/09/01 instruction. The trainer of the training is the Deputy Technical and Safety Manager or another person appointed by the Manager of the Warehouse Logistics Division. Having completed training and filled in the instruction form, one should place it in the "Training/DO" binder in the Warehouse Logistics Division Manager's office. External company workers and managers are obliged to use personal protective equipment.

Warehouses are kept clean in compliance with relevant instructions and cleaning schedules (HACCP). Cleaning protocols together with instructions for cleaning and disinfection of warehouse areas are in individual warehouses. The floor is cleaned using a Karcher cleaning machine. Moreover, there are containers intended for waste segregation (film, cardboard, wood). Warehouses are equipped with three emergency showers supplied with tap water. They are located at gates 2 and 4, and at the end of the warehouse, behind racks. Pallets must be placed symmetrically on racks to ensure that they extend 5 cm beyond the rack at the front and at the back. The maximum height for storing empty IBC containers as blocks is three layers. Materials must be stored in their original, appropriately marked packaging (hazardous materials must adhere to guidelines included in their material data sheets). The location for storage of hazardous materials must be determined in accordance with maximum safety principles. Every day during warehouse rounds it should be verified with particular care whether seals on hazardous materials packaging are intact.

The analysed logistics centre undertook extraordinary measures to reduce direct contact to ensure its continued operation under conditions of COVID-19 threats. There are limitations in place regarding contact between its own employees with third-party workers, couriers and mail carriers. There are separate zones within warehouses for its own workers and external ones. The number of paper settlements has been reduced. Moreover, remote work was implemented in response to the threat, as well as a division of workers between those that are working on site and those working from home. The efficiency of that solution, however, proved to be low once it was employed, since even contact with remote workers was extremely difficult to establish. The managers used it to hide the shortage of work/orders from their workers. This resulted in making some workers go on vacation. A portion of the car fleet was suspended from travelling, and the use of third-party carriers was reduced. No group of workers was made redundant. It was decided, however, that their salary was going to be reduced by 20%.

The operations of logistics centres were simultaneously negatively affected (in mid-March and at the beginning of April) by a small drop in demand for their services. The breaking of international supply chains played an important role in the slump in demand for logistics services. Unexpectedly high levels of interference in the flow of goods (traffic limits, health inspections) and limits on conducting operations abroad because of border closures did not constitute a problem.

Preventive measures for employees and clients of logistics centres to ensure continuation of operations under conditions of COVID-19 threats

The conditions at a logistics company during the pandemic are clearly distinguished based on its dependence on orders submitted by its clients. Severe acute respiratory syndrome coronavirus 2 (SARS-CoV-2) was first detected in China in December 2019, when it was found to cause coronavirus disease (COVID-19) related pneumonia and pneumonitis. By March 2020, COVID-19 had been declared a pandemic. By late March 2020, there had been a worldwide mortality rate of 4.4%, with 19,000 deaths in 430,000 infected individuals in 170 countries (Bonow et al., 2020; Denniss, Chow, Kritharides, 2020), although there has been variation in the indications for testing from country to country, accounting for some of the variation in mortality between countries, besides other factors such as differing demographics (Denniss, Chow, Kritharides, 2020). Patients have typically had a fever and commonly a cough, dyspnoea, fatigue, sore throat and myalgia. While respiratory symptoms have usually predominated, some patients have presented with chest pain or chest tightness and palpitations (Zheng et al., 2020; Huang et al., 2020; Shi et al., 2020; Guo et al., 2020; Denniss, Chow, Kritharides, 2020). Confirmation of the diagnosis involves use of specimen collection for coronavirus ribonucleic acid detection, usually from nasopharyngeal swabs (standard), viral isolation and culture (in limited accredited laboratories) and detection of serum antibodies (Handbook of COVID-19 prevention and treatment, 2020).

The significance of logistics services provided by centres on the logistics services market has increased after the pandemic started. The entire team of people employed at the entity (warehouse workers, drivers, dispatchers and customer service workers) are doing all they can to ensure that logistics processes continue and to support their clients. They are making every effort to ensure that deliveries are performed as safely as possible. A range of security measures was introduced, including, for instance, taking body temperature, providing disinfectants at every entrance/exit at our facilities, security gloves, breaks between shifts at warehouses and including additional disinfection of staff areas. Moreover, a range of preventive measures was implemented, in accordance with recommendations established by the Minister of Health and the Chief Sanitary Inspector.

Evaluation methodology for management of a logistics centre under conditions of COVID-19 threats

The reasoning behind assumptions made for the model

The study focuses on three issues:

- activities undertaken by the logistics centre to ensure its continuous operations under conditions of COVID-19 threats;
- threats to operations at the logistics centre;
- clients' activity (divided into individual sectors) in terms of purchases of logistics services offered by logistics centres.

In Figure 3.1, the research model was presented.

The model for analysis and evaluation will be focused on the analysis and evaluation of management of logistics centres to improve their ability and provide skills for handling COVID-19 threats. The evaluation will verify activities undertaken regarding management of logistics centres under conditions of COVID-19 threats in terms of:

- human and material resources;
- preventive measures against COVID-19's impact on the management of a logistics centre;
- outcomes for the economy;
- the scope of impact of COVID-19 threats on the efficiency of operations of a selected logistics centre conducting its business in Poland.

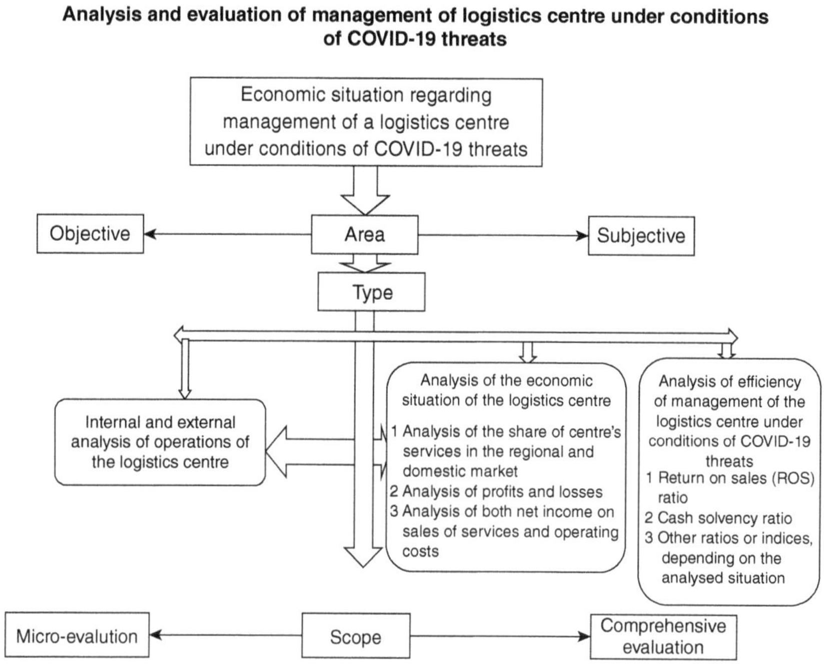

Figure 3.1 A model for analysis and evaluation of management of a logistics centre under conditions of COVID-19 threats

Source: Own study.

Results of an analysis employing the analysis and evaluation model for a logistics centre under conditions of COVID-19 threats

The conducted study is focused on analysing:

- the share of a logistics centre's services in the regional and Polish market;
- profits and losses of the logistics centre;
- net turnover and operating costs;
- evaluation of management of a logistics centre under conditions of COVID-19 threats.

Analysis of the share of logistics centre's services in the regional and Polish market. The share of handling services of a logistics centre in the regional and domestic market was established based on a logistics centre's internal materials. The analysis of the share in the market involved the period from March 2020 to June 2020. The number of handled loads during individual years was determined based on a logistics centre's internal data. The share of the logistics centre in the Polish market during the period from March 2020 to June 2020 is shown in Table 3.1.

Table 3.1 The share of the logistics centre in the market – thousands of tonnes and percentage

Month	*Loads handled by the logistics centre [thousands of tonnes]*	*Loads handled in the regional market [thousands of tonnes]*	*Share in the regional market [%]*	*Loads handled in the domestic market [thousands of tonnes]*	*Share in the domestic market [%]*
March	880.40	2,672.40	32.94	39,332.90	2.24
April	1,244.70	3,390.20	36.71	39,699.50	3.14
May	652.60	3,225,700.00	20.23	40,227.10	1.62
June	1,778.6	3,812.40	46.65	41,192.6	4.32

Source: Own study based on data obtained at the analysed logistics centre.

The share of services provided by the logistics centre during the analysed period from March until June has been gradually rising. In February 2020, the threat of COVID-19 and the expansion of a new handling terminal significantly decreased the centre's handling capacity. The analysed period was also the time when there was a significant drop in the number of handling services performed at the centre. It should be emphasised that the value of handling services performed by the logistics centre has doubled during the March–June period, which allowed it to take over almost 47% of the regional market. Handling at the level of 1,778,600.00 tonnes per month constitutes only about 22% of the handling potential of the centre, which at present amounts to 8,000,000.00 tonnes per month. Currently, the analysed logistics centre is playing a significantly less important role in the domestic market. Throughout the analysed period the centre managed to increase its share in the domestic market from 2.24% to 4.32%, which is far from the number of handling services carried out by the largest handling terminals in the country.

An analysis of profits and losses of the logistics centre

The logistics centre generates income and costs related to acquiring that income, which in turn gives rise to certain profits or, in case of an unfavourable outcome, losses. The breakdown of profits and losses of the logistics centre during the period from March to June 2020 is presented in Table 3.2 and Chart 3.1.

In March 2020 the analysed logistics centre expanded the scope of conducted handling operations, which contributed to the first occurrence of profits that amounted to over PLN 95,000.00. The profit doubled in April 2020, but the trend was interrupted in May 2020. That month, i.e. in May 2020, the losses amounted to almost PLN 900,000.00, which related to investment expenditures intended to expand the road and rail container terminal. June 2020, however, was a time when the profit reappeared and amounted to PLN 190,000.00, which paints an optimistic picture for the future.

Table 3.2 Net profit/loss and dynamics during the March–June 2020 period

Month	*Profit/loss [PLN]*	*Dynamics index [%]*
March	95,348.38	–1,407.37
April	212,236.47	222.59
May	–887,729.35	–418.27
June	188,282.95	–21.21

Source: Own study on the basis from data from the National Court Register (KRS).

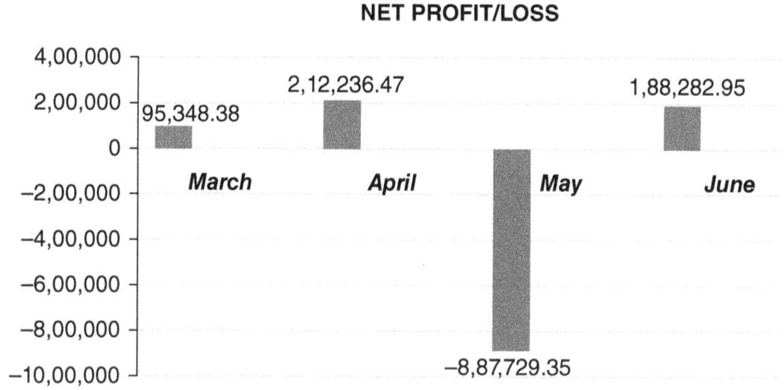

Chart 3.1 Net profit and loss during the March–June 2020 period [PLN]

Source: Own work on the basis from data from the National Court Register (KRS).

Net turnover and operating costs

Net turnover at a logistics centre providing services is income in the form of material benefits obtained or due to a company's operations. Therefore, it is simply the payment for provided services. Cost, on the other hand, is the purposeful use of financial resources to pay for third-party services and workers' salaries, as well as certain expenditures that do not reflect actual use, yet they concern normal operations of a particular unit during that period. Net turnover and operating costs of the logistics centre are presented in Table 3.3 and Chart 3.2.

Despite COVID-19 threats, a significant increase in sales was recorded in March 2020, which was to some extent the result of demand for logistics services and performance of contracts for handling and storage services. Sales of services nearly doubled in April 2020. This was the result of a continuous increase in the centre's handling capability in response to the increased demand for provided services. In May 2020 the sales of services suddenly decreased after a closure of a part of the terminal, which was necessary to perform further investments and expand rail tracks for handling as well as to adjust them to receiving containers. Having reopened the expanded part of the terminal and considering the increasing

Table 3.3 Net turnover and operating costs during the March–June 2020 period

Month	*Net turnover [PLN]*	*Change dynamics [%]*	*Operating costs [PLN]*	*Change dynamics [%]*
March	1,663,147.97	11,696.71	1,310,387.27	10,720.51
April	3,147,139.99	89.23	2,105,944.83	60.71
May	985,747.67	–68.68	1,787,195.45	–15.14
June	3,891.110.22	294.74	3,527,319.09	97.37

Source: Own study based on data from the National Court Register (KRS).

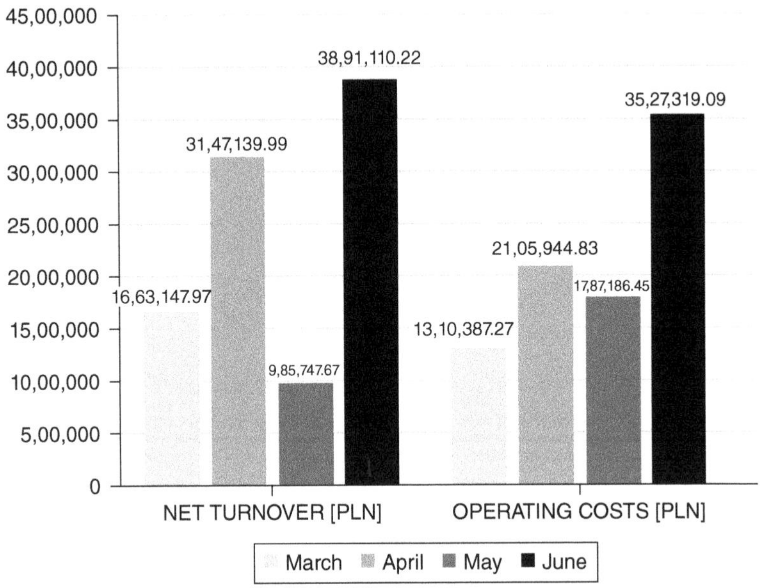

Chart 3.2 Net turnover and operating costs during the March–June 2020 period [PLN]

Source: Own study based on data from the National Court Register (KRS).

demand for services on the market in May 2020, another increase in sales was observed in comparison to March 2020. It was mainly the result of a very good use of the logistics centre's potential.

The handling terminal was opened at the logistics centre in March 2020, the time when the company started providing services. This proved to be a turning point, and the cost of conducted activity amounted to over PLN 1,300,000.00. The following month, April 2020, brought about an increase in costs because of an increase in handling services performed within the centre. In May 2020, however, a small decrease in operating costs was observed, which was the result of a need to retain the employees and operating resources. The subsequent month, June 2020, brought about doubled operating costs, mainly due to putting the rebuilt handling terminal in commission, which caused a significant increase in intensity of work.

Evaluation of management of a logistics centre under conditions of COVID-19 threats

To conduct an evaluation of management of a logistics centre under conditions of COVID-19 threats with regard to specific features of the analysed entity and to consider issues related to obtaining quantitative data, the authors used two ratios: return on sales (ROS) and cash solvency. Nevertheless, the proposal for evaluation of management shows the actual state of activity conducted by the logistics centre in comparison to planned values.

Planned value (PV) is the cumulative planned value as a continuous or periodic function summing the approved budget for accomplishing the scheduled work (activity, work package, or project) as a function of time (Chen, Chen, Lin, 2015, p. 22).

The proposed model for evaluation of management of a logistics centre under conditions of COVID-19 threats allows for determining compatibility with assumed principles and recommendations included in a subject entity's documentation. Moreover, it will enable comparing functionality of a particular entity to other entities that are similar in terms of their size and field of operations and allow an evaluation of the efficiency of the proposed analytical and evaluation procedure under conditions of COVID-19 threats. The proposed model for evaluation of management can be used for other, similar entities once it is adjusted to characteristic features of their activity.

Return on sales ratio

The return on sales ratio provides information on the degree of profitability of sales of services and products provided by the logistics centre. A characteristic feature of that ratio is the fact that the higher it is, the more profitable are the sales of products and services, i.e. it provides information on the degree to which sales are profitable. The ratio is calculated based on the following dependency (3.1):

$$Return\ on\ sales\left(\mathbf{ROS}\right)=\frac{\mathbf{net\,profit}}{\mathbf{net\,sales}}. \qquad (3.1)$$

ROS ratio values during the period from March to June 2020 are presented in Table 3.4 and Chart 3.3.

March 2020 brought a positive value of the return on sales ratio at the level of 6%. A similar result was shown in April 2020, when the ratio increased to 7%, which indicates the potential of the logistics centre. A decrease of the ROS ratio value was recorded in May 2020. This was mainly caused by expenditures incurred to adapt the logistics centre to COVID-19 threats, due to which the

Table 3.4 ROS ratio values during the period from March to June 2020

Month	*ROS*	*Change dynamics [%]*
March	0.06	–111.93
April	0.07	17.63
May	–0.90	–1,435.40
June	0.05	–105.37

Source: Own study.

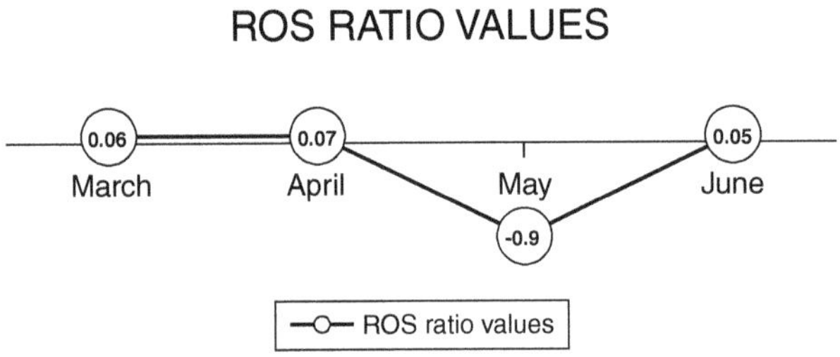

Chart 3.3 ROS ratio values during the March–June 2020 period

Source: Own study.

ratio's value amounted to – 90%. The situation changed in June 2020, when the ROS ratio's value amounted to 5%, which suggests that the trend visible in March and April 2020 will return.

Cash solvency ratio

By employing the cash solvency ratio, one can evaluate the level of an entity's payment capability during a particular period. In this case ongoing payments may be fulfilled using cash available in physical form in the cash register, cash resources deposited in entity's bank accounts and other means of payment, such as bill of exchange, etc. The cash solvency ratio was calculated based on the following dependence (3.2):

$$\textbf{\textit{Cash solvency ratio}} = \frac{\textbf{\textit{financial resources and other financial assets}}}{\textbf{\textit{current liabilities}}}. \quad (3.2)$$

The model value for the ratio is assumed to be 0.2. The assumption of such value relates to the principle consisting in limiting cash resources to the level determined by the scale of variability of income and expenditures involving means of payment at the logistics centre for using debt capital. The higher the value of this ratio, the better the company's ability to quickly pay off its current liabilities. However, too high a value of this ratio means ineffective use of cash (Bartosiewicz, Ozięblo, Zachara, 2018, pp. 116–117). Any increase of the value of the ratio above 0.3 suggests a centre's preference for cash transactions. Cash solvency ratio's values for the logistics centre during the period from March 2020 to June 2020 are shown in Table 3.5 and Chart 3.4.

During the period from March to June 2020 the value of means of payment that the logistics centre had at its immediate disposal was very low. The state of maintained financial resources did not allow for the logistics centre to pay its liabilities on an ongoing basis, considering tasks that it had to perform to prepare for operating under conditions of COVID-19 threats. Moreover, it did not have means of payment at its disposal in case of a possible need to address unexpected situations and those unplanned for by the management of the logistics centre.

Conclusions

Results of performed studies that are shown in this chapter outline the actual state of operations conducted by the logistics centre in comparison to planned

Table 3.5 Cash solvency ratio's values for the logistics centre during the period from March to June 2020

Month	*Cash solvency ratio's value*
March	0.01
April	0.02
May	0.02
June	0.02

Source: Own study on the basis from data from the National Court Register (KRS).

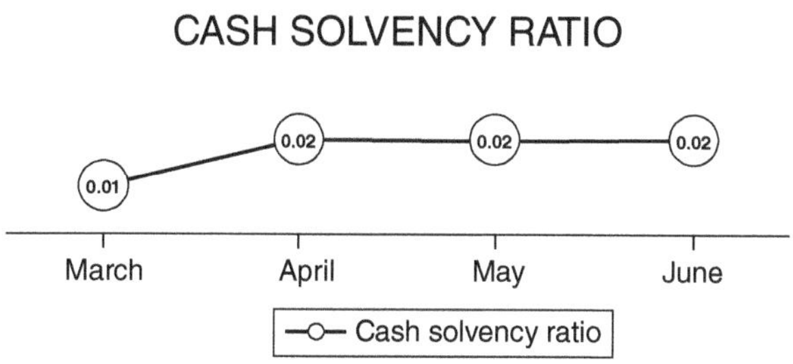

Chart 3.4 Cash solvency ratio's values for the logistics centre during the March–June 2020 period

Source: Own study on the basis from data from the National Court Register (KRS).

values. The proposed model for evaluation of management of a logistics centre under conditions of COVID-19 threats allows for determining compatibility with assumed principles and recommendations included in a subject entity's documentation. Moreover, it will enable comparing functionality of a particular entity to other entities that are similar in terms of their size and field of operations and allow making an evaluation of the efficiency of the proposed analytical and evaluation procedure under conditions of COVID-19 threats.

Conclusions from the study that are of central importance are following:

- the logistics centre did not retire a portion of the car fleet; however, the use of third-party carriers was reduced;
- firms that occupy with trade-in products that were using the logistics centre's services have not only been taking advantage of clients' excessive accumulation of supplies, but they were also making use of their preference to avoid physical contact at retail shops;
- a form of reduction of salaries was employed, yet workers were not made redundant;
- interference in the flow of goods (traffic limits, health inspections) and limits on conducting operations abroad as a result of border closures for logistics centres did not constitute a problem for the analysed logistics centre;
- the centre did not register a decrease in demand for logistics services.

References

Bartosiewicz, S., Oziębło, M. and Zachara, J. (2018). *Centra logistyczne w Polsce: przemiany i rozwój*. Warszawa: Military University of Technology.

Bonow, R.O., Fonarow, G.C., O'Gara, P.T. and Yancy, C.W. (2020). Association of coronavirus disease 2019 (COVID-19) with myocardial injury and mortality. *JAMA Cardiology*, 5(7), 751–753.

Chen, H.L., Chen, W.T. and Lin, Y.L. (2015). Earned value project management: improving the predictive power of planned value. *International Journal of Project Management*, 34, 22–28.

Denniss, A.R., Chow, C.K. and Kritharides, L. (2020), Cardiovascular and logistic issues associated with COVID – 19 pandemic. *Heart, Lung & Circulation*, 29(6), 809–811.

Grzybowska, K. (2010). *Gospodarka zapasami i magazynem cz. 2: zarządzanie magazynem*. Warszawa: Difin.

Guo, T. et al. (2020). Cardiovascular implications of fatal outcomes of patients with coronavirus disease 2019 (COVID-19). *JAMA Cardiology*, 5(7), 811–818.

Handbook of COVID – 19 prevention and treatment (2020). Zhejiang University School of Medicine, www.zju.edu.cn/english/2020/0323/c19573a1987520/page.htm.

Huang, C. et al. (2020). Clinical features of patients infected with 2019 novel Coronavirus in Wuhan. *China Lancet*, 395, 497–506.

Lee, C.K.M., Cao, Y. and Ng, K.K.H. (2017). Big data analytics for predictive maintenance strategies. In Hing Kai, C., Nachiappan, S. and Muhammad Dan-Asabe, A. (Eds.), *Supply chain management in the big data era* (50–74). Hershey: IGI Global.

Lee, C.K.M., Lv, Y., Ng, K.K.H., Ho, W. and Choy, K.L. (2018). Design and application of internet of things based warehouse management system for smart logistics. *International Journal of Production Research*, 56(8), 2753–2768.
Shi, S. et al. (2020). Association of cardiac injury with mortality in hospitalised patients with COVID – 19 in Wuhan, China. *JAMA Cardiology*, 5(7), 802–810.
Zheng, Y., Ma, Y., Zhang, J. and Xie, X. (2020). COVID – 19 and the cardiovascular system. *Nature Reviews Cardiology*, 17, 259–260.

4 Operation of supply chains in the COVID-19 pandemic conditions

Mariusz Gontarczyk, Magdalena Rykała and Jarosław Zelkowski

Introduction

According to its definition, logistics is the process of strategically managing the procurement, movement and storage of materials, parts and finished inventory (and the related information flows) through the organisation and its marketing channels in such a way that current and future profitability are maximised through the cost-effective fulfilment of orders (Christopher, 2016). The wider definition of the optimisation of processes within a supply chain (which also encompass entities in the pipeline such as suppliers and customers) is supply chain management, which is defined as the management of upstream and downstream relationships with suppliers and customers to deliver superior customer value at less cost to the supply chain as a whole (Christopher, 2016). Extending this idea, it has been suggested that a supply chain could more accurately be defined as a network of connected and interdependent organisations mutually and co-operatively working together to control, manage and improve the flow of materials and information from suppliers to end users (Aitken, 1998). Looking at those definitions we must agree that the main goal of supply chain management is providing the end customer with goods under certain conditions. While supply chain management is focused on smooth flow and reducing total costs, the important element of the functioning of the chain is coping with high market volatility and sudden, unpredictable threats sometimes referred to as *resilience*, which is defined as the ability of the supply chain to cope with unexpected disturbances (Christopher, 2016; Scholten, Schilder, 2015). Supply chains which run through many countries on different continents will be the most vulnerable in the event of global disruptions. An example of such a disruption is the COVID-19 pandemic spreading all over the world since the beginning of 2020. On the basis of market observations, the authors of the chapter were tempted to assume that the disruption of the functioning of chains caused by the COVID-19 pandemic has no precedent in modern history and as such significantly differs from threats occurring in everyday operational activities, such as employee absence, failure of the truck or delay in delivery caused by traffic jam, due to the effects it brings to the end customer, and also significantly different from catastrophic threats of different strength and nature such as earthquakes or hurricanes, which have a large impact on the functioning

DOI: 10.4324/9781003285731-4

of many industries, but have usually local character. The threats caused by the COVID-19 pandemic are of a specific nature due to their unpredictability, which means that most of them should be treated more like uncertainty than a risk, in which we are able to determine the effects and probability of occurrence (Ketchen Jr., Craighead, 2020; Esper, 2020; Handfield, Graham, Burns, 2020; Ivanov, Dolgui, 2020; Ivanov, Das, 2020). Due to the global spread of the pandemic, all links in the chain may be at risk of disruption. On example of the February 2020 Volkswagen stoppage, we can observe that even the most efficient supply chain, delivering the product at the lowest cost, can be vulnerable to a sudden drop in market demand (Ashutosh, 2020; Mollenkopf, Ozanne, Stolze, 2020). Also, the most effective and lean supply chain can be suddenly cut off from raw materials by closing mines or the borders of the country from which the raw materials come. A similar situation may apply to virtually every country through which a given chain passes, and the degree of risk in this case can be assumed as proportional to the number of countries, nodes and suppliers of transport services. The situation seems even more complex when we include the time factor. While switching off of the link itself may be preceded by a short announcement, we are not really able to determine when a given link will resume its operation, so we cannot plan the downtime or outage of the respective facility. In case of the pandemic threats proposed by M. Christopher, managing the critical nodes, single supplier, bottlenecks and strategic inventory was not an option due to the unpredictability and extreme volatility of the market and potential threats caused in many cases by the structure of the supply chain itself.

Being aware of the complexity of market processes and the multiplicity of disruption, the authors decided to conduct a simplified analysis of the susceptibility of chains to factors related to epidemic threats. It is a static analysis based on the structure of the chain in a steady state. To solve the research problem, in the next consecutive stages, factors that may affect the chain stability were identified, aggregated into respective categories and then introduced into the fuzzy logic model assuming a positive or negative impact of individual factors on chain sensitivity. The model created based on certain assumptions and limitations can be tested and verified during further research on real chains and will constitute the basis for forecasts and decisions regarding the chain structure.

Assumptions and limitations of the model

The classic model of risk identification should focus on potential threats – events that may occur at certain stages of the analysed chain. It was assumed that it is not possible to define all the events affecting a given chain and their level of probability, or in other words, there are infinitely many of these events. Determining the level of impact of events and their probability depends on data, most of which is not available, which means that we have more uncertainties than risks. Additionally, some of threats are so rare that there is no basis whatsoever to determine their probability, not even to conceptualise them (Bradley, 2014). An additional difficulty is determining which of the events occur simultaneously (here the Monte

Carlo model could be applied, if we have identified all threats, including opportunities). Therefore, it was concluded that a better solution would be to determine the sensitivity of the chain based on its general structure and the tendency of the influence of individual factors on the sensitivity in each category, i.e. make a strategic model. In the model, we consider the general structure of the chain and its elements. The analysis is static, so the basis is the current structure of supply chain and operating conditions. Consecutive iterations of the analysis can be made based on changes of the factors in the steady state.

To the general model of disruption, threats were introduced originating from phenomena typically associated with the COVID-19 pandemic, assuming that the waves predicted in the near future will force us to analyse the susceptibility of the respective supply chains again and again.

The analysis covers the structure of classic relations in the supply chain of a manufacturing enterprise.

These factors are input data that influence the increase of susceptibility of the chain in each category. For example, greater commonality of the raw material causes the susceptibility resulting from the raw material category to be lower. The model encompasses a limited number of factors in each category, assuming that the model can be extended during further analyses. Considering the unpredictability and volatility of the market, it can be assumed that even the deepest analysis of factors does not cover the entire spectrum of categories, factors and threats.

The following categories of factors were selected for the analysis: raw materials, components, suppliers, facilities, location, transportation and customer demand. The individual categories as well as the factors in the selected categories do not drain all the factors affecting chain stability. Factors often overlap, which sometimes strengthens the threats coming from individual categories. For example, threats resulting from the location of sub-suppliers in a distant country may exist in the suppliers, location, transportation or components category, which in fact reflects the actual threats. In many cases, we deal with a situation in which many threats result from one source, and one threat results from several sources, which is characteristic of complex systems.

Raw materials

Ensuring the continuity of supplies of raw materials is of key importance for any manufacturing company. The key importance of continuity of supplies can be observed in logistic systems operating with a strong emphasis on cost reduction – such as "lean philosophy". An example of such systems is the just-in-time production system, which reduces production inventories to a minimum or replaces many suppliers of raw materials with one assumed to be reliable. In this case, any disruption typical for a pandemic, such as border closure or a temporary downtime at a single supplier site would result in the unavailability of raw material, and thus a production disruption. The commonality of the raw material, in turn, is a feature which, in some cases, e.g. when supplies from a single supplier are disrupted, allows the possibility of ordering a substitute from the other suppliers.

In unexpected lockdown situations, commonality will be crucial to restore continuity of production. Commonality should not be confused with availability. Even a resource as common as crude oil may become temporarily unavailable due to reasons such as embargoes. An important factor in case of pandemic threats will be the price of the raw materials, or rather its fluctuations. Although prices are usually rising, it is not so obvious in the case of pandemic threats. At the beginning of 2020, decline in freight and passenger transport resulted in a drop of crude oil prices. In principle, increase in raw material prices will have a negative impact on demand and the related business continuity.

Components

As in the case of raw materials, the supplies of components necessary for production can also make the supply chain more susceptible to common pandemic threats. The more unique the design and production technology, the more vulnerable we are to the negative effects of disruptions. In the past, short power outages in elaborate technologies cases repeatedly led to significantly longer production downtimes. The contamination in semiconductor production at Samsung in recent years is a good example (Anton, 2018; *Minute-long power outage at samsung plant damages millions worth DRAM and NAND*, 2020). In addition to the production technology, the complexity of the product is an important factor. In the case of the automotive products, the lack of at least one of a thousand parts may result in a production outage or disruption of production plan. Due to the fact that a significant part of the production of components takes place in different regions of the world, any unplanned stop in the suppliers' production and transport companies will be of key importance for the continuity of production of goods with a high degree of complexity (Joyce, Hyunjoo, 2020). Alternative suppliers of components, as in case of raw materials, are of a great importance. Having emergency suppliers has often determined many world leaders (Gain, Dunn, 2000). The alternative sub-suppliers also allow us to become independent from temporary supply problems in the event of disruptions related to pandemic threats.

Suppliers

Appropriate relationships with suppliers are an important element of the stability of the supply chain. With all kinds of internal and external conflicts, fierce competition on the market may put the stability of suppliers into question. This phenomenon is very complex in itself because suppliers are often companies operating on a similar scale with their own suppliers, customers and competitors. External conflicts regarding the sharing of the market, patents and lawsuits are typical examples affecting stability of operation. There are also internal conflicts caused, for example, by cultural differences (Górnikiewicz, Gontarczyk, Zelkowski, 2019). Another factor influencing the stability of the chain is the financial situation of suppliers, which may adversely affect supplies. It should be noted that financial stability will be exceptionally dynamic and, in many cases, may result from a pandemic outbreak or significantly worsen because of it. Therefore, the baseline for the analysis should be a situation from before the outbreak. The communication with suppliers is strictly connected with complexity of the supply chain. The complex global supply chains running through different time and climate zones accompanied by cultural diversity are the hallmark of the widespread offshoring trend (Górnikiewicz, Gontarczyk, Zelkowski, 2019; Mudambi, Venzin, 2010).

Facilities

The internal situation of the company has a significant impact on the stability in case of any disruption, and internal problems directly affect the quality of the processes in the company. In case of epidemic threats, human resources and their availability certainly play a key role. The availability of employees and management is important regarding the company's stability and is also related to the location in areas with high or low unemployment and proximity of large urban areas. The epidemic situation will certainly aggravate the problem of the availability of specialists and workers. Relationships between management and employees are also important, and conflicts in this area may cause further threats. Internal conflicts may arise from differences in the perception of the interests of the company and employees, as well as the work culture in case we have employees from different countries and cultures (Górnikiewicz, Gontarczyk, Zelkowski, 2019). In addition to the human factor, the company's infrastructure also plays an important role. Stable, modern and well-protected infrastructure reduces the risk of fires and any other events caused by environmental or human factors. Modern facilities also mean less damage, less maintenance and inspections, which may be difficult to perform in a pandemic.

Location

The location of the business is critical to the operation of the supply chain. The basic criteria used by companies in this case are typical for offshoring, the cost of purchase or manufacture, while the costs connected to the extension of the route and lead times are often underestimated (Christopher, 2016). Threats which are often underrated are the location of production facilities and transportation nodes in the areas of natural disasters. The extension of supply routes also means a greater vulnerability of the supply chains to strikes, social unrest or armed conflicts occurring in different geographic regions, as well as potential outbreaks of infectious diseases. On the other hand, what prompts companies to offshore production is supporting policy of the local authorities, infrastructure development, tax incentives or relief in case of sudden unexpected events. Regardless of the potential profits, the location of production and transportation nodes will play a key role in a pandemic emergency.

Transportation

All goods are transported at some point in their life cycle. Therefore, efficient and reliable transport will be a key process that will ensure the continuity of the supply chain, and thus customer demand will be met. The problem that most often occurs in complex supply chains is the lack of control over its individual stages because we do not own the entire chain. Long-distance transport is often carried out by container ships and by specialised companies for which we are one of a thousand of customers. In most cases, transportation is outsourced, which makes us entirely dependent on the reliability of external transport companies. The mode of transport also has a huge impact on the continuity of the supply chain. When transporting by different modes, whether by land, air or sea, a short stoppage of air traffic is enough to paralyse the entire chain. Likewise, the number of transportation nodes through which a given chain passes leads to a greater risk of disruption of the flow of supplies. In a pandemic, local stoppage or a decrease in the intensity of processes may occur at each transportation node – port, terminal or warehouse.

Customer demand

An important part of the analysis is the introduction of the market demand category. In the event of a pandemic threat, it is the sudden and unpredictable drop in demand that is important for the stability of the supply chain. In case of the large number of customers of the final product, a sudden introduction of quarantine or disruption of activity in a respective area may also result in loss of the number of customers, and significant stocks at the downstream of the chain may become a high operational burden for the company. This is less important in case of having multiple distribution channels such as direct sales or e-shopping. Having a variety of distribution channels of sale is certainly an advantage; however, also important is the ability to quickly switch our sale to e-shopping as a primary channel, which relates to quick employment of additional well-qualified staff. It should also be noted that not all goods are equally susceptible to e-sales, although experience shows that even the car industry has made great progress in this regard. A characteristic reaction of the customers observed in pandemic is the reduction of expenses on exclusive goods, or more precisely those that are not everyday goods, regardless of whether the basis for this type of behaviour is of an economic nature. Of course, the rising demand for everyday goods or goods of basics needs may also result in the supply chain deregulation (Bull Whip Effect), but it can be assumed that the temporary shortages in the retail market are less harmful for the company than a long-term decrease in sales.

In the subsequent stage of the research, the identified factors in each category were analysed in terms of their positive or negative impact on the susceptibility of the supply chain to pandemic disruption threats.

Fuzzy logic in analysis of supply chain susceptibility

As mentioned before, the primary role of logistics is to keep the continuity of supplies. In January 2020, in the report prepared by DHL Resilience360 entitled "The Novel Coronavirus: Impact on Supply Chain Operations amid the Lunar New Year" (Wilding, Dohrmann, Wheatley, 2020), it was assumed that the outbreak of the pandemic would cause serious disruptions not only in transport but also at every stage of the supply chain. At the beginning of March 2020, most European countries set up the lockdown. Restaurants were closed, air traffic was suspended, international road transport had difficulties at the borders and was struggling with a reduced number of orders, while employees were assigned to work remotely. Many industries suffered, and the introduced legal regulations and restrictions related to the number of people per 1 m^2 and, among others, the 2-meter distance between employees, resulted in a sudden reorganisation of the activities of enterprises (production, distribution and trade). It is estimated that around one million automotive (DHL – Post-Coronavirus Supply Chain Recovery) workers have been made redundant in Europe. The resilience of supply chains has been put to the test; thus business operations must be transformed in the short and long term, as they must be adapted not only operationally but also strategically.

To determine the susceptibility of the supply chain to disruptions caused by epidemic-nature threats, selected elements of the supply chain have been analysed (for each category three factors, as the input data has been assigned constituting the assumptions for building a fuzzy logic model).

Fuzzy systems are used where there is insufficient knowledge about the mathematical model governing a given phenomenon and where creating such a model becomes unprofitable or even impossible (Brzezinski et al., 2017; Kijek, Rykała, Zelkowski, 2019). To develop the model, identified factors were analysed in terms of determining their impact on the stability of the supply chain.

To develop the fuzzy model, the input factors must be determined as stimulants or destimulants. Stimulants are variables which when increasing cause the increasing of the value of the dependent variable (positive correlation), while the increase of destimulant values affect the output data negatively (negative correlation) (Table 4.1). For example, in the Suppliers category a higher number of internal or external conflicts increases the chain's vulnerability to disruptions, while in the Facilities category a greater number of available employees undoubtedly has a negative impact on destabilisation, i.e. the chain is less prone to disruptions. Translating this into the COVID-19 situation, we say that many infected or quarantined employees or potential employees may cause the outage of the respective link.

The use of fuzzy logic allows modelling of complex systems indirectly by modelling their individual components, i.e. subsystems. It results from the necessity to determine the exponentially increasing number of rules, increasing with the number of system inputs. In an analysed case, dividing the system into seven fuzzy models makes it possible to describe in detail the phenomena occurring in each subsystem. Then the subsystems should be connected by introducing inference elements whose purpose is the final assessment of the impact of individual inputs on the entire system. The discussed result was obtained by applying a weighted average from the outputs of individual subsystems. It is a consequence of the observation that the sensitivity of the system to the outputs of individual subsystems is varied, which requires taking it into account when modelling. The outputs from individual subsystems are treated as partial results, which, after

Table 4.1 Stimulant and destimulant analysis

ID	*Factor/Input to the system*	*Trend*	*Category/ /Subsystem*	*Susceptibility*
A1	Availability	↑	Raw materials	↓
A2	Commonality	↑		↓
A3	Price	↑		↑
B1	Technology	↑	Components	↑
B2	Complexity	↑		↑
B3	Alternative sources	↑		↓
C1	Conflicts	↑	Suppliers	↑
C2	Finances	↑		↓
C3	Communication	↑		↓
D1	Human resources	↑	Facilities	↓
D2	Internal relations	↑		↓
D3	Facility construction	↑		↓
E1	Location (disaster area)	↑	Location	↑
E2	Social unrest	↑		↑
E3	Support policy	↑		↓
F1	Transportation provider	↑	Transportation	↑
F2	Number of transportation modes	↑		↓
F3	Transition nodes	↑		↓
G1	Number of customers	↑	Customer demand	↓
G2	Number of distribution channels	↑		↓
G3	Exclusiveness	↑		↑

Source: Own study.

considering the weights, are summed up and constitute the final rating of the system (Figure 4.1).

Each of the mentioned fuzzy models has three inputs (in the standardised range [0, 1]) with triangular/trapezoidal membership functions, which were selected due to their universal application and lower computational complexity than Gaussian functions. The implemented subsystems are Takagi-Sugeno (T-S) models, which in turn were selected due to the "sharp" nature of the outputs, as opposed to the Mamdani models. In case of outputs in T-S models, linear functions or constant values are used. The proposed solution uses the second option, i.e. three characteristic constants: 0 – decrease (sensitivity decreases), 0.5 – neutral (no change), 1 – increase (sensitivity increases) (Figure 4.2). After designing the architecture of fuzzy models (inputs, membership functions, outputs), sets of rules (about 180 in total) were defined based on expert knowledge supported by an in-depth analysis of the state of the problem.

To determine the weights for individual subsystems, an expert survey was carried out among the logistics employees of individual supply cells. On their basis, the method of arranging objects by features (the so-called Bord's conduct) was used. The key is to select the "most favourable" object (the highest value of indications) and the "least favourable" (the smallest number of indications assigned). Table 4.2 presents an analysis of the criteria priorities. On its basis, the average weights of the final stage of processing categories (Chart 4.1) were determined.

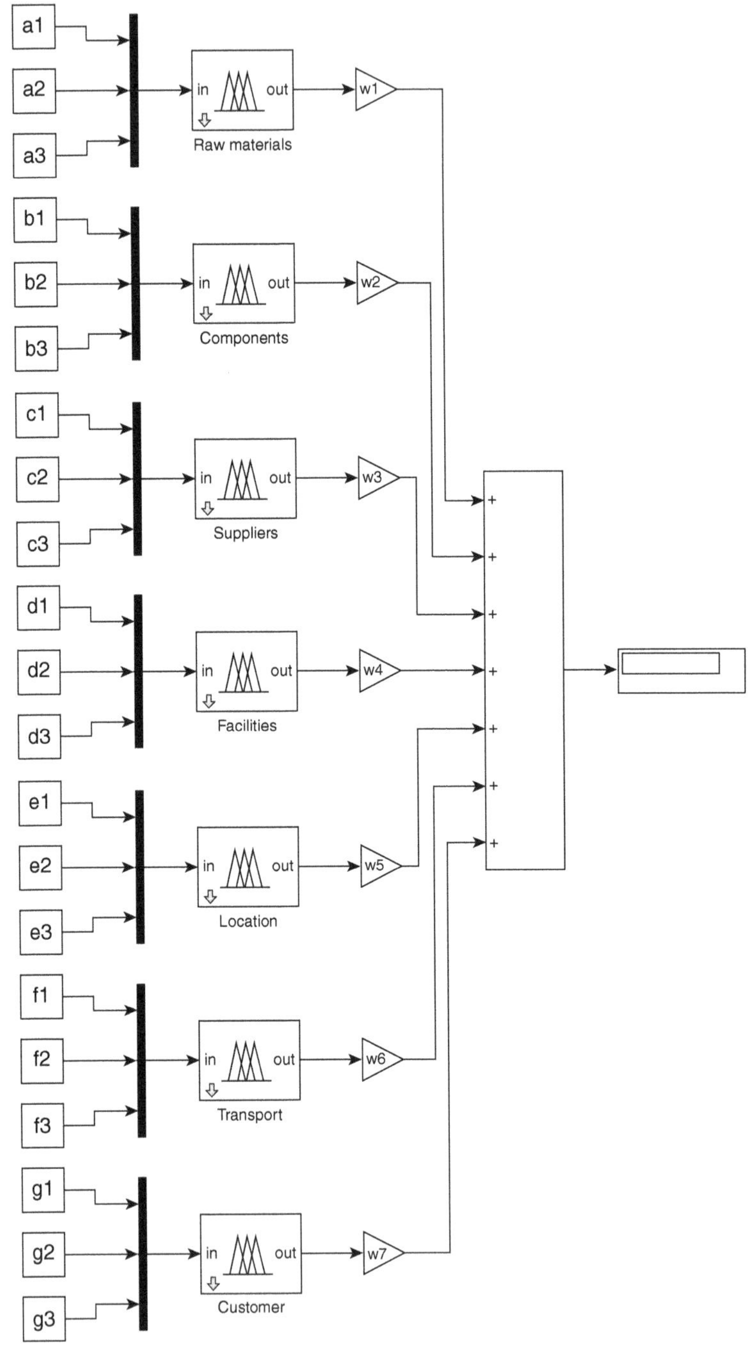

Figure 4.1 Simulink model of the system

Source: Own study.

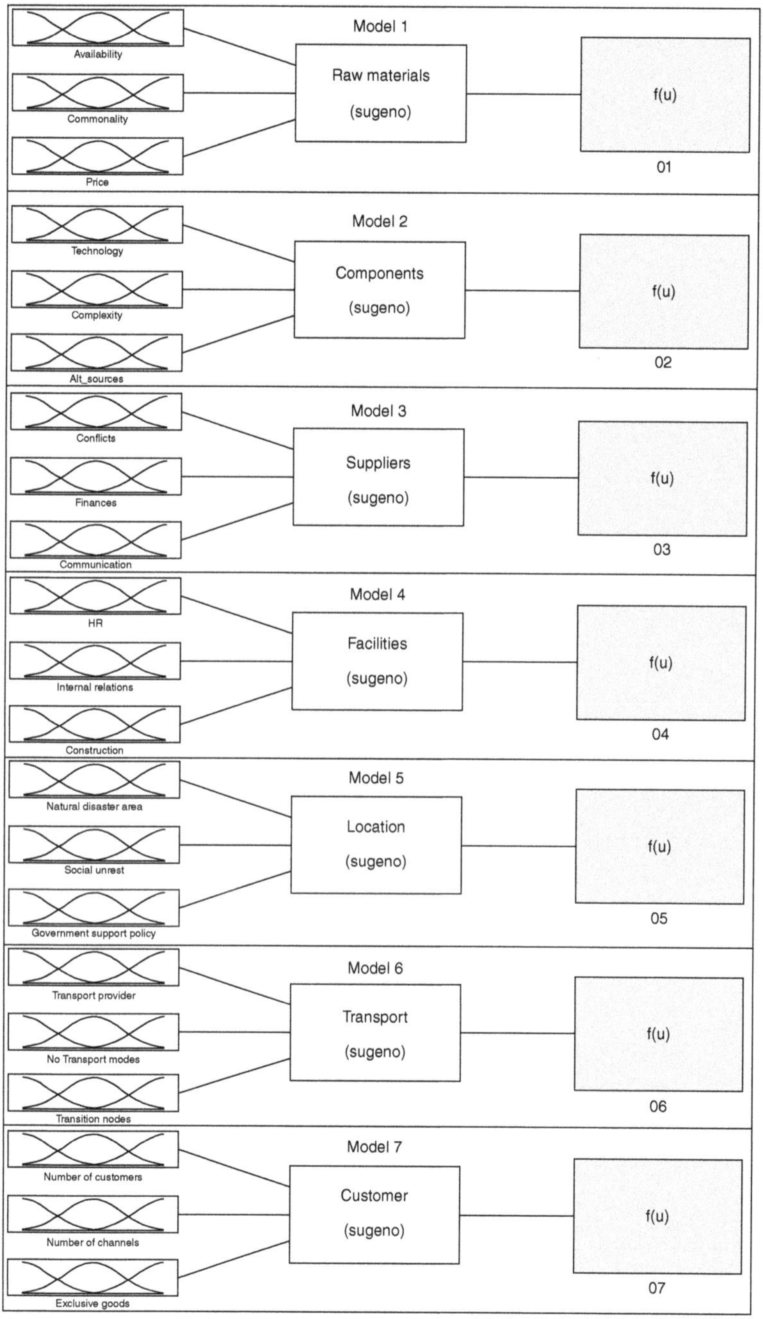

Figure 4.2 The architecture of fuzzy models 1–7 created in Fuzzy Logic Toolbox

Source: Own study.

Table 4.2 Analysis of criteria priorities

	Raw materials	*Components*	*Suppliers*	*Facilities*	*Location*	*Transport*	*Customer*	*Number of indications*	*Priority of importance*
Raw materials	(–)	1	3	4	5	6	1	2	3
Components	(–)	(–)	3	4	5	6	2	1	4
Suppliers	(–)	(–)	(–)	3	5	6	3	4	2
Facilities	(–)	(–)	(–)	(–)	5	6	7	2	3
Location	(–)	(–)	(–)	(–)	(–)	5	7	5	1
Transport	(–)	(–)	(–)	(–)	(–)	(–)	6	5	1
Customer	(–)	(–)	(–)	(–)	(–)	(–)	(–)	2	3

Source: Own study.

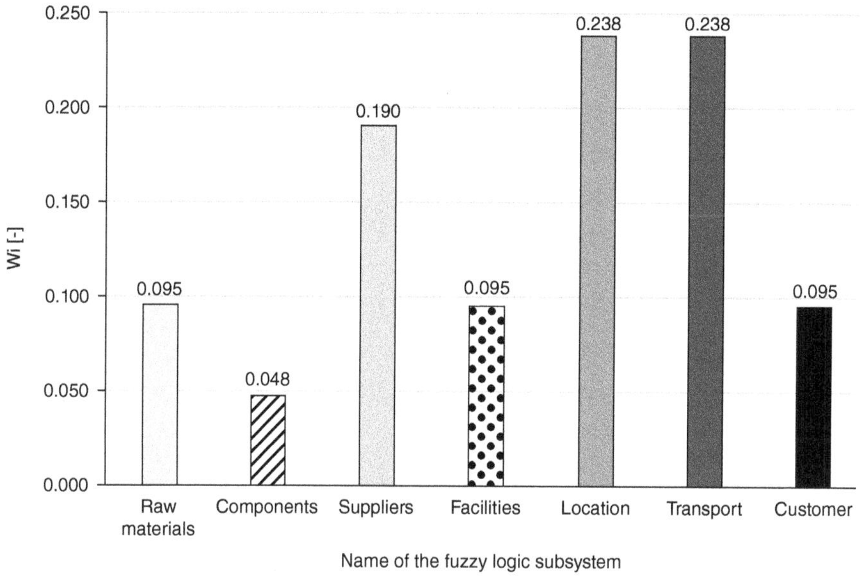

Chart 4.1 Weights of the fuzzy logic models

Source: Own study.

Based on the obtained results, the most important system is Location and Transport (five indications each), which translates into a weight value equal to 0.238. On the other hand, the lowest number of indications (and thus 4th place in the ranking of criteria priorities) was awarded to the Components model, with a weight of 0.048.

All presented models and calculations were made in the Matlab/Simulink software with the use of Fuzzy Logic Toolbox.

Discussion

To verify the developed model, three scenarios were prepared. The expected result of the model is to obtain values similar to the system outputs – three characteristic constants: 0 – decrease (sensitivity decreases), 0.5 – neutral (no change), 1 – increase (sensitivity increases). The purpose of this test is to compare chain behaviour under different scenarios. For this purpose, input values are presented for each entry in the supply chain. Scenario 1 assumes an optimistic variant, where we cannot observe any disturbances in the system (Chart 4.2). The situation presents, among others, the variant in which the raw material is characterised by high availability and commonality, where there is no problem with employees, the location of individual links in the supply chains is not in the area of natural disasters and there is no phenomenon of social unrest. Scenario 2 assumes slight system disturbances (Chart 4.3). In turn, scenario 3 assumes a pessimistic variant

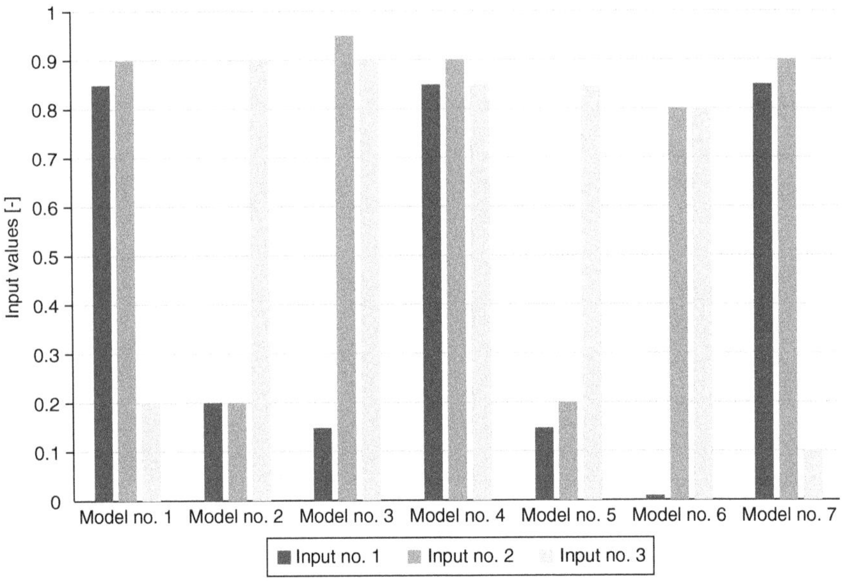

Chart 4.2 Scenario 1 – the optimistic variant

Source: Own study.

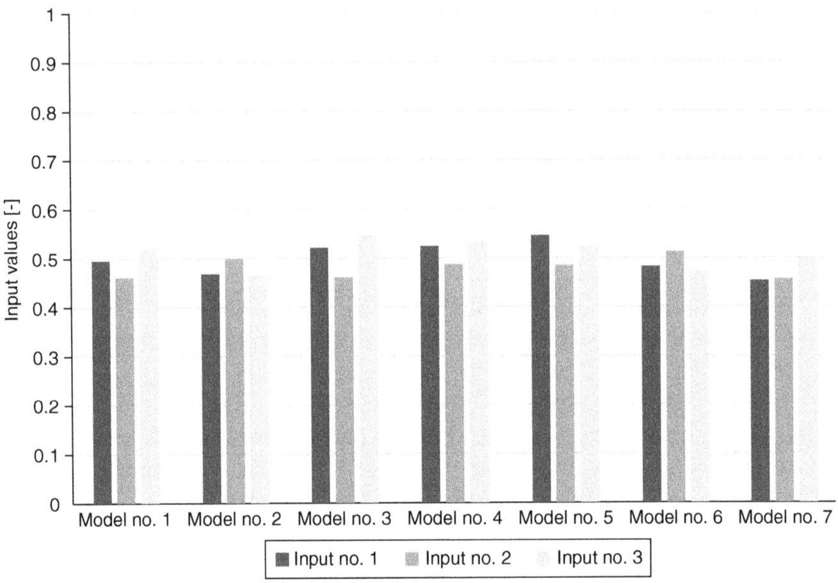

Chart 4.3 Scenario 2 – variant with slight disturbance

Source: Own study.

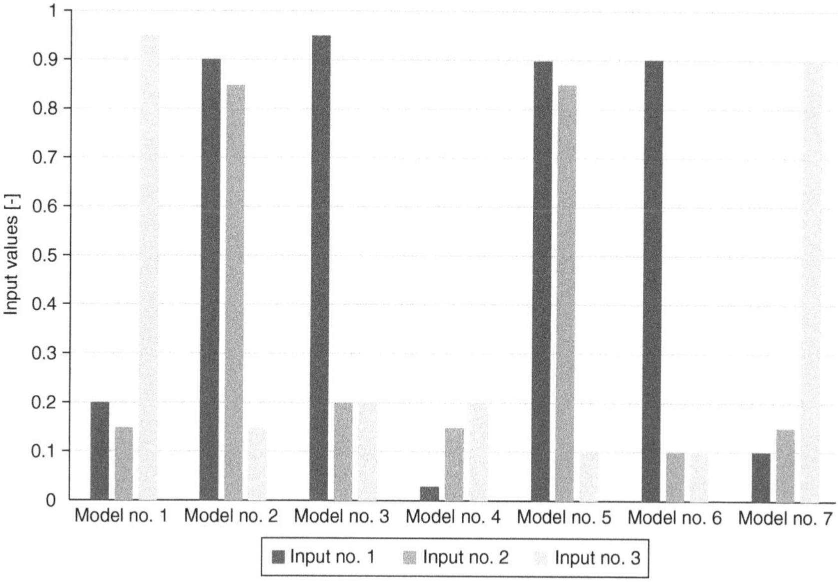

Chart 4.4 Scenario 3 – pessimistic variant (e.g. COVID-19 pandemic)

Source: Own study.

(e.g. epidemic state) where disruptions occur at each stage of the supply chain (Chart 4.4).

Based on the simulations, the model was verified. The assumed input values of the individual scenarios (Charts: 4.2, 4.3, 4.4) were put into the model and the final outputs of respective scenarios are presented in Chart 4.5. We can observe that in case of scenario 1, the final result is approximately 0.23; in the case of scenario 2, it is approximately 0.5; and in the case of scenario 3, it is approximately 0.75.

The obtained results confirm the accuracy of the proposed model: the score within the range [0, 0.25] indicates a decrease in sensitivity; the score of about 0.5 indicates no change in sensitivity; a score within the range [0.75, 1] indicates increased sensitivity of the chain.

Conclusions

The number and frequency of disruptions undoubtedly affect the normal functioning and stability of supply chains (Carvalho et al., 2011). By increasing the number of negative impacts, the chains lose their full capacity to meet needs. One poorly prospering link can contribute to the disruption of the entire chain, so it is necessary to look for solutions that will eliminate their weaknesses and effectively react to the negative effects of disruptions. The article identifies potential factors

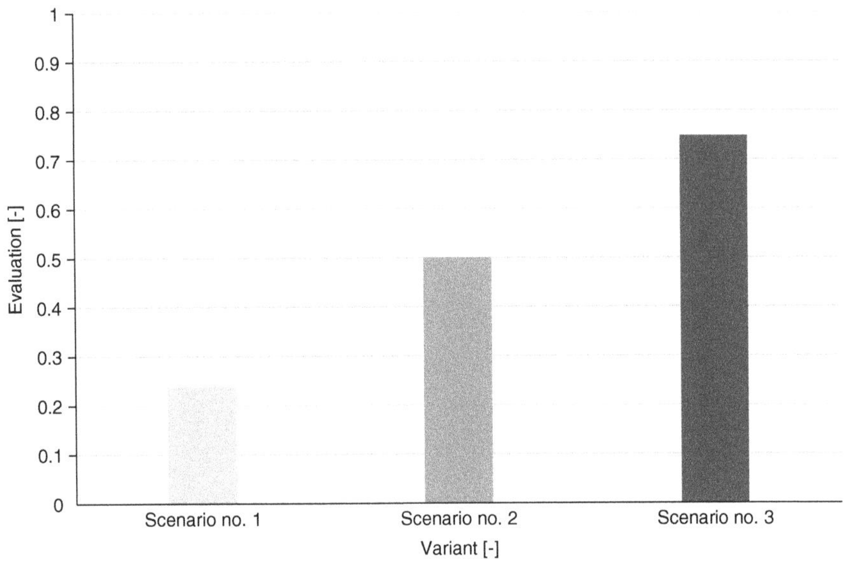

Chart 4.5 Results of scenarios 1–3

Source: Own study.

affecting chain stability, with particular emphasis on epidemiological disorders (e.g. COVID-19). In addition, threats were categorised to provide input to a fuzzy logic supply chain behaviour model. The model was built of seven subsystems (categories), each of them with three factors (inputs). An analysis of the importance (Bord's procedure) of individual subsystems was performed based on an expert survey conducted among employees of the logistics industry.

The proposed model was verified using three scenarios: the optimistic variant, the slightly disturbed variant and the pessimistic variant (e.g. the COVID-19 pandemic). The obtained results confirm the accuracy of the proposed solution. The authors proposed three of the most important sets of inputs to each subsystem. The direction of further research may be an extension of the proposed model and its validation, taking into consideration more factors and data due to current observation of pandemic developments and its impact on real supply chains.

The world after the coronavirus will not be the same. People's everyday lives will change, and their consumer behaviour will also change. Therefore, to achieve business success in such a difficult time, it is essential to evaluate supply chains for greater resilience, flexibility and reliability (Pettit, Croxton, Fiksel, 2019). The use of new innovative technologies, such as robotics and automation, IoT or the analysis of data using the innovative tools and models may be key to salvation (Grzelak, Zdunek, 2017; Typiak, Rykała, 2018).

References

Aitken, J. (1998). *Supply chain integration within the context of a supplier association: case studies of four supplier associations*, http://dspace.lib.cranfield.ac.uk/handle/1826/9990.

Anton, S. (2018). *Power outage at Samsung's fab destroys 3.5% of global NAND flash output for March*, www.anandtech.com.

Ashutosh, P. (2020). *Coronavirus keeps VW's China factories shut*, www.dw.com/en.

Bradley, J.R. (2014). An improved method for managing catastrophic supply chain disruptions. *Business Horizons*, 57(4), 483–495.

Brzezinski, M. et al. (2017). Fuzzy modeling of evaluation logistic systems. *Proceedings of the 21th International Conference, Transport Means*, 377–382.

Carvalho, H. et al. (2011). Supply chain resilience: a simulation study. *Annals of DAAAM & Proceedings*, https://scholar.google.com/citations?view_op=view_citation&hl=tr&user=7knmm8YAAAAJ&citation_for_view=7knmm8YAAAAJ:9yKSN-GCB0IC.

Christopher, M. (2016). *Logistics & supply chain management*. London: Pearson.

Esper, T.L. (2020). Supply chain management amid the coronavirus pandemic. *Journal of Public Policy & Marketing*, 40(1), 101–102.

Gain, B. and Dunn, D. (2000). Nokia stays firmly on the path while its competitors stumble. *Electronic Buyers' News*, 1235, 4–5.

Górnikiewicz, M., Gontarczyk, M. and Zelkowski, J. (2019). Zarządzanie ryzykiem w logistyce w warunkach różnic kulturowych. *Gospodarka Materiałowa i Logistyka*, 5(CD), 783–793.

Grzelak, M. and Zdunek, P. (2017). Process optimization of order fulfillment. *Systemy Logistyczne Wojsk*, 46, 68–77.

Handfield, R.B., Graham, G. and Burns, L. (2020). Corona virus, tariffs, trade wars and supply chain evolutionary design. *International Journal of Operations & Production Management*, https://eprints.whiterose.ac.uk/161923/1/PDF_Proof%20%282%29.PDF.

Ivanov, D. and Das, A. (2020). Coronavirus (COVID-19/SARS-CoV-2) and supply chain resilience: a research note. *International Journal of Integrated Supply Management*, 13(1), 90–102.

Ivanov, D. and Dolgui, A. (2020). Viability of intertwined supply networks: extending the supply chain resilience angles towards survivability. A position paper motivated by COVID-19 outbreak. *International Journal of Production Research*, 58(10), 2904–2915.

Joyce, L. and Hyunjoo, J. (2020). *Hyundai to halt South Korea output as China virus disrupts parts supply*, www.reuters.com.

Ketchen, Jr., D.J. and Craighead, C.W. (2020). Research at the intersection of entrepreneurship, supply chain management, and strategic management: opportunities highlighted by COVID-19. *Journal of Management*, 46(8), 1330–1341.

Kijek, M., Rykała, Ł. and Zelkowski, J. (2019). Rozmyta metoda wyboru kierowcy do realizacji zadań transportowych. *Gospodarka Materiałowa i Logistyka*, 5, 15–24.

Minute-long power outage at samsung plant damages millions worth DRAM and NAND (2020). www.techpowerup.com.

Mollenkopf, D.A., Ozanne, L.K. and Stolze, H.J. (2020). A transformative supply chain response to COVID-19. *Journal of Service Management*, 32(2), 190–202.

Mudambi, R. and Venzin, M. (2010). The strategic nexus of offshoring and outsourcing decisions. *Journal of Management Studies*, 47(8), 1510–1533.

Pettit, T.J., Croxton, K.L. and Fiksel, J. (2019). The evolution of resilience in supply chain management: a retrospective on ensuring supply chain resilience. *Journal of Business Logistics*, 40(1), 56–65.

Scholten, K. and Schilder, S. (2015). The role of collaboration in supply chain resilience. *Supply Chain Management: An International Journal*, 20(4), 471–484.

Typiak, A. and Rykała, Ł. (2018). Research of an omnidirectional mecanum-wheeled platform with a fuzzy logic controller. *Journal of Kones*, 25(1), 423–432.

Wilding, R., Dohrmann, K. and Wheatley, M. (2020). *Report post-coronavirus supply chain recovery: a DHL perspective on the impact of the COVID-19 pandemic on supply chains and logistics*, www.dhl.com/content/dam/dhl/global/core/documents/pdf/glo-core-post-covid-eme-white-paper.pdf.

5 Material inventory management during the COVID-19 pandemic

Paweł Ślaski

Introduction

There is no need to convince anyone in Poland or the rest of the world about the need to maintain inventories of selected goods. The recent difficult time of the COVID-19 pandemic and the epidemic state that has been introduced is a clear sign of this. The shortage of medical supplies to prevent the spread of the virus, especially surgical masks, overalls, protective gloves, disinfectants and respirators indicates the urgent need for systemic changes in the management of these items. However, it should be noted that the scale of the current crisis is unprecedented in present times, and even the best-developed contingency plans and system changes may prove inadequate. The pandemic makes it clear that in times of crisis it is difficult to make rational decisions in the form of finding alternative suppliers or implementing new processes. However, it is certain that companies will try to implement their risk mitigation tools before any disruption occurs in the supply chain.

Shortages of goods are only some of the consequences of the global disruption of the supply chain caused by the COVID-19 pandemic visible for consumers. Disruptions in the flow of products may result from a lack of workers in the logistics industry, but they may also be a consequence of government action, such as restrictions on the unloading of goods at seaports or suspension of air transport.

Economics experts believe that the pandemic has motivated many companies to find solutions that can become permanent practice over time. One of them is increased e-commerce. It generates demand for logistics services, which in turn requires facilities for storage, order picking and distribution of goods to customers. The experts also identified the key actions that will shape the economy during the pandemic. These include:

1 gathering optimal inventory – companies need to stock their goods and components, so the main focus is on supply chain resilience;
2 the spread of the e-commerce industry – the increase in purchases over the internet creates a demand for warehouses serving e-commerce. The owners of online shops will locate the goods closer to the recipients and thus shorten the delivery time.

DOI: 10.4324/9781003285731-5

Objective and test methods

The objective of this chapter is to develop a model for the control of material stocks, the assumptions and structure which are in line with the current situation of the crisis related to the COVID-19 pandemic. The following research methods and tools were used:

- modelling in compliance with the BPMN notation;
- process analysis;
- inventory management model (optimal production batch).

The research concerned the possibility of using BPMN modelling and selected optimisation methods and tools to develop a model of inventory management in a crisis. The study also included an analysis and evaluation of supply chain disruptions mainly related to delays in the execution of orders, accumulation of surplus inventories and supply shortages.

A novelty in the publication is the mapping of the supply chain using BPMN modelling and the application of classical methods of inventory optimisation. Companies that invest in such solutions benefit in the event of disruption because they can make an efficient analysis of the impact of a given phenomenon on the supply chain in the coming days or weeks. When companies know where the disruption will come from and which products will be affected by the disruption, they have time to immediately implement strategies to avoid these risks and mitigate their effects by, for example, purchasing or controlling the distribution of inventories.

Analysis of the global supply chain during the COVID-19 pandemic based on the example of Amazon UK

The United Kingdom is Europe's largest and the world's third-largest e-commerce channel retail market. Already in 2019, sales in this channel reached 21% of total organised retail sales. According to a report by Edge by Ascential, 97% of the inhabitants of the British Isles have access to the internet, which equals 66 million people. It is the largest European online population after Germany. Up to 78.6% of the country's population can be easily reached with digital content, as daily web use has become the norm in all age groups. Penetration of the e-commerce market is progressing rapidly in such an environment. In 2014, this channel generated 13% of the total revenues of organised retail, and in 2019 it was 20.9%, which is about $101 billion. By 2024, online sales will already account for about 25.5% of total retail sales. UK's online retail will progressively take market shares away from stationary retail, supported by the operation of leading pure play players (trading only online) who are expanding their own range of products into further categories, developing marketplace sales platforms for other companies. Online sales in the British Isles will continue to be based on the 1P model (first party – selling only products from their own offer), which is used by both Amazon and the largest retail chains: Sainsbury's, Tesco, Walmart and John Lewis. In 2019, the 1P model accounted for 69.4% of total sales in the e-commerce channel wiadomoscihandlowe.pl (report from 31.10.2019).

As a result of the COVID-19 pandemic, global supply chains have undergone major changes. Companies dependent on global sourcing have faced difficult crisis management choices due to supply chain disruptions. A bright example of the company's functioning under the conditions of the COVID-19 pandemic is Amazon – a giant of the global e-commerce market. Amazon is the UK's market leader in e-commerce, and it accounted for 30.1% of total sales in 2019 at $30.4 billion (Table 5.1).

Amazon, which runs the world's largest online store, started to accumulate and increase stocks as early as February 2020 to prevent problems that could arise from the spread of the coronavirus. It provided suppliers with five additional days to send products to its warehouses and stated that it waived charges for late deliveries. At the same time Amazon contacted Chinese suppliers and placed "last-minute" orders to replenish inventories of the goods produced there. The company has abandoned late delivery surcharges, which was a good strategy to secure the supply chain, especially since about 40% of its products come from wholesale suppliers, and most of them use factories in China.

Amazon has also informed its customers that they may have to wait longer for their orders, and some popular household items have run out due to excess orders for basic everyday items. Delays in delivery also affected orders placed by customers using the Amazon Prime same-day delivery service, used by more than 150 million users worldwide. After the lockdown, Amazon invested $1.5 billion in the development of the same-day delivery service, improving warehouse operations, among other things. It tries to meet the logistical challenge and supply chain disruptions, even though some factories in China and other countries are stopping production. Amazon has taken additional precautions in logistics centres – it has increased the frequency of disinfection of loading and unloading points and warehouses. It also changed the validity of shipments. Priority is given to orders

Table 5.1 Gross e-commerce sales in the UK in 2019 in billions of USD

No.	*United Kingdom Gross e-commerce sales in 2019 [billions of USD]*	
1	Amazon	30.4
2	eBay	9.8
3	Sainsbury's	4.6
4	Tesco	4.5
5	Walmart	3.9
6	John Levis	3.6

Source: Own study based on wiadomoscihandlowe.pl (Report, 2019).

related to household goods, as well as medical and other products for which there is a high demand.

COVID-19 pandemic material inventory management model

The presented analysis and evaluation of the e-commerce industry based on the example of Amazon UK allowed the author to develop a model for the management of material inventory in the global supply chain during the pandemic. The key elements of this model are measures to ensure that the optimal size of material resources is determined at each stage of the flow of goods in the supply chains to protect the public against COVID-19. The structure of the model should also be considered from an economic point of view, especially as the global economy during the lockdown period was severely affected by the immobilisation of production and the closure of factories, shops, shopping centres and other public facilities.

Assumptions and structure of the model

The model was developed in compliance with the BPMN notation, which is a standard developed by the Object Management Group (OMG). The purpose of the notation is to provide information to describe business (logistics) processes in a manner that is transparent and understandable both for the company's strategists and analysts and the programmers responsible for IT support and technical implementation. A special feature of the BPMN notation is its universality. As a standard used to describe processes, it is recognised by many organisations in Poland and worldwide and is present in most of the modelling tools and practically all BPMSs (Business Process Management System) available on the market (Drejewicz, 2017).

Model structure

The proposed model consists of two stages. The first one consists of an analysis and assessment of supply chain disruptions. The second concerns the proposal to improve inventory management in pandemic conditions (Figure 5.1).

The first stage of disruption included three dynamic phenomena destabilising the sustainable supply chain, i.e.: Forrester (bullwhip), Burbidge and Houlihan effect (Miłosz, Miłosz, 2014).

The Forrester effect, also known as the bullwhip effect, consists in transferring changes in delivery volumes resulting from structure and dynamic properties and from ineffective ordering strategies. In the processes of information and material planning, due to inappropriate algorithms for controlling inventory levels (safety stock), excessive inventory volumes are accumulated, which generate excessive maintenance costs. The impact of stockpiling depends on the size of the company; larger companies seem to be more vulnerable due to a centralised purchasing strategy, better inventory control and a diverse supply base. For smaller

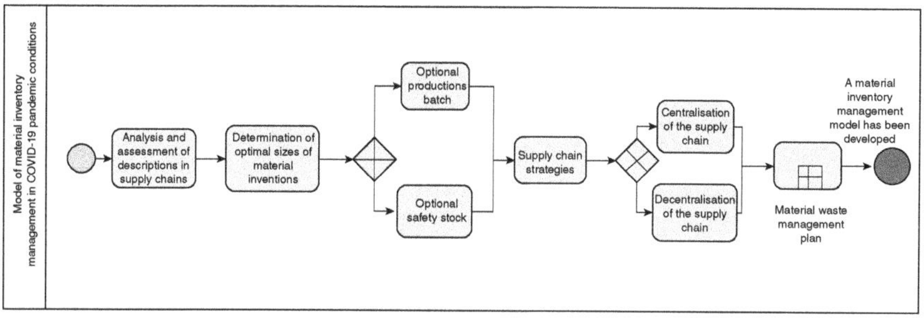

Figure 5.1 Model of material inventory management in COVID-19 pandemic conditions

Source: Own study in BPMN notation.

companies, stockpiling can contribute to the problem of dynamic demand. Variability is difficult to accept because smaller companies do not have the flexibility required to maintain a reasonable level of product availability when demand shock occurs (Forrester, 1961; Miłosz, Miłosz, 2014). A good solution to mitigate the scale of the described effect is to select appropriate procurement strategies, reduce delays in the chain by using electronic data exchange channels and change the structure of decision-making processes (e.g. implementation of VMI *Vendor Managed Inventory*, VMI and CPFR *Collaborative Planning, Forecasting and Replenishment*).

The Burbidge effect, on the other hand, is the use of a classic ordering apparatus based on economic size. This phenomenon is also connected with group ordering of goods and the scale effect in the production process. The synchronisation of group ordering over time results in a steep periodic increase in the volume of orders in a sustainable supply chain with a subsequent equally steep decrease (Miłosz, Miłosz, 2014).

The last worth paying attention to is the Houlihan effect (Houlihan, 1985). It concerns the reaction of company strategists to temporary shortages or delays in deliveries. In such a case, decision-makers plan orders above current needs to replenish security inventories, as increased inventories are created at individual links in the chain. This leads to a reduction in orders, which exacerbates the destabilising effect through the temporary disappearance of flows of goods (Miłosz, Miłosz, 2014).

A good solution to eliminate these disruptions may be to invest in monitoring global suppliers. New technologies, such as artificial intelligence or the use of appropriate notations for mapping processes in the supply chain, make it possible to easily monitor suppliers. The first online supply chain mapping platform was developed at the Massachusetts Institute of Technology in 2008. Modern supply chain mapping is the process of engaging companies and suppliers to document the exact source of every process involved in bringing goods to the market.

In the event of such disturbances, a legal analysis of agreements with customers and suppliers, and especially with logistics service providers, is also important. In the face of the COVID-19 pandemic, entrepreneurs and their business partners have had problems with the timely execution of agreements, so it is important to consider those customer agreements that are subject to severe penalties for late delivery and to note what are the provisions in the event of a crisis situation and which agreements can be terminated at short notice.

The second stage concerns the economic aspects of supply chains and describes activities related to the optimisation of the volume of maintained material stocks in individual links. It consists of four basic measures set in a sequential manner. These include:

- determining the optimal production batch;
- determining the size of the safety stock;
- adopting a strategy for the management of material stocks in the supply chain;
- waste management.

In times of the pandemic, and especially during the lockdown, manufacturing companies were forced to close their operations. Some of the companies were liquidated, and those that survived struggled to hire employees and ensure a minimum of business operation. The production stoppage also resulted in shortages of deliveries in logistics chains and delays in the execution of orders to customers due to the limited functioning of transport companies. The material reserves, especially of essential resources including medical resources, kept in warehouses to secure the continuity of production and distribution processes were used in the first period of the COVID-19 pandemic.

Therefore, it seems reasonable to answer the question: How large should the batches produced and maintained in sales warehouses be to secure the needs of customers at an appropriate cost?

To solve this problem, the methodology of the "optimal production batch" can be used. The classic optimal production batch model is based on the optimal delivery volume model (Economic Order Quantity – EOQ) (Axsäter, 1996; Arslan, Turkay, 2013; Battini, Persona, Sgarbossa, 2014; Eppen, Martin, 1988; Lee, Rim, 2019; Lewis, 1975). Determining the optimal production batch refers to the situation when the transfer of finished products from the production phase to the sales warehouse takes place successively and continuously secures the needs of customers. In this case, average inventory levels will be lower than for one-off delivery. The average inventory size for this case can be expressed via the formula (5.1):

$$\bar{Z} = \frac{Q}{2}\left(1 - \frac{P}{m}\right) \tag{5.1}$$

Where:

Q – delivery volumes;
P – annual demand;
m – annual production capacity.

For the average inventory size determined in this way, total inventory costs will be (5.2):

$$RKZ = \frac{Q}{2}\left(1 - \frac{P}{m}\right)c \cdot u_r + \frac{P}{Q} \cdot k_z \tag{5.2}$$

Where:

c – unit price of production;
u_r – annual inventory maintenance cost factor;
k_z – unit cost of conversion of production of the product.

By calculating the first order derivative after the variable Q and equating the equation to zero, $\frac{dŁKZ}{dQ} = 0$, by analogy to Wilson's formula for economic order quantity (EOQ), the optimal production batch can be determined from the formula (5.3) (Maddah, Jaber, 2008):

$$Q_{opt} = \sqrt{\frac{2 \cdot k_z \cdot P}{c \cdot u_r\left(1 - \frac{P}{m}\right)}} \tag{5.3}$$

The presented methodology (Ślaski, 2017) of the optimal production batch enforces another measure related to determining the size of the safety stock of the goods.

These inventories are planned and gathered in order to secure the continuity of logistics processes, eliminate market demand uncertainty and mitigate the effects of natural disasters, economic crisis and other threats (Krzyżaniak, 2002; Sharma, Malhotra, 2015).

The optimum safety stock size can be determined from the formula (5.4):

$$Z_b = \omega \cdot \delta_{pt} \tag{5.4}$$

$$\delta_{pt} = \sqrt{\delta_p^2 \cdot T + \delta_t^2 \cdot P^2} \tag{5.5}$$

Where:

Z_b – safety stock;
ω – security factor (related to the level of customer service);
σ_{pt} – standard deviation of demand forecasts in the inventory replenishment cycle;
σ_p – standard deviation of the demand forecast;
σ_t – standard deviation of the replenishment cycle time;
T – replenishment cycle time;
P – average demand.

The size of this inventory depends on the irregularity of demand in the market as well as the level of customer service. For first-aid goods and medical devices, the level of customer service should aim at 100%. The safety stock also considers the time of order completion (replenishment of inventory) together with its variability (e.g. delays in deliveries) (Brown, 1959).

Maintaining safety stock in each link of the supply chain results in the adverse effects described in the first part of the model. Therefore, this inventory should be properly allocated using the empirical strategy of centralisation and decentralisation.

The empirical rule has been applied for the optimal distribution of the safety stock. The problem of centralising security inventories in supply chains requires appropriate assumptions:

1 the time series do not show trends or seasonality, so the observed quantities are random;
2 the recording of demand during the period considered concerns regional warehouses;
3 the average values of demand and its variability are approximately the same for all warehouses.

Since the size of the safety stock is determined from the formula (5.4), it can be assumed that:

$$\delta_{p(1+2+3+\cdots n)} \approx \sqrt{\delta_{p1}^2 + \delta_{p2}^2 + \delta_{p3}^2 + \cdots \delta_{pn}^2} \quad (5.6).$$

Thus:

$$Zb_{(1+2+3+\cdots n)} \approx \omega \cdot \sqrt{\delta_{p1}^2 + \delta_{p2}^2 + \delta_{p3}^2 + \cdots \delta_{pn}^2} \quad (5.7)$$

and:

$$Zb_{(1+2+3+\cdots n)} \approx \sqrt{Zb_1^2 + Zb_2^2 + Zb_3^2 + \cdots Zb_n^2} \quad (5.8).$$

Therefore, the formula defining the rule (5.8) determines the size of the safety stock in the company's central warehouse, the so-called centralisation of stocks (5.9):

$$Zb_c = Z_{bi} \cdot \sqrt{n} \tag{5.9}$$

Where:

Zb_c – safety stock at the company's central warehouse;
Zb_i – safety stock of the i-th regional warehouse;
n – number of regional warehouses.

The transformation of the formula (5.9) allows for the decentralisation of the safety stock, i.e. moving it to regional warehouses serving local markets. What is important here is that the level of customer service in both cases does not change (Sarjusz-Wolski, 2000).

In the difficult economic conditions of the pandemic, it is important to remember about waste management. Appropriate regulations for the transport and disposal of waste are established by the relevant services and are laid down by legislation and normative acts. The appropriate symbol of the waste management plan presented in the model (Figure 5.1) shows the complexity of the problem. Proper waste management, especially of medical supplies during the pandemic, requires the system organisers to properly organise the selective collection, transport and disposal of this group of hazardous items.

Recommendations and conclusions

During the pandemic, there is a growing demand for certain medicinal and other healthcare products that can support the healing process. Effective inventory management and knowledge of the actual level and location of a particular assortment begin to play a greater role in this situation. The developed model meets these expectations; it also fits into the concept of "lean management" recommended by economists for use in the COVID-19 pandemic conditions.

The measures presented in the model related to the determination of the optimal production batch and the size of safety stock eliminate the problems associated with excessive transport, inventories and overproduction. Skilful support for these activities through the introduction of e.g. the "5S" concept will enable the employees of companies, mainly manufacturing ones, to maintain a sanitary regime and an appropriate distance, thus improving work comfort (Fabrizio, Tapping, 2006; Grycuk, 2012; Takashi, 2004).

The pandemic has caused huge disruptions in the global supply chain, and governmental actors and businesses are expected to make the right decisions to safeguard the population against the virus and ensure the supply of products that are key for the market economy.

Polish law meets such needs by monitoring the flow of medicines in the country and creating mechanisms to prevent their illegal export, not only in times of the pandemic. An example of such a system is Integrated System for Monitoring of Medicinal Products Trade (ISMMPT). More and more hospitals are taking steps to rationalise their internal processes for the distribution of healthcare products to reduce the response time to patient needs and increase the economic efficiency of hospital functioning. To this end, solutions using barcode scanning and electronic documents are being implemented more and more often (Gawrońska, 2020).

References

Arslan, M.C. and Turkay, M. (2013). EOQ revisited with sustainability considerations. *Foundations of Computing and Decision Sciences*, 38(4).

Axsäter, S. (1996). Using the deterministic EOQ formula in stochastic inventory control. *Management Science*, 42(6).

Battini, D., Persona, A. and Sgarbossa, F. (2014). A sustainable EOQ model: theoretical formulation and applications. *International Journal of Production Economics*, 149.

Brown, R.G. (1959). *Statistical forecasting for inventory control*. New York: McGraw-Hill.

Drejewicz, S. (2017). *Zrozumieć BPMN modelowanie procesów biznesowych*. Gliwice: Helion.

Eppen, G.D. and Martin, R.K. (1988). Determining safety stock in the presence of stochastic lead time and demand. *Management Science*, 34(11).

Fabrizio, T. and Tapping, D. (2006). *5S for the office: organizing the workplace to eliminate waste*. New York: CRC Press.

Forrester, J. (1961). *Industrial dynamics*. Cambridge: MIT Press.

Gawrońska, A. (2020). *Logistyka w czasach zarazy: medycyna w dobie epidemii*. Poznań: Instytut Logistyki i Magazynowania.

Grycuk, A. (2012). Metoda 5S w praktyce lean management. *Zarządzanie Jakością*, 2.

Houlihan, J.B. (1985). International supply chain management. *International Journal of Physical Distribution & Materials Management*, 27(3), 17–18.

Krzyżaniak, S. (2002). *Basics of inventory management in examples*. Pozna: Biblioteka Logistyka, ILiM.

Lee, C.J. and Rim, S.C. (2019). A mathematical safety stock model for DDMRP inventory replenishment. *Mathematical Problems in Engineering*, https://downloads.hindawi.com/journals/mpe/2019/6496309.pdf.

Lewis, C.D. (1975). *Demand analysis and inventory control*. Lexington, MA: Saxon House.

Maddah, B. and Jaber, M.Y. (2008). Economic order quantity for items with imperfect quality: revisited. *International Journal of Production Economics*, 112(2).

Miłosz, M. and Miłosz, E. (2014). Negatywne efekty w łańcuchach logistycznych: modele i przykłady. *Logistyka*, 3.

Sarjusz-Wolski, Z. (2000). *Sterowanie zapasami w przedsiębiorstwie*. Warszawa: PWE.

Sharma, S. and Malhotra, A. (2015). Safety stock calculations and inventory analysis: a practical approach for the FMCG case in a South-East Asian country. *International Journal of Advanced Logistics*, 4(3).

Ślaski, P. (2017). *Inventory management in logistic systems*. Warszawa: WAT.

Takashi, O. (2004). *The 5S's: five keys to a total quality environment (Terjemahan)*. Jakarta: Penerbit PPM. www.wiadomoscihandlowe.pl.

6 Sustainable waste management in COVID-19 circumstances

Dorota Krupnik and Bogusław Rogowski

Introduction

The state of threat caused by the COVID-19 pandemic has put pressure on many sectors and industries, including waste management. The problem of protecting against the SARS-CoV virus has also had an impact on this area. Proper waste management is one of the most important public services. The EU member states produce, on average, approximately 0.5 Mg of municipal waste per capita per year. Therefore, preventing disruptions in the waste management system, including separate collection and recycling of waste, is of great importance for health, safety, the environment and the economy. The EU legal regulations for waste management offer some possibility of adjustment in the face of identified risks to human health and the environment. However, it is the responsibility of each member state to implement these laws.

Unexpectedly, new problems arose due to changes in waste streams, increasing amounts of medical waste, difficulties in collecting waste (including hazardous waste), shortage of staff, safety procedures, work organisation and logistics. The waste management sector as well as management boards of companies had to face some difficult decisions and procedures regarding occupational health and safety due to bacteriological hazards. During the pandemic, the necessity arose to adapt the way waste is processed due to the potentially increased amounts of infectious and quarantine waste. In the light of such threats, new problems and questions emerge, including those regarding the storage of waste before it is released to a facility, the incineration of extra waste and the storage of non-processed waste in the event of an epidemiological emergency.

These problems turn into challenges that the waste management sector must respond to in order to ensure its sustainable development. What is essential is that temporary, ad hoc measures to improve waste collection and treatment for the time being do not turn into permanent solutions. A systemic approach to waste management is required, which would be based on the provisions of standardisation documents as well as on responsibility extended to all elements of the waste supply chain, at all management levels. Currently, it is imperative to design a system that would supply the waste management sector with additional funding and crisis-proof solutions. Within a systemic approach, one should search for

DOI: 10.4324/9781003285731-6

universal solutions, where tools for monitoring waste management processes can be used without any harm to health or the environment. In addition, small local, specialised and decentralised recycling facilities should be promoted. *This is possible due to the presence of significant competition between numerous business entities dealing with waste management.* It also facilitates a response to changing conditions in a balanced and flexible manner and helps bring crisis situations under control.

The purpose of this chapter is to analyse and assess the functioning of sustainable waste management in COVID-19 circumstances and to propose solutions for a waste management system that would prevent or mitigate crises in terms of adverse environmental impact. The conducted research was based on a combination of quantitative and qualitative data on sustainable waste management during crises. The collected empirical material came from sample entities operating in the waste management chain, from waste producers, through recyclers, to consumers of finished products. The size of the research sample is representative for the respective group. The formulated research objective – consistent with the topic of the chapter – assumes an innovative approach.

A diagnosis of the current state of the waste management sector under circumstances of sustainable development is helpful in finding the answers to the research problems formulated. How and to what extent did COVID-19 affect the way waste management systems work and are managed? What actions should be taken, and what tools should be used in the waste management sector to neutralise the consequences of the crisis? What approach and systemic solutions would allow for a balanced and flexible response to the changing circumstances of the waste management sector? The presented research problems have been formulated in such a way as to clarify and specify the purpose of the research.

Along with the research purpose and research problems, the following working hypothesis was formulated: effective functioning of sustainable waste management under circumstances of epidemiological threat is difficult due to the limitations and procedures imposed to combat SARS-CoV. Only the implementation of universal, standardised systemic solutions to monitor sustainable waste management processes as well as dedicated final recycling facilities can guarantee security without harm to health or the environment.

Both theoretical and empirical methods were adapted and used for the purposes of the research and consisted in an analysis of normative documents and system documentation of the examined entities, an audit through direct and indirect interviews with authorised specialists and experts, observation of processes and actions, inference and generalisation based on the collected data and practical experience of the authors in terms of the waste management sector.

Analysis of the existing legal environment of the Polish waste management system at the time of the COVID-19 pandemic

Waste management and transport is regulated by international, EU and domestic legal acts, as well as normative documents, including agreements, codes of conduct, and technical standards and specifications. The implementation of the set directional objectives of the concept of "recycling society" in the waste management law consists in: 1) ensuring the segregation of waste at the source, and 2) collecting and recycling priority waste streams (Duczmal, 2008). The basis for this approach was the Thematic Strategy on the prevention and recycling of waste, adopted by the European Commission on December 21, 2005 (COM, 2005, p. 666), which defines two approaches to waste management:

- linking the waste policy with the policy on the re-use of materials in the manufacturing processes;
- close connection between materials, products and waste in the production processes.

Although in recent years the perspective on the generation of waste in terms of a full product life cycle has expanded to include the processes of its implementation and exploitation (Figure 6.1), it does not consider new threats that may possibly arise, such as viral contamination of waste (e.g. with SARS-CoV-2 that causes COVID-19). Therefore, it is necessary to take this aspect into account while developing and implementing the concept of a full product or service life cycle.

In waste management policy, this should be reflected in a greater emphasis on the stages of concept and design and a focus on issues such as the selection of materials and raw materials in terms of their efficiency, minimising the use of harmful substances, reducing emissions, reducing energy consumption, energy recovery, reducing the amount of waste, reducing water consumption, as well as selecting appropriate methods of re-use, recovery, recycling and disposal (ISO 14006, 2020). On the other hand, procedures should be implemented for each waste category, and a separate waste stream from contaminated sources should be identified. This should also apply to new legal and normative solutions in terms of the process of excluding certain materials from the scope of the waste directive. Such actions would also address "by-product" and "end-of-waste" mechanisms (Consolidated Waste Directive, 2018). Moreover, reference to eco-design sets the directions for creating such environmentally friendly solutions in terms of production and product (Kosieradzka-Federczyk, 2013).

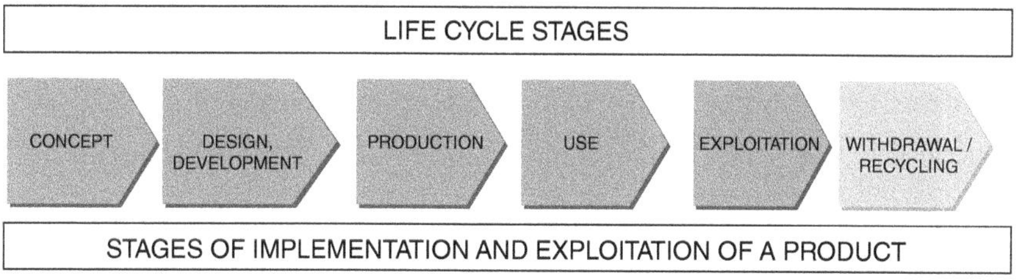

Figure 6.1 Product life cycle stages

Source: Own study based on: AAP 48 ed.B, NATO system life cycle processes, NSA 2013.

Basic waste management is regulated by the following EU legal documents: the Waste Framework Directive (2008/98/EC) and the Hazardous Waste Directive (91/689/EEC). The provisions of these documents emphasise the environmental objectives, as defined in Art. 174 of the Treaty on the Functioning of the European Union and focus on the impact of generated waste, as well as its management throughout the entire life cycle of the product. However, except for medical and veterinary waste, no mention is made of the possibility that waste may be virally contaminated.

Regardless of the adopted detailed solutions for the development of the waste management system, several legal acts have been adopted concerning individual waste streams, including hazardous ones, such as fuel oils, PCB/PCT, batteries, packaging waste, asbestos-containing waste, decommissioned vehicles, electrical and electronic waste, warfare agents and explosives. A structured list of major EU and domestic legislation as well as domestic guidelines on waste management is presented in Table 6.1.

The analysis of the listed documentation shows the importance of a rational management of natural resources and minimisation of the stored waste, with simultaneous optimisation of the processes of its production. The legislation in question also emphasises the role of waste as a valuable raw material and energy source suitable for reuse.

The objectives that the EU intends to achieve by introducing legal regulations are the implementation of the proximity principle and the effective management of waste by the regions which generated it (self-sufficiency). This forces the member states to develop and maintain their own waste management systems, including for hazardous waste. The adopted objectives were aimed at curbing the uncontrolled transboundary movement of waste within the EU (Kosieradzka-Federczyk, 2013, p. 47).

Despite the unfavourable opinion of the European Economic and Social Committee, on November 20, 2013, Decision No. 1386/2013/EU of the European Parliament and of the Council of 20 November 2013 on a General Union Environment Action Programme to 2020 'Living well, within the limits of our planet' was adopted. This seventh edition of the programme obliges the EU institutions and individual member states to take measures to achieve the programme's priority objectives and obliges all public entities to work together with businesses, social partners, European society and citizens to ensure the programme's effective implementation. The priorities of the programme include:

- protection, preservation and improvement of the EU's natural capital;
- transformation of the European Union into a resource-efficient, green and competitive low-carbon economy;
- protection of EU citizens from environmental pressures and threats to their health and well-being;
- maximisation of benefits from environmental legislation, improvement of knowledge and evidence base in the field of the environment and climate protection;

Table 6.1 List of the most important legal documents in the field of waste management

No.	*Type of document*	*Source*
BASIC EUROPEAN UNION DOCUMENTATION		
1	Thematic strategy on the prevention and recycling of waste of December 21, 2005	COM (2005) 666
2	Guidelines of the European Commission for Waste Prevention Programmes of 2012	European Commission: 'Preparing a Waste Prevention Programme' Oct. 2012
3	Directive (EU) 2018/851 of the European Parliament and of the Council of 30 May 2018 amending Directive 2008/98/EC on waste	OJ L 312 of 02.11.2008
4	Council Directive 94/31/EC of 27 June 1994 amending Directive 91/689/EEC on hazardous waste	OJ L 150/109 of 14.06.2018
5	Directive 2008/1/EC of the European Parliament and of the Council of 15 January 2008 concerning integrated pollution prevention and control	OJ L 24 of 29.1.2008, p. 8–29, as amended)
6	Commission Directive 2014/103/EU of 21 November 2014 adapting for the third time the Annexes to Directive 2008/68/EC of the European Parliament and of the Council on the inland transport of dangerous goods to scientific and technical progress	OJ L 335 of 22.11.2014, p. 15
7	Commission Decision of 18 December 2014 amending Decision 2000/532/EC on the list of waste pursuant to Directive 2008/98/EC of the European Parliament and of the Council	European Waste Catalogue (EWC) OJ L 370/44 of 30.12.2014
8	Commission Regulation (EC) No. 1418/2007 of 29 November 2007 concerning the export for recovery of certain waste listed in Annex III or IIIA to Regulation (EC) No. 1013/2006 of the European Parliament and of the Council to certain countries to which the OECD Decision on the control of transboundary movements of wastes does not apply	Amended by regulations no.: 740/2008, 967/2009, 837/2010, 661/2011, 674/2012, 57/2013, 519/2013, 733/2014
9	Decision No. 1386/2013/EU of the European Parliament and of the Council of 20 November 2013 on a General Union Environment Action Programme to 2020 'Living well, within the limits of our planet'	(OJ L 354 of 28.12.2013, p. 171)
DOCUMENTS CONCERNING THE TYPES OF WASTE STREAMS		
10	Council Directive of 22 December 1986, amending Directive 75/439/EEC on the disposal of waste oils	OJ L of 12.02.1987
11	Council Directive 96/59/EC of 16 September 1996 on the disposal of polychlorinated biphenyls and polychlorinated terphenyls (PCB/PCT)	OJ L 243 of 24.09.1996, p. 31, as amended

(*Continued*)

Table 6.1 (Continued)

No.	*Type of document*	*Source*
12	Council Directive 78/176/EEC of 20 February 1978 on waste from the titanium dioxide industry	OJ L 54/19 of 25.02.1978, p. 19, as amended
13	Directive 2006/21/EC of the European Parliament and of the Council of 15 March 2006 on the management of waste from extractive industries and amending Directive 2004/35/EC – Statement by the European Parliament, the Council and the Commission	OJ L 102 of 11.04.2006, str. 15, as amended
14	Council Directive 86/278/EEC of 12 June 1986 on the protection of the environment, and in particular of the soil, when sewage sludge is used in agriculture	OJ L 181/6 of 04.07.1986, p. 6, as amended
15	Directive (EU) 2018/852 of the European Parliament and of the Council of 30 May 2018 amending Directive 94/62/EC on packaging and packaging waste	OJ L.2018.150.141 of 30.05.2018.
16	Council Directive 1999/31/EC of 26 April 1999 on the landfill of waste	OJ L 182 of 16.07.1999, p. 1, as amended
17	Directive 2006/66/EC of the European Parliament and of the Council of 6 September 2006 on batteries and accumulators and waste batteries and accumulators and repealing Directive 91/157/EEC	OJ L 266 of 26.09.2006, p. 1, as amended
18	Directive 2000/53/EC of the European Parliament and of the Council of 18 September 2000 on end-of-life vehicles	OJ L 269 of 21.10.2000, p. 34, as amended
19	Directive 2002/96/EC of the European Parliament and of the Council of 27 January 2003 on waste electrical and electronic equipment (WEEE)	OJ L 37 of 13.02.2003, p. 24–39 and L 345 of 31.12.2003, p. 106, as amended
20	Directive (EU) 2018/849 of the European Parliament and of the Council of 30 May 2018 amending Directives 2000/53/EC on end-of-life vehicles, 2006/66/EC on batteries and accumulators and waste batteries and accumulators, and 2012/19/EU on waste electrical and electronic equipment	OJ L.2018.150.93 of 30.05.2018
21	Directive 2008/56/EC of the European Parliament and of the Council of 17 June 2008 establishing a framework for community action in the field of marine environmental policy (Marine Strategy Framework Directive)	OJ L 164 of 25.06.2008, p. 19
22	Directive (EU) 2015/1535 of the European Parliament and of the Council of 9 September 2015 laying down a procedure for the provision of information in the field of technical regulations and of rules on Information Society services (It also concerns the provision of information about medical and veterinary waste.)	OJ L 241 of 17.09.2015, p. 1.

No.	*Type of document*	*Source*
23	Directive 2010/75/EU of the European Parliament and of the Council of 24 November 2010 on industrial emissions (integrated pollution prevention and control)	OJ L 334 of 17.12.2010, p. 17, as amended
DOCUMENTATION ON FACILITIES		
24	Directive 2000/76/EC of the European Parliament and of the Council of 4 December 2000 on the incineration of waste	OJ L 332 of 28.12.2000, p. 91, as amended
25	Council Directive 1999/31/EC of 26 April 1999 on the landfill of waste	OJ L 182 of 16.07.1999, p. 1, as amended
26	Regulation of the Minister of the Environment of March 21, 2006, on the recovery or disposal of waste outside facilities and devices	Journal of Laws No. 49, item 356
BASIC DOMESTIC DOCUMENTATION		
27	Act of 14 December 2012 on waste	Journal of Laws of 2013, item 21, as amended
28	Act of 13 June 2013 on the management of packaging and packaging waste	Journal of Laws of 2013, item 888 as amended
29	Act of September 13, 1996, on maintaining cleanliness and order in municipalities	Journal of Laws of 1996 No. 132 item 622 (Journal of Laws of 2020, item 1439 – consolidated text)
30	Act of 11 May 2001 on the obligations in the field of management of certain waste and the product fee	Journal of Laws of 2007, No. 90, item 607, as amended
31	Act of 20 January 2005 on the recycling of end-of-life vehicles	Journal of Laws of 2013, item 1162
32	Act of 29 July 2005 on waste electrical and electronic equipment	Journal of Laws of 2013, item 1155
33	Act of 10 July 2008 on extractive waste	Journal of Laws of 2013, item 1136
34	Act of April 24, 2009, on batteries and accumulators	Journal of Laws No. 79, item 666, as amended
35	Regulation of the Minister of the Environment of 29 December 2014 on the waste catalogue	Journal of Laws No. 112, item 1923
36	Regulation of the Minister of Health of October 5, 2017, on the detailed method of handling medical waste	Journal of Laws of 2017, item 1975
37	Regulation of the Minister of the Environment of 13 January 2014 on the document confirming the neutralisation of infectious medical or veterinary waste	Journal of Laws of 2014, item 107
38	Regulation of the Minister of Economy of 19 March 2010 amending Regulation on requirements for waste incineration	Journal of Laws of 2010 No. 61, item 380
39	Regulation of the Minister of the Environment of 29 December 2016 on the detailed method of separate collection of selected waste types	Journal of Laws of 2017, item 19

(*Continued*)

Table 6.1 (Continued)

No.	*Type of document*	*Source*
40	Regulation of the Minister of Health of 24 July 2015 on types of medical and veterinary waste acceptable for recovery	Journal of Laws of 2015, item 1116
41	Regulation of the Minister of Climate of 2 January 2020 on the waste catalogue	Journal of Laws of 2020, item 10
42	Order of the Minister of Climate and Environment of 12 October 2020 on the establishment of a group to support the construction of combined heat and power plants fired with high-calorific types of municipal waste	Journal of the Ministry of Climate and Environment of October 20, 2020, item 4
43	Order of the Minister of Climate of 3 September 2020 on entrusting the Chief Inspector of Environmental Protection with supervision over a separate national centre for the Basel Convention on the control of transboundary movement and disposal of hazardous waste	Journal of the Ministry of Climate and Environment of September 7, 2020, item 46
44	Guidelines of the Minister of Climate and the Chief Sanitary Inspector on the handling of waste generated during the SARS-CoV-2 coronavirus infection and the COVID-19 caused by it (during the pandemic/epidemic)	09.04.2020

Source: Own study.

- securing green investments and support for sustainable cities;
- incorporation of a more coherent environmental policy to address international environmental and climate challenges more efficiently.

One of the key elements of the programme is the adaptation of systemic solutions in the field of waste management to progressing climate change, which are related to many other environmental aspects such as soil protection, sustainable urban environment, sustainable protection of waters and marine environment, etc. The programme also presents a vision of the year 2050, showing citizens enjoying a good quality of life, with simultaneous consideration for ecological limitations of our planet, resource-efficient economy, restoration of biodiversity and low-carbon approach paving the way for a global development. In accordance with the EU legal requirements, by 2030 Europeans should be recycling 70% of municipal waste and 80% of packaging waste, and by 2025, they should stop landfilling recyclable waste. This poses a significant challenge, especially for less technologically developed countries.

After years of experience in waste management, one might venture the observation that by joining the EU, many obligations resulting from the adopted EU acquis were imposed on Poland. The EU law is directly applicable in all member states through the imposition of Community provisions on domestic legislation by issuing regulations equivalent to domestic legal acts of parliament. Therefore, the issues related to environmental protection, with particular emphasis on waste management, are regulated by numerous legal acts in which EU law has been transposed. The most fundamental act in terms of waste is the Act of 14 December 2012 on waste, which sets out the principles of waste management in accordance with sustainable development, and in particular the principles of waste prevention or reduction of the amount of waste generated. In addition, there are several acts on individual waste streams, such as batteries, end-of-life vehicles, waste electrical and electronic equipment, etc. Pursuant to individual acts, specific issues are regulated by relevant regulations, e.g. requirements for waste incineration and storage. The most important European and domestic legal acts are presented in Table 6.1.

Considering the current state of threat, the most relevant are those related to hazardous waste streams, such as medical or veterinary waste. It should be emphasised that fundamental changes regarding medical waste were introduced by the aforementioned 2012 act on waste, which stresses the importance of compliance with the principles of waste management in a manner that protects human life and health, as well as the environment. Medical waste was defined as a type of waste generated during provision of health services and medical research or scientific experiments. From the point of view of epidemiological issues and work safety, the need to supervise medical waste management is one of the main reasons for the use of a special management system for this group of waste, especially in the current state of COVID-19 threat.

The Waste Framework Directive 2018/851 of 30 May 2018, clearly sets out the current priorities for handling all types of waste, including medical waste. A detailed hierarchy of waste management determines the order of priorities for the processes related to waste management, including:

- prevention (avoiding or reducing generation of waste);
- preparation for re-use;
- recycling;
- other methods of recovery, e.g. energy recovery;
- disposal.

In the case of hazardous waste management – its collection, transport, storage and disposal – the directive obliges EU member states to make every effort to comply with Community laws. Based on these guidelines, the handling of waste is regulated in each country by relevant provisions of law. The act on waste, along with the Regulation of the Minister of Health of 5 October 2017 on the detailed method of handling medical waste, set out the rules for the collection and temporary storage of medical waste, classified according to the Regulation of the Minister of the Environment of 29 December 2014 on the waste catalogue. They also impose several new obligations on waste producers. Healthcare centres that generate waste and its recipients are obliged to keep quantitative and qualitative records of waste according to legally specified documentation, prepared according to specific templates. In this regard, the Guidelines of the Minister of Climate and the Chief Sanitary Inspector introduced in April 2020 on the management of waste generated during the occurrence of SARS-CoV-2 coronavirus infections and the COVID-19 disease caused by the virus (during the pandemic) are of particular importance. The regulations impose on state and local government entities, as well as households, new, unprecedented obligations in terms of handling contaminated waste.

In addition, in accordance with the Regulation of the Minister of Health of 24 July 2015 on the types of medical waste and veterinary waste, the recovery of which is acceptable, a new method of classification of waste subject to recovery applies, as shown in Table 6.2.

At the same time, the Regulation of the Minister of Climate of 2 January 2020 on the waste catalogue includes a full classification of all types of waste depending on their source, including medical and veterinary waste. The latter (excluding kitchen and restaurant waste not related to health care or veterinary care) is classified in the waste catalogue as group 18.

The pandemic, along with the dynamic changes brought in its wake, including in the legal system, has had a significant impact on the well-established system of recovering individual waste streams, not only in the field of municipal, medical and veterinary waste, but also other waste streams generated in areas contaminated with SARS-CoV. The restrictions imposed one after the other – including legal solutions – result in a significant increase in the total amount of infectious or contaminated waste that can be disposed of only by thermal treatment in closed facilities without the possibility of simultaneous incineration with other types of waste. These requirements generate enormous costs and exacerbate the problems related to the shortage of adequate and efficient technical facilities, as well as appropriately adapted infrastructure. In addition, the principle of proximity – in force due to other regulations – which requires the processing of waste in the place where it was generated, further complicates the problem.

The difficulties mentioned here, as well as other problems, pose a real threat of disruption in the continuity of the entire waste management system or at least some of its elements and processes. Therefore it is important to take preventive measures and corrective actions, based on practical experience in terms of the functioning of the system in the circumstances of a pandemic. It is also advisable to diversify the methods of implementing the process of the system management by entities that are not permanent parts of the decision-making and executive structures of the system, including from such areas as science, public-private partnership and business. Only well-coordinated actions can effectively counteract the escalation of threats and provide a new perspective and innovative approach in the process of development and improvement of the existing waste management system, in the circumstances of the current threat of the SARS-CoV-2 infection. The legal and administrative experience gained will allow to better prepare the system for similar forms and types of threats in the future. From an academic point of view, it is assumed that the conducted research will make a useful contribution to the development of safety sciences.

Table 6.2 List of medical and veterinary waste from group 18, including infectious waste

No.	*Code*	*Medical and veterinary waste*
18 01 WASTE FROM PERINATAL CARE, DIAGNOSIS, TREATMENT AND PREVENTIVE CARE		
1	18 01 01	Surgical and treatment instruments and their remnants (except for 18 01 03)
2	18 01 04	Types of waste other than those mentioned in 18 01 03 (e.g. cloth dressings or plasters, bed linen, disposable clothes, diapers)
3	18 01 06*	Chemicals, including chemical reagents, containing hazardous substances
4	18 01 07	Chemicals, including chemical reagents other than those mentioned in 18 01 06
5	ex 18 01 10*	Dental amalgam waste (excluding infectious waste)
6	ex 18 01 81	Peloids left after medical treatments other than those mentioned in 18 01 80 – post-treatment mud
18 02 WASTE FROM VETERINARY RESEARCH, DIAGNOSIS, TREATMENT AND PREVENTIVE CARE		
7	18 02 01	Surgical and treatment instruments and their remnants (except for 18 02 02)
8	18 02 03	Types of waste other than those mentioned in 18 02 02
9	18 02 06	Chemicals, including chemical reagents other than those mentioned in 18 02 05

Source: Own study based on the Regulation of the Minister of Health of 24 July 2015 (Journal of Laws of 2015, item 1116).

General principles of the functioning of the waste management system in Poland in light of the COVID-19 pandemic

The waste management system in Poland functions in accordance with the EU strategy of sustainable development. The pillars of this development were presented in a UN Resolution in 2015 as the 2030 Agenda. The objectives of sustainable development of the economy and societies focus on the circular economy, in which the waste management system plays a key role (Schroeder, Anggraeni, Weber, 2019, p. 90; Pikoń, 2018, p. 230). The general principle of the circular economy resembles a loop, where the generated waste becomes a raw material again. This idea is illustrated in Figure 6.2.

Taking this into account, one can distinguish three main driving factors of the circular economy in relation to waste management (Lacy, Rutqvist, 2015, p. 18):

- limited resources;
- technological development;
- socio-economic opportunities.

It is assumed that the economy in its current state uses too many resources and is characterised by a short-sighted approach. The introduction of new technologies

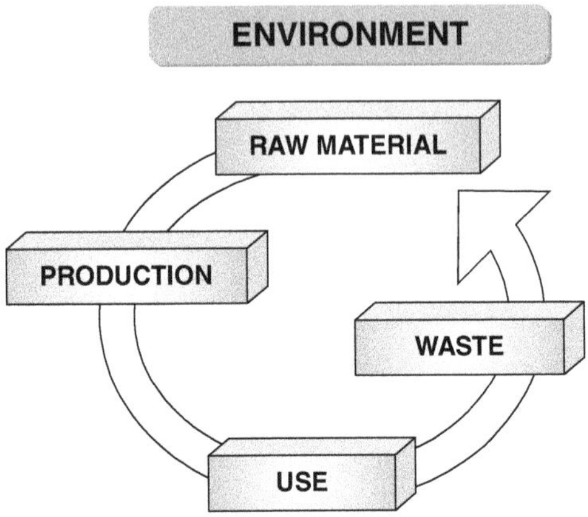

Figure 6.2 Diagram of waste management in a closed cycle

Source: Own study based on: Pikoń, 2018, p. 30.

will allow the consumption of resources and the generation of waste to be reduced, while also enhancing environmental awareness and encouraging customers to use the products to the maximum extent. The implementation of the principles of the circular economy requires the adoption of clearly defined rules to act as guidelines or a code of good practice for all aspects of socio-economic life. Do the developed rules consider crisis situations, such as the state of epidemiological threat that people around the world are currently facing? After analysing these rules (Pikoń, 2018, pp. 55–59) in terms of their applicability in the current situation related to the declared global pandemic, it can be concluded that many of them are not appropriate. The relationships and interdependencies between the principles of the circular economy, with particular emphasis on the generation of waste, are shown in Figure 6.3.

Many of these principles at individual stages of the product life cycle are not applicable in the event of an epidemiological threat, for instance, the principle of material efficiency or the principle of optimisation of energy consumption, the use of resources and generation of waste. Considering an increased, general demand for personal and collective protective equipment against microbes, the rules applicable under normal conditions can no longer be applied. The same is true for the principle of avoiding harmful substances – the systematic use of disinfectants is required, which are not neutral for the environment and increase the amount of packaging waste. Only the principles of resistance to external factors and continuous improvement of processes are still applicable in the current situation, although it should be reconsidered whether these principles can be applied in isolation from other principles, which would constitute a violation of the holistic approach promoted in relation to the circular economy.

The current, unprecedented situation leads to an increased generation of waste, including hazardous waste classified under code 18 (Regulation, 2020). The same

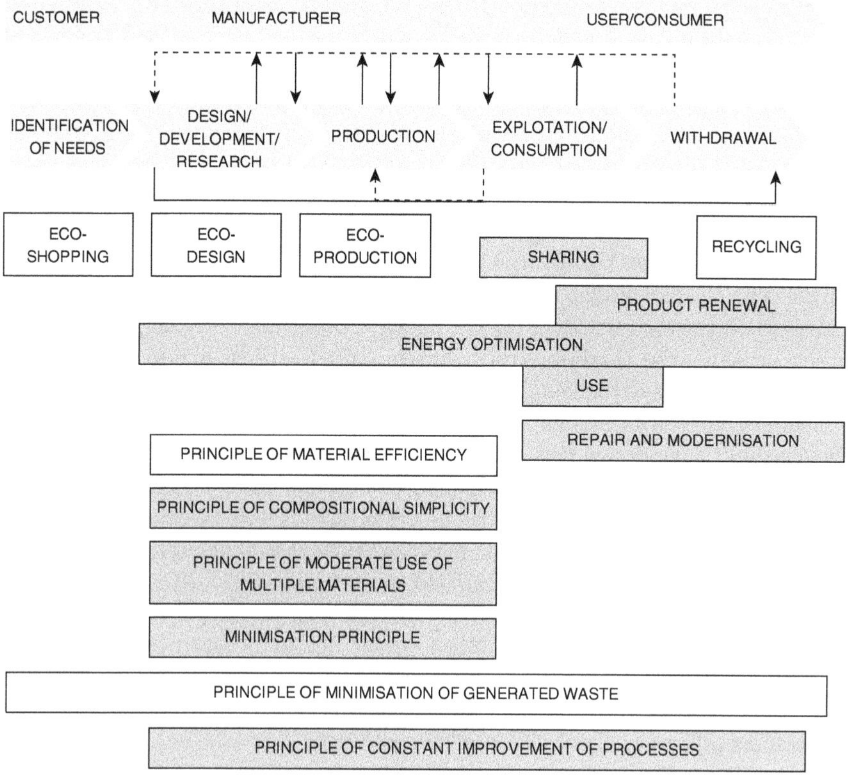

Figure 6.3 Diagram of the principles and functioning of the circular economy

Source: Own study based on: Pikoń, 2018, p. 37.

conclusions can be drawn from an analysis of the EU plan for a circular economy (Announcement, 2015, pp. 15–20). When specifying the rules, potentially dangerous situations were not considered, and the associated risks were not sufficiently examined and assessed. Particular attention should be paid to certain sectors and industries (e.g. medical, waste and recycling industries) facing difficult challenges in the context of the circular economy, including those related to waste management.

Two issues should be of fundamental importance in the waste management system:

- the protection of the natural environment;
- economic efficiency consisting in the use of raw materials from waste as well as the material and energy efficiency of waste management.

Environmental and economic instruments should play a key role in achieving the objectives of waste prevention and management. Since waste retains a certain value, for instance as a raw material or source of energy, it can be considered from an economic point of view. This does not apply to situations of crisis, emergencies, martial law and other situations where the economy and environmental protection must give priority to the protection of human health and life.

The principles delineating a long-term strategy of waste management are included in EU decisions, programmes and directives. Directive (EU) 2018/851 of the European Parliament and of the Council of 30 May 2018 on waste, mentioned in Chapter 1, aims to create a circular economy, with principal emphasis on the entire life cycle of products, and seeks ways to save resources and minimise the amount of waste. However, it does not mention exceptional situations, such as the state of epidemiological threat. The former should be addressed in amendments to the provisions referred to in Chapter 1, especially regarding the so-called waste package. The conditions related to the COVID-19 pandemic limit the possibility of saving and reducing the consumption of resources.

Microbiological threats have affected the approach to the waste management systems and have drawn particular attention to hazardous, including infectious, waste. The question is how to define this type of waste due to its extreme harmfulness to human health and life. The act on waste defines it as the category indicated in the waste catalogue, specified in the regulations issued under Art. 4 sec. 3, as hazardous waste, subject to Art. 22.7 (Journal of Laws 2020.797, effective from 1 August 2020). In this case, one must also consider municipal waste generated by households or other waste producers which, due to its nature or composition, is similar to household waste (e.g. unsorted [mixed] waste). Due to the common use of personal protective equipment, large amounts (e.g. face masks, disposable gloves and others) can be found in municipal waste.

A detailed analysis of the current legislation regarding waste in Poland in light of the COVID-19 pandemic, is presented in Chapter 1. Emphasis is placed on waste management, along with logistic processes related to its collection, transport and treatment, as well as supervision of these processes. However, the Regulation of the Minister of Climate, amended at the end of 2019, on the criteria for defining infectious waste, generally does not bring any radical changes, but rather raises doubts as to an unambiguous definition of the terms in the face of COVID-19. The document reads: ‘For the waste suspected to contain living microorganisms or their toxins, which are known or highly suspected to cause diseases in humans or other living organisms, indicator microorganisms should be selected, which are representative of the group of organisms responsible for this property of the waste. According to the selected indicator group, it is recommended to use tests for qualitative or quantitative analysis of the microorganisms’.

The regulation provides for specific procedures for handling:

- infectious medical waste generated while combatting the consequences of COVID-19;
- waste generated while combatting the consequences of COVID-19, other than infectious medical waste, including municipal waste.

This raises the question of what kind of waste is mentioned in the amendment. Does the amendment introduce new regulations? After the analysis of the definition of "medical waste" included in the Act on waste, "infectious waste" included in the regulation and the concept of "combatting the consequences of COVID-19" mentioned in the special act, one might conclude that infectious medical waste generated in the course of combatting the consequences of COVID-19 should be understood as waste generated in connection with the provision of health services and the medical research and scientific experiments conducted, and at the same time in connection with fighting the spread of infections, as well as preventing and combating the consequences of COVID-19. The question remains as to whether the regulation applies to waste contaminated with SARS-CoV-2 (or other viruses). If the criterion is the presence of living microorganisms or their toxins, then such a record does not include viruses, since – as stems from basic principles of biology – all living organisms have a cell structure, nourish, breathe and transfer their genes in the process of reproduction. Viruses, viroids and prions do not have these characteristics. They do not have a cell structure; therefore, they cannot be classified as living organisms (Lederberg, McCray, 2015, p. 8; Villarreal, 2005, pp. 56–61).

But as it happens in the relative world of science, by adopting a specific definition of life, SARS-CoV-2 can be considered as a living microorganism or its toxins, as specified in the regulation. As mentioned earlier, the waste generated in connection with COVID-19 includes not only infectious medical waste, but all other types of waste generated while fighting the virus, preventing its spread, implementing preventive measures and combating the consequences of COVID-19 (e.g. waste generated in places where infected people are isolated). But does this category also include waste from places where people who are still healthy or asymptomatic are quarantined? Is such waste infectious? Just in case, it is suggested that this type of municipal waste be indiscriminately allocated to a separate stream, which would be subject to processing in a similar way to infectious waste. The hazardous nature of this type of waste is presumed on a preventive basis, without examining knowledge-based facts. The provisions clearly and precisely specify that the disposal of infectious medical waste generated while combatting the effects of the COVID-19 pandemic involve combustion processes, understood as:

- waste incineration by oxidation at a temperature equal to or higher than 850°C;
- thermal processing of waste other than indicated earlier, including pyrolysis, gasification and plasma processing, provided that the substances generated during these processes are subsequently incinerated.

But what about methods of neutralising waste generated while combatting the consequences of the COVID-19 pandemic other than infectious medical waste?

These types of waste have not been considered. Since they belong to the category of municipal waste, the following alternatives are available:

- transferring mixed municipal waste other than those of mechanical and biological treatment and separating fractions that can be wholly or partially recovered;
- landfilling or incineration of municipal waste without preliminary processing.

In the case of waste (including municipal waste) generated while combatting the consequences of the COVID-19 pandemic other than infectious medical waste, another problem is its selective storage before undergoing treatment processes. How should waste be handled during the coronavirus pandemic? In places where municipal waste is collected, it is suggested that such waste (e.g. tissues, gloves, face masks, etc.) be tightly sealed in plastic bags and disposed of in mixed-waste containers. There is no mention of any separate collection of such waste, for instance in specially designated containers for that purpose. The risk can hardly be said to be minimised, since the sealed bags end up in the same containers anyway. In addition, the problem is further complicated by the morphological system of waste, which depends on the structure of families and their state of health (not only related to COVID-19, but also, for instance, to increased, seasonal outbreaks of flu).

Who is responsible for the organisation of municipal waste management in Poland? The legislation indicates local governments of individual municipalities as the entities responsible for the organisation of municipal waste collection from property owners, as well as for organisational and investment processes. The organisation of the municipal waste management system in Poland is presented in Figure 6.4.

The framework directive emphasises the need to create waste recovery and disposal facilities using the best technologies available (Pinasseau et al., 2018). This means that the basis of the waste management system should be a variety of technologies and technological processes facilitating the management of collected municipal waste, recycling, thermal processing or energy recovery. Other forms of waste recovery are also considered acceptable, including those that require pre-treatment (separation of individual fractions), which then allows the waste to be neutralised by processing. Through these regulations, local governments have a significant impact on the method of municipal waste management, and, in particular, on establishing fees for those services (Styś, Witwicki, 2013, p. 6). The legal regulations include a statutory prohibition on the processing of certain types of municipal waste outside the waste management region in which it was generated. This applies to:

- mixed municipal waste;
- residues left after sorting and the mechanical-biological treatment of municipal waste, if they are intended for landfilling;
- green waste.

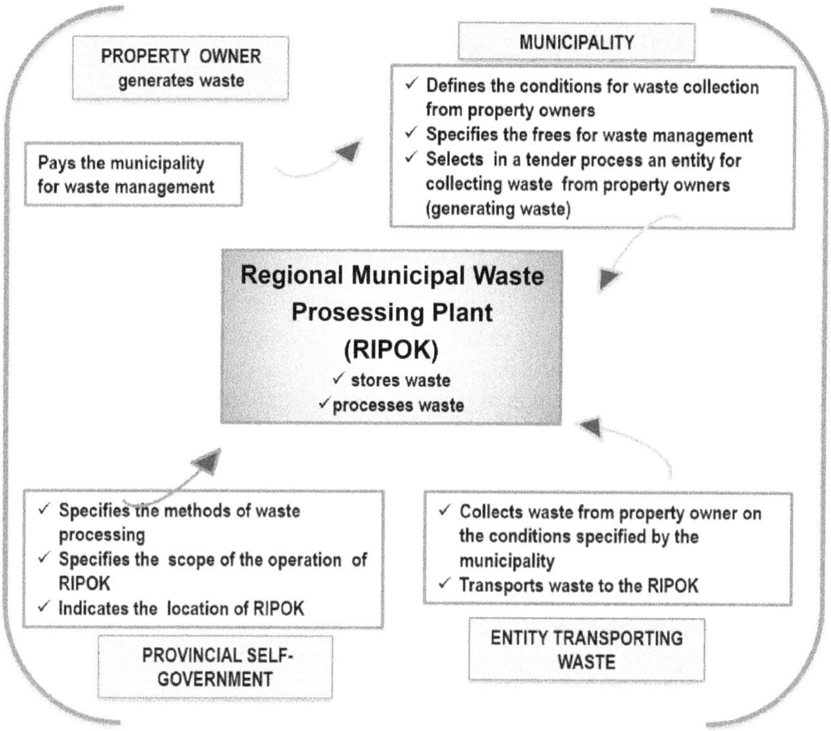

Figure 6.4 A simplified diagram of the organisation of the municipal waste collection and processing system in Poland

Source: Styś, Foks, 2014, p. 15.

From the point of view of entities operating in the municipal waste management sector (e.g. local governments), the most important tasks include:

- organisation of municipal waste collection for processing;
- ensuring the construction, maintenance and operation of Regional Municipal Waste Processing Plants.

These projects can be implemented in three ways (Styś, Foks, 2014, pp. 24–25):

- by organising tenders to select an entity that will be responsible for the construction, maintenance or operation of the facilities;
- by selecting the entity referred to based on public-private partnership;
- by selecting the entity on a concession basis.

When analysing the types of industrial and domestic waste, the most optimal method of their management should be considered, as shown in Figure 6.5, in accordance with the waste management hierarchy:

- preventing waste generation;
- preparation for re-use;
- recycling;
- other recovery processes;
- neutralisation.

One of the key high-priority methods is the prevention of waste generation, for example by reusing or reducing the amount of waste produced. If waste generation cannot be prevented, it should be subjected to the recovery process, e.g. by recycling. If this is not possible due to technological limitations or is not justified for ecological or economic reasons, such waste should be subjected to other recovery processes, e.g. energy recovery. Separate waste collection is at least expected for categories of waste such as paper, metal, plastic and glass. If, for various reasons, other methods of waste management are not possible, such waste is disposed of, for instance by incineration. Only waste with potentially recoverable streams is subjected to disposal, while landfilling should be used only when other forms of disposal are not possible. The Waste Framework Directive 2008/98/EC introduces the obligation to develop waste management plans and waste prevention

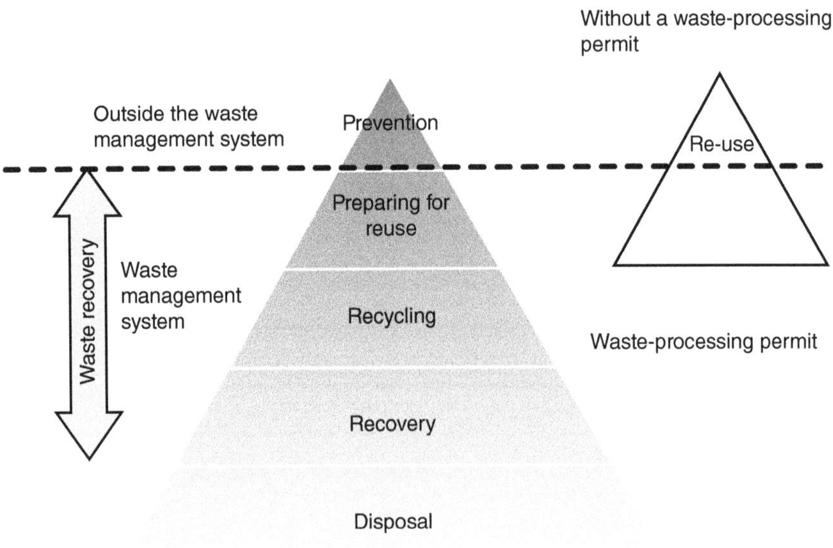

Figure 6.5 Waste management hierarchy

Source: GIOŚ 2013 National Waste Prevention Program, p. 115.

programmes with clearly delineated available preventive measures and waste prevention objectives (National Waste Management Plan, 2022, pp. 5–6).

The principles of waste management depend on its morphological composition and sources. The definition of waste in the Framework Directive is of primary importance here, as it is being used as a reference for legal documents in other areas of environmental legislation, e.g. Landfill Directive, Industrial Emissions Directive, Waste Shipment Regulation, etc.

The most general classification of waste (Figure 6.6) specified in the Regulation divides it into two groups: hazardous waste and non-hazardous waste.

Such a classification of waste requires a basic explanation in the context of the discussed issue. The group of non-hazardous waste includes municipal waste, generated through broadly understood industrial activity and its infrastructure, packaging waste, etc. Hazardous waste also includes part of the municipal waste generated in households and through business activities, including PCBs, oils, medical waste, including infectious and veterinary waste, batteries, electrical and electronic equipment, waste containing asbestos, out-of-date plant protection chemicals, packaging, and others. In accordance with Art. 20 on hazardous waste generated in households, by January 1, 2025, member states are obliged to introduce separate collection for hazardous waste generated in households and ensure its processing in accordance with Art. 4 and 13, and to ensure that it does not contaminate other municipal waste streams.

Pursuant to the act on waste, waste management is understood as the collection, transport and processing of waste, including supervision over such

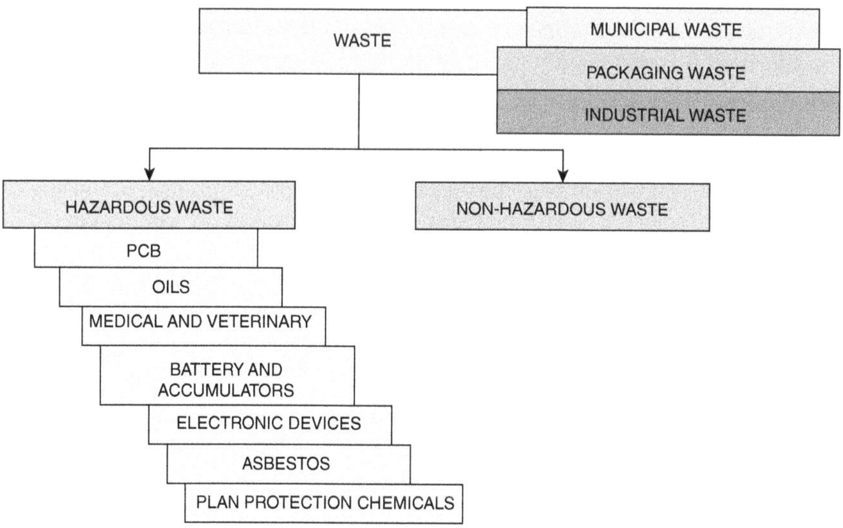

Figure 6.6 General classification of waste

Source: Own study.

processes and over waste disposal sites. For this reason, great importance is attached to the successive implementation and improvement of the principles defining the EU strategy in terms of waste management, including (Klatka, Kuźniak, 2012, p. 16):

- prevention of waste generation – measures undertaken to prevent and reduce the generation of waste; recycling and landfilling should only be used when the generation of waste could not have been prevented;
- recycling of waste – if waste generation could not have been prevented, it should be recovered or disposed of in a way so as not to endanger human health and the environment;
- maximum limitation of waste landfilling – waste landfilling should only be used as a last resort;
- restoration – taking measures aimed at restoring degraded areas to an optimal condition;
- safe transport of waste – increasing safety and reducing the risks related to the transport of waste.

Waste is managed appropriately, provided that the types of waste are correctly identified based on a detailed analysis of their sources. The classification should reflect sources and paths of waste generation, its hazardous properties and components. Waste catalogues define the groups, subgroups and types of waste, along with codes and a list of hazardous waste. There are many regional and international classifications, but the standard, international classification of waste distinguishes 27 basic groups of waste. The current European waste classification is compliant with the EUROSTAT methodology (Guidance on Classification, 2010). It was adopted by the European Commission in 2010. In turn, the Polish waste classification is based mainly on documentation prepared by the European Economic Commission (EEC).

The basis for the classification of waste in Poland is the waste catalogue introduced by the Regulation of the Minister of Climate of 2 January 2020 *on the waste catalogue*. The regulation classifies types of waste into 20 groups, according to their sources. Group 18, which includes infectious waste, is presented in detail in Chapter 1.

What is fundamental for proper waste management is the implementation of the following processes, one by one, which together make up the waste management system:

1 identification of types of waste and their appropriate classification depending on their properties, composition, nature and degree of hazard they pose, based on the current waste classification;
2 selective collection of waste, i.e. its segregation into groups, in a given place and time, on the basis of developed and implemented procedures, taking into account technological limitations and processing capabilities;

3 internal transport to the place of temporary storage – storage before waste is subjected to disposal or transported to the disposal site;
4 storage in places where the waste was generated;
5 selection of waste recovery or disposal technology depending on the level of hazard posed by a given type of waste;
6 external shipment of waste to the target place of management (landfill, incineration plant, recovery site);
7 reporting.

The functioning of the waste management system (Figure 6.7) involves the physical flow of waste streams and information relevant for the purposes of reporting.

These include the processes of:

- collection (sorting, packing, labelling);
- internal transport;
- storage;
- external shipment;
- processing – target destination (recovery or disposal);
- information and reporting.

The waste management system requires the implementation of technical and organisational solutions in terms of these processes, especially in medical facilities during the COVID-19 pandemic. The types of waste generated in medical facilities are illustrated in Figure 6.8.

In addition to municipal waste and non-hazardous medical waste, medical facilities also generate hazardous waste (drugs), chemical reagents, microbiological cultures, human remains, blood and secretion, materials contaminated

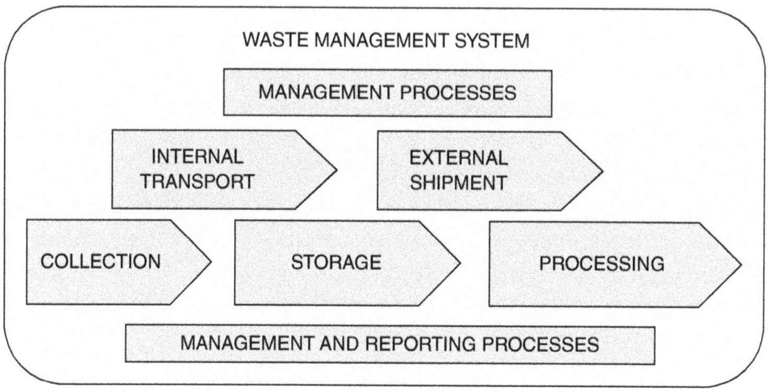

Figure 6.7 Processes in the general waste management system

Source: Own study.

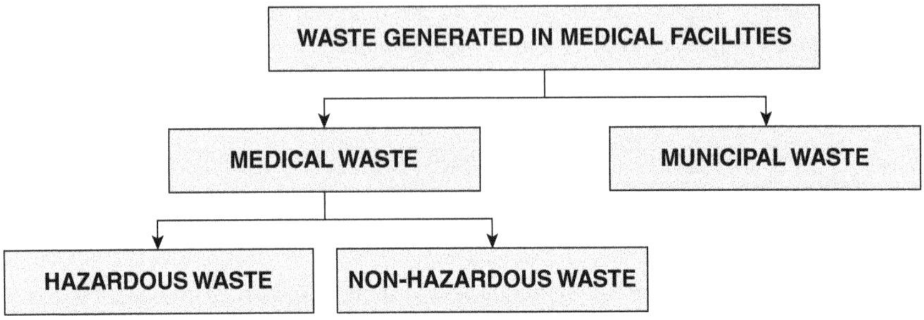

Figure 6.8 Types of waste generated in medical facilities

Source: Own study.

with blood and secretion, biological waste, dressings, gloves, sponges and tools such as pipettes, syringes, needles, scalpels, etc., used for treatment. As indicated by research, the likelihood of the presence of infectious agents in such an environment is estimated at 81–98% (Grabowski, Wielgosiński, 2008). In addition, these risks should be considered when organising logistical operations in medical facilities. For this reason, strict waste management procedures have been imposed on medical waste producers, which they may either perform on their own or entrust to another entity with appropriate facilities and permits to collect or process waste.

What is fundamental for proper waste management is the implementation of the following processes, one by one, which together make up an integrated waste management system:

- identification of types of waste and their appropriate classification depending on their properties, composition, nature and degree of hazard they pose, based on the current waste classification;
- selective collection of waste, i.e. its segregation into groups, in a given place and time, based on developed and implemented procedures, taking into account technological limitations and processing capabilities;
- internal transport to the place of temporary storage – storage before waste is subjected to disposal or transported to the disposal site;
- storage in places where the waste was generated (i.e. in a given medical facility);
- selection of waste recovery or disposal technology depending on the level of hazard posed by a given type of waste;
- external shipment of medical waste to waste management facilities according to the technology adopted.

Medical waste is collected at the place where healthcare services are provided, for example in hospitals, hospices, specialist clinics, outpatient clinics, research institutes and laboratories, health resorts, rehabilitation and treatment centres, health clinics, treatment rooms, and diagnostic laboratories. Individual waste streams are collected separately, depending on their type and characteristics, to facilitate further processing (recovery or disposal). The collection criteria are presented here:

- waste with codes: 18 01 02*, 18 01 03* and 18 01 82*, except for items with sharp edges, is collected in opaque red, sealable, disposable polyethylene foil bags, which are durable and resistant to moisture and chemicals;
- waste with codes 18 01 06*, 18 01 08*, 18 01 10*, except for items with sharp edges, is collected in opaque yellow, sealable, disposable polyethylene foil bags, which are durable and resistant to moisture and chemicals;
- waste with codes 18 01 01, 18 01 04, 18 01 07, 18 01 09, except for items with sharp edges, is collected in disposable, opaque polyethylene foil bags of a colour other than red or yellow, which are durable and resistant to moisture and chemicals or in reusable containers.

Other regulations regarding the collection process are as follows:

- bags are placed on racks or in rigid containers (disposable or reusable) to prevent contamination of people who come into contact with these items;
- medical waste with sharp edges is collected in rigid disposable containers, resistant to moisture, punctures or cutting;
- containers or bags are filled to 2/3 of their volume to enable their secure sealing;
- if a bag or container is damaged, it should be placed in a larger container or bag;
- it is prohibited to open disposable containers or bags once they have been sealed;
- containers or bags should be replaced at least every 72 hours;
- each container and bag containing medical waste should have a visible label with the waste code, the address of the waste producer and the date it was sealed.

Pursuant to the Act on waste, in some cases temporary storage of waste is required prior to its transportation, recovery or disposal. Medical waste has strictly defined storage conditions:

- medical waste with code 18 01 02*, including body parts and blood containers, is stored only at a temperature of up to 10°C, and the storage time should not exceed 72 hours;
- other types of waste with codes: 18 01 03* and 18 01 82*, 18 01 06*, 18 01 08*, 18 01 10* should be stored at a temperature ranging between 10°C and

18°C if their properties allow, but not longer than 72 hours, while at a temperature of up to 10°C – no longer than 30 days;
- medical waste with codes: 18 01 01, 18 01 04, 18 01 07, 18 01 09 should be stored for as long as its properties allow, but no longer than 30 days.

The Regulation of the Minister of Health specifies the conditions that rooms and refrigeration equipment must meet in regard to the detailed manner of handling and storage of medical waste.

Internal transport of medical waste from the place where it was generated to the storage, disposal or collection site shall be carried out by dedicated means of transport, such as open or closed trolleys (depending on whether hazardous or non-hazardous waste is moved). For small amounts of waste, closed containers can be used for internal transport. Means of internal transport of medical waste and reusable containers should be disinfected and washed after each use in storage areas intended for this purpose. Detailed requirements regarding internal transport of waste are specified in the regulations mentioned earlier.

Medical waste, due to its activity and infectiousness, requires appropriate processing methods, and the choice of methods depends on the properties and types of hazardous substances they contain (Wandrasz, 2000, p. 15). The current legal regulations prohibit medical waste recovery and require the disposal of infectious medical waste by thermal treatment in hazardous waste incineration plants. Another variant of medical waste management assumes its disposal at the site where it was generated (e.g. in a hospital), with the use of methods alternative to thermal treatment. In accordance with applicable law, alternative methods are subject to the same requirements as thermal methods in terms of the composition and properties of waste after processing, i.e. the waste should be rendered non-infectious, and the total organic carbon content should be reduced to 5%. Alternative methods such as autoclaving, thermal disinfection, thermal-chemical disinfection or microwave processing do not meet the second requirement. Consequently, alternative methods can currently be used only as an interim solution in medical waste processing. The step that should follow disinfection (sterilisation), required to comply with legal regulations, is subjecting the waste to thermal transformation, preferably in municipal waste incineration plants (Marczak, 2012).

External shipment of hazardous medical waste is carried out in accordance with the regulations applicable to the transport of dangerous goods. It is regulated by strict legal requirements, the most important of which is the European Agreement concerning the International Carriage of Dangerous Goods by Road (ADR). Vehicles used for the shipment of waste must also meet the requirements of separate regulations (e.g. traffic law, transport of dangerous goods, etc.). The entity responsible for waste shipment (including hazardous waste) must hold an appropriate permit to carry out the activity in the field of waste transport. Such a permit is issued by the starosta competent for the seat or place of residence of the waste holder. The entity ordering the shipment of waste is obliged to indicate to the service provider the target destination of waste and the entity to which the waste should be delivered (Act on Waste, 2012; ADR Agreement, 2019).

Practical aspects of waste management during the COVID-19 pandemic

The basis for a practical approach to waste management under the COVID-19 project are the EC guidelines on waste management (EC Guidelines, 2020). The document was developed with the support of the European Centre for Disease Prevention and Control (ECDC). According to ECDC, standard waste management procedures can ensure sufficient safety against SARS-CoV-2 infection. The guidelines also mention that household waste does not play a fundamental role in the transmission of SARS-CoV-2 or other respiratory viruses (ECDC Report, 2020). In terms of the protection against coronavirus infection at work, the European Agency for Safety and Health at Work has issued guidelines on this matter (Chapter 3). According to specialists, the continuity of the provision of municipal waste management services, including separate waste collection and recycling in accordance with EU law, should be ensured.

Preventing disruptions to selective waste collection is important to ensure that the infrastructure for the collection and processing of mixed waste is not overloaded, which could pose a potential threat of further disruptions to the division of tasks in terms of waste collection. The provision, which says that people who are suspected or have been diagnosed with coronavirus should have a separate bag for used wipes, face masks, gloves and similar waste, and should dispose of it into mixed waste containers, seems somewhat unclear. No special system for the collection or disposal of such waste has been provided for (ECDC Report, 2020).

There are no regulations that would require separating the stream of municipal waste contaminated with COVID-19. In the event of disorganisation of the waste collection system, e.g. due to staff shortages, it is recommended to ensure the continuity and sufficient frequency of mixed waste and bio-waste collection, and to limit the frequency of collection of dry secondary raw materials, e.g. waste electrical and electronic equipment (WEEE), batteries or bulk waste.

On the other hand, waste generated in connection with the provision of healthcare services, in laboratories and in the course of other actions involving COVID-19 patients, should be collected and processed in accordance with EU legislation regarding waste (in particular Directive 2008/98/EC on waste and its Art. 17, 23, 24 and 25 on hazardous waste and permit requirements), as well as with domestic legislation applicable to this category of infectious waste, taking into account the most recent guidelines provided by ECDC. These guidelines apply to waste generated during cleaning of healthcare facilities, which should be treated as category B infectious clinical waste (UN3291), as well as other types of waste potentially contaminated with COVID-19.

When storing waste, it is advisable to use closed containers and place them in a secure area with access restricted to authorised personnel only. The inner and outer surfaces of the containers should be cleaned with an appropriate disinfectant. Sufficient occupational health and safety precautions should also be taken, including occupational risk assessment for workplaces potentially at risk of SARS-COV-2 coronavirus. High risk of exposure to known or probable sources of SARS-CoV-2 is related to the following professions:

- healthcare providers and hospital staff;
- medical transport workers (ambulance drivers);
- funeral services staff;
- healthcare professionals (e.g. doctors, nurses, dentists, paramedics) who perform aerosol-generating procedures (e.g. intubation, certain dental procedures or invasive sampling) on patients who have been diagnosed or are suspected to be infected with COVID-19;
- medical or laboratory staff collecting samples from patients who have been diagnosed or are suspected to be infected with COVID-19;
- solid waste and sewage management system staff, cleaning staff, home repair services workers;
- social workers who have contact with people who may be spreading the virus.

Bearing in mind the high risk of exposure for these professional groups, to ensure the continuity of waste management services, the European Agency for Safety and Health at Work has presented a list of good practices recommended for the waste management sector (osha.europa.eu, 2020), which include:

- adjusting work organisation for the staff to avoid the transmission of the virus between teams (e.g. introducing social distancing, limiting the number of employees in the same place/room);
- ensuring the availability and proper use of appropriate equipment, personal protective equipment and disinfecting products;
- ensuring strict compliance with increased hygiene standards (e.g. frequently changing and cleaning personal protective equipment and workwear; replacement of protective gloves in the event of damage or potential contamination; regular disinfection of devices, vehicle cabins and clothes);
- ensuring that in places where wearing masks is normally obligatory, procedures for putting on and taking off personal protective equipment are strictly followed, thus avoiding accidental contact and contamination;
- if possible, ensuring special working conditions for vulnerable groups, such as elderly workers and people with chronic health problems.

Despite the amendment to the legal requirements and best practices, not all provisions seem clear. What is lacking is specification on handling waste generated by persons quarantined or isolated at home (or in other places). Regarding this issue, the Minister of Climate (Regulation, 2019) and the Chief Sanitary Inspector (Guidelines, 2020) issued joint guidelines on the management of waste generated during the SARS-CoV-2 coronavirus infection and COVID-19 caused by the virus (during the pandemic). However, the document contains some imprecise provisions. For instance, point C – guidelines for people in isolation – says that bags with waste should be moved to a place intended for waste collection and put in a dedicated, labelled container which, if possible, should be provided by the waste recipient. What is recommended (though not obligatory) is to provide bags in a specific colour marked as "C", which, once filled, should be placed in another, ordinary bag. However, there is no mention about special containers.

A solution that could minimise the risks and shorten the municipal waste logistic chain as much as possible could be achieved by introducing certain changes to the special act:

- the local authorities should inform the entity responsible for collecting municipal waste about locations where people are currently quarantined or isolated (there is an amendment in the GDPR provisions);
- the waste collection entity should supply the places of quarantine or isolation with special containers or bags for the collection of waste;
- waste from these places should be transported with special vehicles;
- the waste management hierarchy does not apply to waste from places of quarantine or isolation;
- waste collected from these places should be sent straight to the incinerator for thermal processing.

The suggested solutions closely resemble the principles for handling infectious medical waste. The amendment allows for the storage and thermal processing of municipal waste produced by people in quarantine or isolation without preliminary processing. This, however, is allowed as an exception, not as a rule.

In practice, both healthcare facilities and other places where hazardous waste (including infectious waste) is generated and temporarily stored should have appropriate waste-handling instructions to ensure proper waste management. An example of such an instruction applicable to individual logistic processes for non-hazardous waste (code 18 01 01), as well as hazardous waste (code 18 01 02*), is presented in Table 6.3.

When developing procedures or instructions for handling waste, especially during the COVID-19 pandemic, several basic principles should be considered:

- changes in the waste-processing methods;
- occupational health and safety;
- application of the principles of logic, common sense and good practices.

The situation related to the COVID-19 pandemic raises many doubts and questions. Even though one always has to consider a bacteriological hazard when handling municipal waste, the question is what should be considered as infectious waste, and what as mere municipal waste? How should the collection process be organised, and where should waste generated during quarantine be sent? What should be the procedures for municipal waste incinerators? Should

Table 6.3 Instructions for handling medical waste with codes 18 01 01 and 18 01 02*

Waste code	*Collection process*	*Internal transport process*	*Storage process*	*External shipment process*
18 01 01	COLLECTION POINT: operating rooms, sterile processing department, endoscopy units, treatment rooms. Medical waste is collected selectively in 2, 3, 5-litre, reusable, stiff plastic containers, resistant to punctures, of a colour other than red and yellow, or in 10, 20-litre opaque polyethylene bags, resistant to moisture and chemicals, black or blue in colour. *(The regulations regarding equipping racks and containers with lids opened with a foot pedal lever and marking them with codes for collected waste were extended.)* Labelling with an indelible black marker – waste code, name of the waste producer, sealing date and time, also date and time of opening. Temporary storage in a designated and inaccessible room (in warehouses, sluice rooms, etc.). Replacement of the container as required, but at least every 72 hours *(every 24 hours)*.	Waste from the place of temporary waste collection is transported with an open trolley or in a container intended for medical waste; the loading part of the trolley should be disinfected after each transport of waste in a separate section of the waste storage room; in addition, disinfection is carried out in the event of damage to the containers/bags and spilling of waste; transport staff should use personal protective equipment, including protective gloves resistant to puncture, grey protective apron, full footwear. ***(A ventilation system in places designated for disinfection, washing and storage of means of internal transport of medical waste and reusable containers is required.)***	Waste is collected selectively and stored in a warehouse for non-hazardous waste in a designated, marked location intended only for medical waste; the storage time cannot exceed 30 days.	Waste is transferred to an external entity authorised for waste transport; regulations for non-hazardous waste apply; waste is subsequently passed on for recovery or disposal; a waste transfer card should be filled in and kept in the records.

18 01 02*	Operating rooms, treatment rooms, diagnostic laboratories – medical waste is collected selectively in 30- or 60-litre opaque red disposable polyethylene bags, or in 2, 3, 5 or 10-litre disposable, tightly sealed, stiff plastic containers resistant to punctures, which, once filled, should be placed in a red disposable bag and put closest to the workstation with free access to it. *(The regulations regarding equipping racks and containers with lids opened with a foot pedal lever and marking them with codes for collected waste were extended.)* Labelling of containers or bags with an indelible black marker – waste code, name of the waste producer, sealing date and time, also date and time of opening. the bag/container should be sealed once it is filled to 2/3 of its capacity (it should not be reopened afterwards) and immediately shipped away after treatment or, if required, stored in a hazardous waste warehouse or refrigerated at a temperature of up to 10°C; waste should be shipped away at least every 72 hours (*every 24 hours*).	Waste from the place of temporary waste collection is transported with a closed trolley or in a tightly sealed container intended for medical waste; the trolley should be disinfected after each transport of waste with disinfectants intended for large surfaces, on the basis of hygiene procedures applicable for the hazardous waste warehouse, in a section designated for this purpose; in addition, disinfection is carried out in the event of damage to the containers/bags and spilling of waste; the bags should not be thrown violently; they should be carried by the sealing in an upright position; putting hands underneath the bags should be avoided; transport staff should be vaccinated against hepatitis B, and use personal protective equipment, including protective gloves resistant to puncture, grey protective apron, full footwear. ***(A ventilation system in places designated for disinfection, washing and storage of means of internal transport of medical waste and reusable containers is required.)***	Waste is collected selectively and stored in a hazardous waste warehouse equipped with refrigeration devices, in a designated area, separated from other waste, at a temperature up to 10°C; storage time should not exceed 72 hours; refrigeration rooms and equipment should be made of materials that are easy to wash and disinfect; a washbasin and gravity ventilation should be provided; a calibrated thermometer should be placed inside the refrigeration equipment and temperature reading should be performed once a day and recorded in a special log; refrigeration rooms and equipment should be secured against access by unauthorised persons; employees are obliged to wash and disinfect their hands each time they put waste in the warehouse; after each collection of waste from the warehouse, the refrigeration devices and rooms should be disinfected and washed, which should be registered in the log.	Waste is transferred to an external entity authorised for hazardous waste transport (a permit is required); regulations for the transport of hazardous items apply; waste is passed on only for disposal; a waste transfer card should be filled in and kept in the records.

Source: Own study based on: Krupnik, 2015.

Selective Municipal Waste Collection Points be closed during a pandemic? At the beginning of COVID-19, the Waste Management Employers' Union, the Polish Chamber of Waste Management, the National Waste Management Chamber, the Boards of Regional Municipal Waste Processing Plants and the OHS Coalition pointed out that the industry did not have any special regulations regarding waste management in such circumstances. A sanitary disaster was anticipated in connection with mass infections of employees or the need to impose quarantine on waste treatment and collection facilities. Even though the pandemic has now been ongoing for 9 months, the same questions and doubts have been raised, despite the fact that waste collection is carried out on a daily basis and the amounts and types of waste do not exceed the existing capabilities of the plants.

Conclusions and discussion

The conducted research and the presented system and standardisation solutions could allow for a quick diagnosis of the state and functioning of the waste management system in crisis situations and for the creation of a universal, systemic approach to waste management, based on system procedures and standardisation documents, as well as extended responsibility for all participants in the waste supply chain, at all management levels. In the face of a crisis, these solutions are aimed at protecting human health and life and may have practical implications for all participants of the waste supply chain during the COVID-19 pandemic, and once it is over, they may be used as preventive measures. The solutions may be applied by companies operating in the field of waste management, entities collecting, transporting and processing waste, waste recyclers and representatives of municipal waste management plants and facilities.

References

AAP 48 ed.B (2013). *NATO system life cycle processes*. NSA, https://tssodyp.ssb.gov.tr/genel/ReferansDokumanlar/AAP-48%20NATO%20System%20Life%20Cycle%20Processes-Mart%202013.pdf.

Act on Waste (2012). Ustawa z dnia 14 grudnia 2012 r. *o odpadach* (Dz. U. z 2020 r., with changes).

ADR Agreement (2019). European agreement concerning the international carriage of dangerous goods by road ADR applicable as from 1 January 2019. https://unece.org/transport/publications/european-agreement-concerning-international-carriage-dangerous-goods-road.

Announcement (2015). Komunikat Komisji do Parlamentu Europejskiego, Rady, Europejskiego Komitetu Ekonomiczno-Społecznego i Komitetu Regionów (2015). *Zamknięcie obiegu – plan UE dotyczący gospodarki o obiegu zamkniętym*. Bruksela: Komunikat Komisji do Parlamentu Europejskiego.

COM (2005). *666 final thematic strategy on the prevention and recycling of waste*. http://eurlex.europa.eu/legalcontent/EN/TXT/?uri=CELEX:52005DC0666.

Consolidated Waste Directive (2018). DYREKTYWA PARLAMENTU EUROPEJSKIEGO I RADY (UE) 2018/851 z dnia 30 maja 2018 r, Dz.U.UE.L.2018.150.109.

Directive (EU) 2018/851 of the European Parliament and of the Council of 30 May 2018 *amending directive 2008/98/EC on* waste, *official journal of the European Union* (Dz.U.UE.L.2018.150.109).

Duczmal, M. (2008). *Nowa dyrektywa ramowa w sprawie odpadów* 2008/98/WE, OiŚ 2008, nr 6, s. 28–37.

EC Guidelines, C. (2020). COVID-19. 1753 *final regarding border management.*

GIOŚ (2013). *Krajowy program zapobiegania powstawaniu odpadów*. Opole: GIOŚ.

Grabowski, Z. and Wielgosiński, G. (2008). *Odpady medyczne i weterynaryjne – warunki unieszkodliwiania. Materiały szkoleniowe*. Warszawa: MŚ.

Guidance on Classification (2010). *Guidance on using the European Waste Catalogue (EWC) to code waste*. Luxembourg: Eurostat.

Guidelines (2020). Wytyczne Ministra Klimatu i Głównego Inspektora Sanitarnego w sprawie postępowania z odpadami wytwarzanymi w czasie występowania zakażeń koronawirusem SARS-CoV-2 i zachorowań na wywoływaną przez niego chorobę COVID-19 (w czasie trwania pandemii/epidemii).

ISO 14006:2020–8 *Environmental management systems – guidelines for incorporating ecodesign.*

Klatka, J. and Kuźniak, M. (2012). *Gospodarowanie odpadami komunalnymi. Poradnik dla gmin.* Warszawa: Wolter Kluwer.

Kosieradzka-Federczyk, A. (2013). Priorytety unii europejskiej w gospodarowaniu odpadami. *Współczesne Problemy Zarządzania*, 1, 47–63.

Krupnik, D. (2015). Selected issues relating to the collection, storage, transport medical waste in Poland. *GMiL*, 5.

Lacy, P. and Rutqvist, J. (2015). *Waste to wealth: the circular economy advantage*. New York: Palgrave Macmillan.

Lederberg, J. and McCray, A. (2015). Ome sweet 'omics – a genealogical treasury of words. *The Scientist*, 15(7), 8.

Marczak, H. (2012). Prawne i ekonomiczne uwarunkowania gospodarki odpadami medycznymi. *Inżynieria Ekologiczna*, 30, 74–84.

National Waste Management Plan (2022). UCHWAŁA Nr 88 RADY MINISTRÓW z dnia 1 lipca 2016 r. w sprawie Krajowego planu gospodarki odpadami 2022. M.P.2016.784.

National Waste Prevention Program (2013). *Krajowy program zapobiegania odpadom.* Opole: GIOŚ.

Osha (2020). www.osha.europa.eu/en/highlights/covid-19-guidance-workplace.

Pikoń, K. (2018). *Gospodarka obiegu zamkniętego w ujęciu holistycznym.* Gliwice: Wydawnictwo Politechniki Śląskiej.

Pinasseau, A. et al. (2018). *Dokument referencyjny dotyczący najlepszych dostępnych technik (BAT) dla przetwarzania odpadów*. Spain, https://docplayer.pl/8261017-Garbowanie-skor-dokument-referencyjny-dotyczacy-najlepszych-dostepnych-technik-bat-dla.html.

Raport ECDC (2020). *Infection prevention and control in the household management of people with suspected or confirmed coronavirus disease (COVID-19)*, www.ecdc.europa.eu/en/publications-data/infection-prevention-control-household-management-covid-19.

Regulation (2019). Rozporządzenie Ministra Klimatu z dnia 24 grudnia 2019 r. *w sprawie warunków uznania odpadów za posiadające właściwości zakaźne oraz sposobu ustalania tych właściwości*, Dz.U. 2020, poz. 3.

Regulation (2020). Rozporządzenie Ministra Klimatu z dnia 2 stycznia 2020 r. *w sprawie katalogu odpadów* (Dz.U.2020 poz. 10).

Schroeder, P., Anggraeni, K. and Weber, U. (2019). The relevance of circular economy practices to the sustainable development goals. *Journal of Industrial Ecology*, 23(1), 77–95.

Styś, T. and Witwicki, B. (2013). *Nowy system gospodarowania odpadami komunalnymi w Polsce. Wybrane aspekty* (54). Warszawa: Instytut Sobieskiego.

Styś, T. and Foks, R. (2014). *Rynek gospodarowania odpadami komunalnymi w Polsce. Perspektywa 2030*. Warszawa: Instytut Sobieskiego.

Villarreal, L.P. (2005). Czy wirusy są żywe. *Świat Nauki*, 1(161).

Wandrasz, J. (2000). *Gospodarka odpadami medycznymi*. Poznań: Polskie Zrzeszenie Inżynierów i Techników Sanitarnych.

7 Motor transport modelling using a simulation program and artificial neural networks

Mieczysław Pawlisiak, Tomasz Waśniewski and Arkadiusz Jóźwiak

Introduction

Nowadays, road transport is the most common mode of transporting people and goods of all kinds. For this purpose, passenger cars, buses of varying capacity and trucks are mainly used. In some cities, trolleybuses are used to transport people. The path to attaining the contemporary position of road transport began in the 21st century. It was back then that, along with the development of the crude oil refining method and the invention of combustion ignition "diesel" engine, the first motor vehicles were constructed, primarily used for passenger transport. Along with the technical and technological progress, a dynamic development of all motor vehicles took place, and today almost every cargo can be transported using a motor vehicle. A vehicle's two fundamental features are an additional factor contributing to the mass use of road transport for cargo and passenger transport in Europe (Jóźwiak, Owczarek, Prochowski, Świderski, 2020). First is speed, resulting from the possession of vehicles with appropriate quality and a well-developed road network. The second feature is the flexibility to adapt to specific conditions or expectations of the passenger or customer. Because of these developments before the outbreak of the COVID-19 pandemic, more than half of cargo and passenger transport in the European Union countries were transported using road transport. Therefore, we are looking for tools for effective modelling of road transport, considering specific requirements. Currently, these requirements are determined by the COVID-19 situation.

Statistical data

The data from November 2019 shows that road transport performed carriage at the level of 1,924,995 tonne-kilometres when implementing cargo transport in the European Union countries. Country specific data is included in Table 7.1.

The data provided shows that European road cargo transport increased by 0.2% between 2017 and 2018. At the same time, cross-border and cabotage transport, which account for 11.5% of total transport performance, decreased by 4.5% in 2018 compared to the results obtained in 2017. On the other hand, a decrease by 4.1% was recorded in inter-trade transport, and the share of cabotage transport in

DOI: 10.4324/9781003285731-7

Table 7.1 Cargo road transport in the European Union countries in 2018 in million tonne-kilometres /tkm/ and changes in relation to 2017[1]

No.	*Entity*	*Domestic transport*	*International transport*	*Cabotage transport*[2]	*Inter-trade transport*[3]	*Total cargo transport*	*Changes compared to 2017*
1	European Union			186 782	45 442	1 924 995	+0.2%
2	Belgium	Pf.	10 073	1 057	962	Pf.	–
3	Bulgaria	7 734	8 572	9 626	Pf.	Pf.	–
4	Czech Republic	23 543	14 972	464	Pf.	Pf.	–
5	Denmark	12 069	Pf.	Pf.	241	14 992	–3.3
6	Federal Republic of Germany	276 151	35 802	1 532	3 287	316 772	+1.2
7	Estonia	1 686	Pf.	Pf.	Pf.	5 775	–
8	Ireland	9 401	1 456	243	Pf.	Pf.	–
9	Greece	15 392	Pf.	Pf.	Pf.	29 279	+3.2
10	Spain	158 476	73 531	Pf.	4 268	Pf.	–
11	France	161 941	10 791	379	Pf.	Pf.	–
12	Croatia	4 235	5 692	186	2 522	12 635	+6.8
13	Italy	111 741	12 070	597	Pf.	Pf.	–
14	Cyprus	865	26	Pf.	Pf.	892	+8.0
15	Latvia	3 459	6 339	Pf.	4 278	Pf.	–
16	Lithuania	3 642	11 016	3 885	15 047	43 590	–
17	Luxembourg	–	–	–	–	–	–
18	Hungary	12 797	15 265	1 069	8 634	37 948	–4.4
19	Malta	–	–	–	–	–	–
20	Netherlands	33 814	28 973	1 862	3 910	68 559	+1.5
21	Austria	16 914	7 105	549	1 195	25 763	–0.8
22	Poland	114 692	125 663	16 637	58 911	315 874	–5.8
23	Portugal	10 530	15 802	1 112	5 518	32 963	–3.6
24	Romania	14 358	20 048	3 725	20 631	58 762	+7.4
25	Slovenia	2 256	9 685	991	9 294	22 225	+6.8
26	Slovakia	6 477	16 095	1 263	11 750	35 586	+0.5
27	Finland	25 790	Pf.	122	Pf.	28 345	–
28	Sweden	40 662	2 521	211	Pf.	Pf.	–
29	Great Britain	151 973	6 510	223	431	159 137	–

Source: Own study based on: https://ec.europa.eu/eurostat/web/covid-19/overview.

the performance of transport decreased by 6.4% in the analysed period. The data in Table 7.1 also shows that the Federal Republic of Germany, as one of the most important countries in European road transport /16.5% of transports carried out in the EU in tkm/, was ahead of Poland, whose share in the European cargo transport market reached 16.4% in 2018. It can also be noted that there are countries such as Cyprus with an increase of 8.0%, Romania with an increase of 7.4%, and Slovenia and Croatia with an increase of 6.8% each, which are in the stage of a significant growth in the performance of road cargo transport. On the other hand, there are countries that recorded a decrease in the amount of road cargo transport in the analysed period. These are Poland – decrease by 5.8%, Hungary – decrease by 4.4%, Portugal – decrease by 3.6% and Denmark – decrease by 3.3%. It is also worth noting that only Croatia and Cyprus recorded an increase in all modes of transport, with an increase of 6.8% and 8.0%, respectively, recorded in total transport. On the other hand, Poland recorded a decrease in all modes of transport, with an overall decrease of 5.8%. It is also interesting that Lithuania, Italy, Croatia and Austria recorded a very strong increase in cabotage, with the largest declines in this type of transport recorded in Finland, Great Britain, Belgium and the Czech Republic. The situation regarding cargo carriage with motor transport in individual countries is complex and diversified. The only trend noticeable over the years is the general increase in cargo transport throughout the European Union. It is not very high, but increases are recorded every year (Chart 7.1).

When analysing cargo carriage with motor transport in the territory of the European Union, it is important to look at this issue taking into consideration the length of transport routes. The distance of goods transportation measuring from 150 to 1,999 km recorded the largest increase in 2018. The details are presented in Table 7.2.

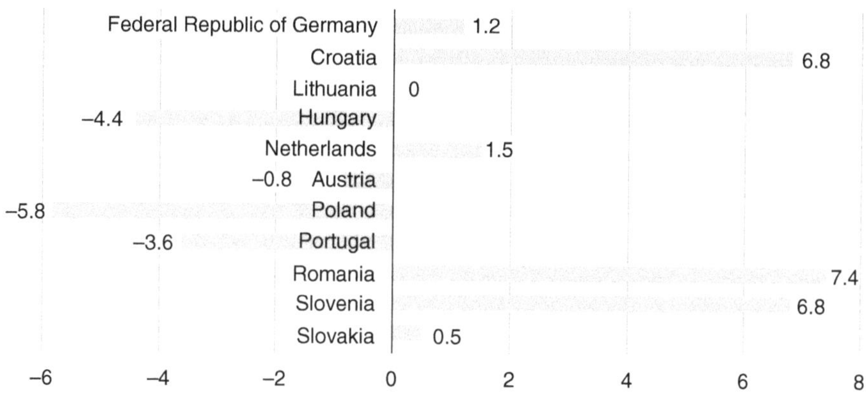

Chart 7.1 Changes in cargo carriage with motor transport in percentage points in selected EU countries in 2018 (based on Table 7.1)

Source: Own study.

Table 7.2 The increase in the volume of goods transported with motor transport depending on the length of the transport route

No.	*Specification – length of the transport route [km]*	*Increase [%]*
1	150–299	16.5
2	300–499	17.4
3	500–999	14.1

Source: Own study based on: https://ec.europa.eu/eurostat/web/structural-business-statistics/global-value-chains/international-sourcing.

The data contained in Table 7.2 clearly indicates that the transport of goods along a route of 150 kilometres or more is gaining more and more popularity in Europe, and it is probably the result of ordinary economic calculation. Whatever is profitable both for the entrepreneur and the customer thrives.

Motor transport plays an extremely important role in passenger transport. It can be even said that it is dominant in many countries. The obtained data from 2016 shows that passenger cars performed the greatest amount of transport work/passenger kilometres. For the entire European Union, it accounts for approximately 82.9%, considering all forms of land transport. In turn, the share of coaches, buses and trolleybuses at that time was at the level of 9.4%.

The passenger car was the most important means of passenger transport in Lithuania and Portugal, where nearly 90% of all passenger transport was carried out by passenger cars. On the other hand, in Slovakia, the Czech Republic and Hungary, the share of passenger cars in passenger transport did not exceed 75% of the total land transport carriage. In the case of Hungary, this results from the fact that in this country the share of coaches and buses in passenger transport was the highest and reached 21.7%. It can also be noted that the coach, bus and trolleybus transport enjoyed the least popularity in the Netherlands and did not exceed 3%. In addition, railway transport, which is not very popular for passenger transport in the European Union, should be perceived as complementary to land transport. Nevertheless, the highest share of railway in passenger transport was recorded in Austria /12.1%/ and the Netherlands /11.0%/. However, the share of railway in passenger transport in Switzerland was much higher, about 19.8% of all passenger transport. At the same time, the share of railway in passenger transport reaching the level of 2% was recorded in Estonia, Slovenia, Greece and Lithuania (https://ec.europa.eu/eurostat/web/structural-business-statistics/global-value-chains/international-sourcing).

The situation in road transport changed completely in 2020. It resulted from the occurrence of a disease commonly known as coronavirus or COVID-19 at present. The pandemic spreading around the world has caused changes in the way societies function. This in turn has led to an economic stagnation and reduction in the transport of passengers and goods. Closed borders and the requirement to remain in quarantine during certain periods led some industries to a complete stagnation. This mainly applies to international goods exchange and, as an example, to the tourism industry.

At present, for reasons of time, there is no reliable comprehensive data on the volume of cargo and passenger carriage using motor transport (Świderski, 2009). The search for the data on the decrease in the performance of transport tasks may be conducted by following the example of one-month-long transport of broadly understood fuels. Data on changes in fuel demand comparing March to April 2020 in the European Union countries is shown in Table 7.3.

From the point of view of the research conducted, it is a significant fact that the EU Member States have taken various measures to slow down the spread of COVID-19. These measures translated directly into the use of fuels in land transport, including motor transport. The measures taken by individual countries began

Table 7.3 Changes in the volume of fuel demand in the European Union countries in March–April 2020

No.	*Country*	*Gasoline thousand tons*		*Diesel fuel thousand tons*		*LPG thousand tons*		*Heating oil thousand tons*		*Kerosene thousand tons*	
		[thousand tons]	*[change compared to March]*	*[thousand tons]*	*[change compared to March]*	*[thousand tons]*	*[change compared to March]*	*[thousand tons]*	*[change compared to March]*	*[thousand tons]*	*[change compared to March]*
1	Belgium	53	–59%	953	–20%	201	+ 1%	454	+7%	68	–41%
2	Bulgaria	19	–32%	93	–46%	22	–27%	2	0 %	9	–31%
3	Czech Republic	92	–12%	325	–13%	19	–39%	3	–57%	8	–47%
4	Denmark	81	–11%	346	+1%	5	0%	20	+11%	15	–67%
5	Federal Republic of Germany	1010	–20%	3892	–14%	314	+1%	227	+14%	251	–62%
6	Estonia	22	–8%	55	–17%	1	–50%	22	+57%	2	–50%
7	Ireland	18	–65%	211	–37%	12	–33%	1	–80%	122	–40%
8	Spain	97	–65%	1659	–31%	159	–35%	491	–1%	39	–87%
9	France	221	–58%	2370	–29%	280	–19%	99	–9%	120	–70%
10	Croatia	19	–39%	122	–14%	8	–11%	3	–25%	1	–75%
11	Italy	164	–55%	1111	–30%	157	–30%	210	–20%	54	–68%
12	Cyprus	8	–58%	47	–41%	3	–50%	45	–13%	2	–82%
13	Latvia	11	–8%	93	–10%	5	–17%	0	0	1	–80%
14	Lithuania	17	+6%	143	–5%	9	–18%	12	–33%	4	–33%
15	Luxembourg	6	–70%	84	–45%	0	0	0	0	40	+3%
16	Hungary	87	–16%	258	–9%	41	0	0	0	2	–82%
17	Malta	4	0	33	–35%	3	+50%	167	–8%	7	+17%
18	Netherlands	221	–22%	521	–19%	288	–1%	707	–2%	93	–58%
19	Austria	61	–33%	557	–14%	11	+175%	16	–33%	8	–80%
20	Poland	246	–22%	1268	–16%	188	–2%	88	–4%	9	–79%
21	Portugal	36	–45%	256	–30%	80	+1%	82	–8%	8	–89%
22	Romania	49	–57%	412	–26%	29	–31%	15	0	2	+100%
23	Slovenia	22	–8%	66	–34%	7	–22%	10	–23%	1	0
24	Slovakia	33	–11%	116	–13%	11	–31%	21	–9%	1	–50%
25	Finland	83	–13%	345	–5%	81	–5%	23	–8%	14	–74%
26	Sweden	154	–14%	465	+18%	64	–26%	167	–25%	30	–14%

Source: Own study based on: https://ec.europa.eu/eurostat/web/products-eurostat-news.

in mid-March and were in full force throughout April 2020 (Świderski, Jóźwiak, Jachimowski, 2018).

The preliminary data from April shows that the decline in demand for the implementation of transport tasks, which was observed in March, is still visible, and in some countries, it is deepening and has spread across the entire European Union (Gandini, Studer, Borghetti, 2015).

Analysing the data contained in Table 7.3 and converting it into real values, it can be noticed that in April 2020, because of the restrictions caused by the COVID-19 pandemic, gasoline deliveries were decreased in all EU countries. In comparison to March, the largest decrease was observed in France /-311,000 tons, 58%/, the Federal Republic of Germany /-250,000 tons, 20%/, Italy/ -203,000 tons, 55%/ and Spain /-179,000 tons, 65%/.

The deliveries of gas and diesel fuel also decreased in most of the EU member states. The largest decrease in absolute terms compared to March was observed in France /-983,000 tonnes, 29%/, Spain /-737,000 tonnes, 31%/, the Federal Republic of Germany /-640,000 tonnes, 14%/ and in Italy /-485,000 tons, 30%/.

It can be noticed that the data presented in Table 7.3 shows that in April 2020, gasoline and diesel fuel deliveries throughout the European Union decreased by 34% and 21%, respectively, compared to March. A larger decrease by 46% and 25%, respectively, was noted when taking as a starting point the month of January 2020, when no restrictive measures had been introduced yet (https://ec.europa.eu/eurostat/web/products-eurostat-news).

The simulation model of transport in Europe

Road transport in Europe during the pandemic recorded a decrease in the provision of services. This stemmed from the lack of transport procedures during emergencies such as COVID-19. This problem may be solved by the construction of simulation models based on spatial simulation programs. Spatial simulation programs allow for building models from ready-made modules which can be freely configured or programmed according to the needs. These types of solutions allow tests of several variants and selection of the best one in a short time. Various solutions which can be easily applied are embedded in simulation programs (Siskos, Grigoroudis, Matsatsinis, 2005).

In the model 11 senders and 4 recipients were applied along with the possibility of mirroring the entire transport in the European Union. The construction of an immense model calls for time and computing power which the computer must be equipped with. In some simulation programs, small models can be built, and tests may be run on them. In the model proposed, 11 senders mirror the international transport. The parameters subjected to tests were speed, distance and safe distance between the vehicles called *collision*. The speed values that were tested ranged from 5 to 25 m/s, assuming that the distance between vehicles can be in the range of 50 to 2500 m. Based on these two parameters, the optimal distance that ought to be kept between the vehicles is determined. Figure 7.1 shows the network of connections between senders and recipients. The grey circles are the nodes which

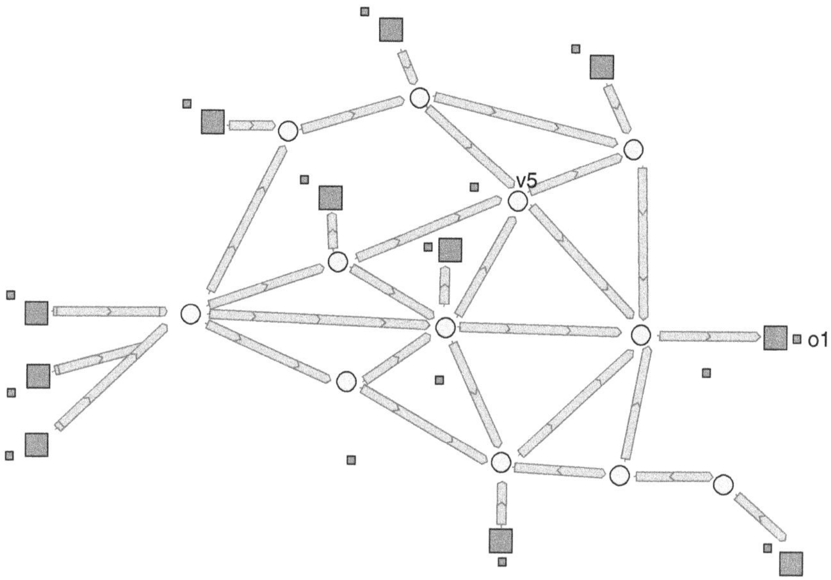

Figure 7.1 Network of connections in the model

Source: Own study.

can be programmed. Each of these nodes was programmed with an appropriate algorithm. The nodes are responsible for directing traffic according to the assumptions of the model (Sedgewick, Wayne, 2017; Hu, Chen, 2012).

The speed, which is an important parameter for the transport of goods and has a significant impact on supply, was studied. If the driver moves at high speed, this forces him or her to be more vigilant and concentrated. This type of situation makes the driver tired sooner, and at the same time driving too slowly causes fatigue. In the model under study, the speed and distance between vehicles was simulated. The two parameters studied with the use of three types of algorithms – speed and distance – will produce the result determining which algorithm will provide the most optimal solutions.

The selected optimal speed and distance will guarantee the safety of the passage and will be comfortable for the driver. The tested model mirrors a system that should control traffic between vehicles to regulate stops in places which allow for appropriate distance between vehicles and drivers and eliminate situations in which a collision could occur (Owczarek, Jóźwiak, 2019).

The graphic form of the model with the use of three algorithms is presented in Figure 7.1.

The advantage of the model is the graphic representation of the situation Figure 7.2.

The model uses three algorithms. The first algorithm mirrors the real movement in the model, where vehicle drivers choose the shortest route. The second

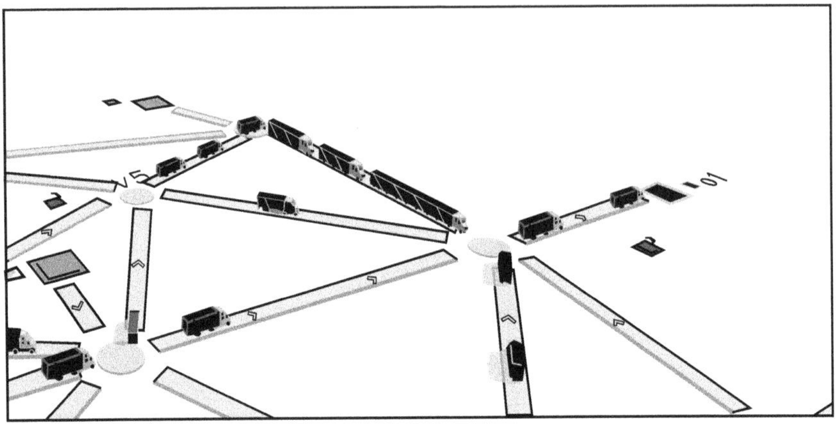

Figure 7.2 3D graphic representation in the network of connections

Source: Own study.

algorithm is a random selection of a route satisfying the distance and speed requirements; in this algorithm, if it is not possible to select both suitable parameters, it chooses one with the best fit. The third algorithm plans the route and selects it to adapt to traffic conditions.

The first algorithm (Chart 7.2) shows the real movement of vehicles. Speed values are varied, which means that drivers are in a hurry due to various traffic situations: 15% are speed values between 4 and 6 m/s (15 and 21 km/h); 12% are 10–12 m/s (36–43 km/h); 16–18 m/s (57–65 km/h) and 24–26 m/s (86–93 km/h). There are different speed values in the algorithm, but only those with the highest percentage rate are considered.

The second algorithm (Chart 7.3) shows the speed values in the range of low and medium speed. The highest share of speed is 17% for the speed of 14–16 m/s, with the speed of 6–8 m/s, which is low speed, accounting for 16%; the speed in the range of 12–14 m/s, which continues the speed range from 12–14 m/s, accounts for 11%.

In the third algorithm (Chart 7.4), we can see that the speed values which occur are high, with an indicator of 17% speed in the range from 24–26 m/s; the range 4–6 m/s accounts for 16%. The speed of 10–12m/s accounts for 13%. When examining the algorithms in terms of speed, we notice that the safe passage criteria for trucks are not met by any of the algorithms.

Another parameter that was tested is the safe distance between vehicles.

The range from 50 m to 2500 m was adopted as the safe distance. In the first algorithm, the element tested represents 20% for the distance between 600–800m, successive percentage parameters for 15% and 19% for the distance between 50–400m (Chart 7.5).

However, the second algorithm (Chart 7.6) for 47% adopted 600–800m as the safest distance. In turn, the range from 50–200m accounts for 11%. The remaining percentage parameters are within the range of 2–8 percentage points (Chart 7.5).

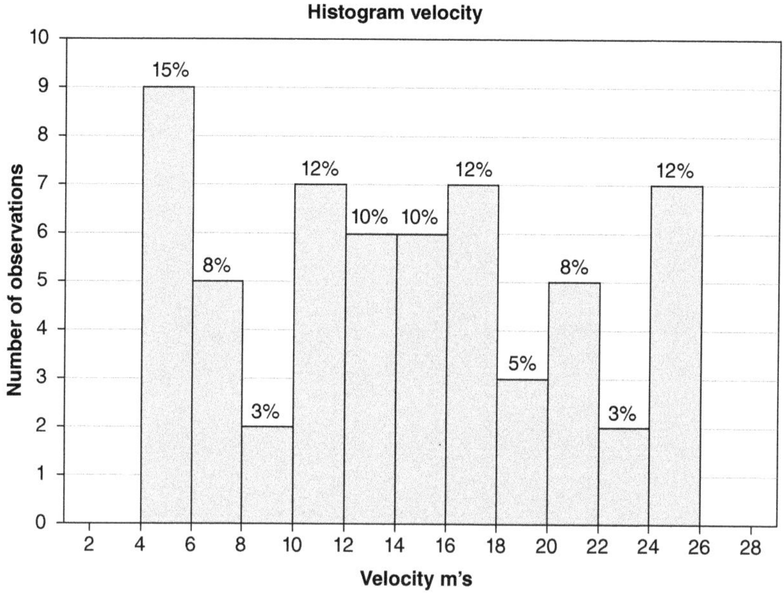

Chart 7.2 Speed for the first algorithm

Source: Own study.

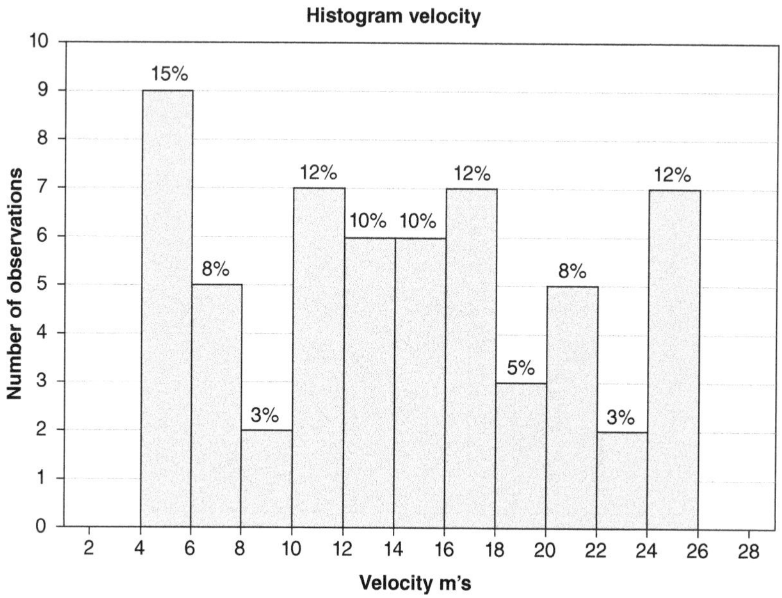

Chart 7.3 Speed for the second algorithm

Source: Own study.

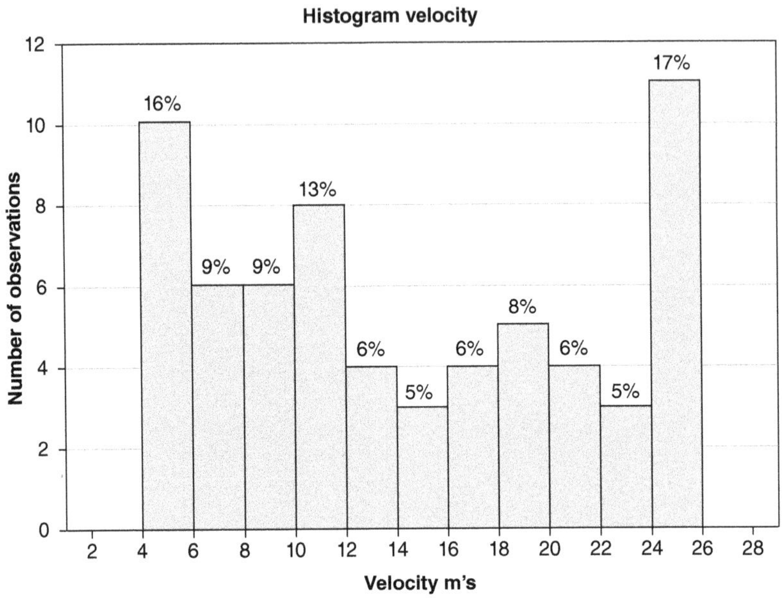

Chart 7.4 Speed for the third algorithm

Source: Own study.

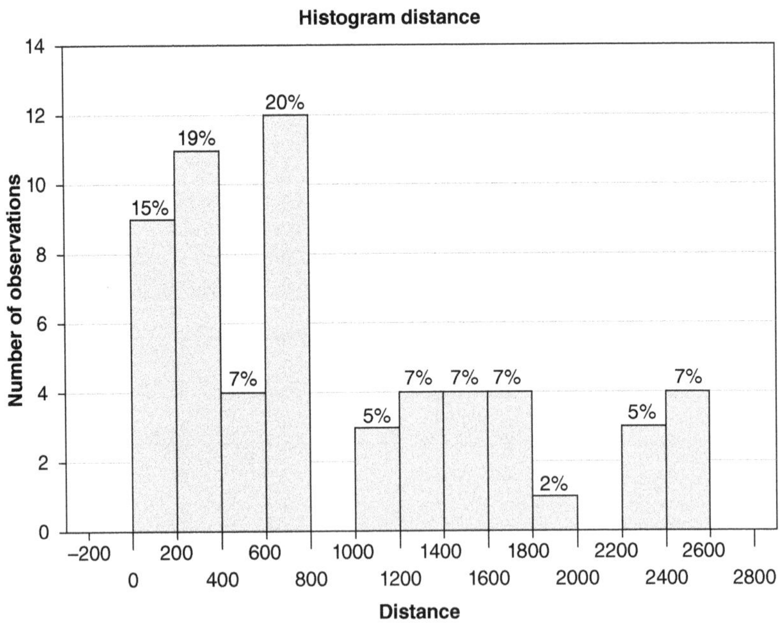

Chart 7.5 First algorithm distances

Source: Own study.

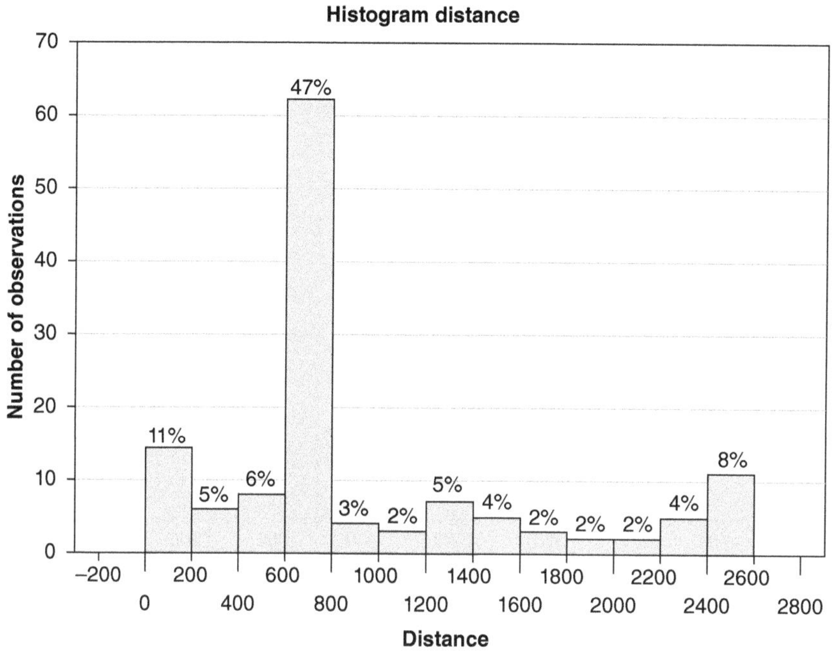

Chart 7.6 Second algorithm distances

Source: Own study.

The tested third algorithm (Chart 7.7) provides four solutions for the distance between vehicles ranging from 50 to 800 meters. For the distance 50–200 meters it is 9%; for the distance 201–400 it is 20%; for the distance 401–600 meters it is 17%, with the last case being 22%. This type of solution will allow greater flexibility in spacing vehicles.

The third parameter that was tested determines whether there are cases in which vehicles did not keep the required distance while driving. For the first (Chart 7.8) algorithm, the cases where the distance between vehicles was not exceeded reached 61%, which equals 36 different solutions.

However, the second algorithm (Chart 7.9) yields 71% of cases without exceeding the distance, which equals 94 different solutions.

The third algorithm yields 69% (Chart 7.10) of cases without exceeding the distance between the vehicles while driving, which equals 44 different solutions.

It can be said that the best solution is the second algorithm, which is tasked with adjusting the speed and distance so that there will be no collisions. As can be seen from the results, there are as many as 71% of cases in which 94 solutions are available for this example. This type of solution shows that the tool in the form of a simulation program allows for quick implementation of results to verify the best solutions.

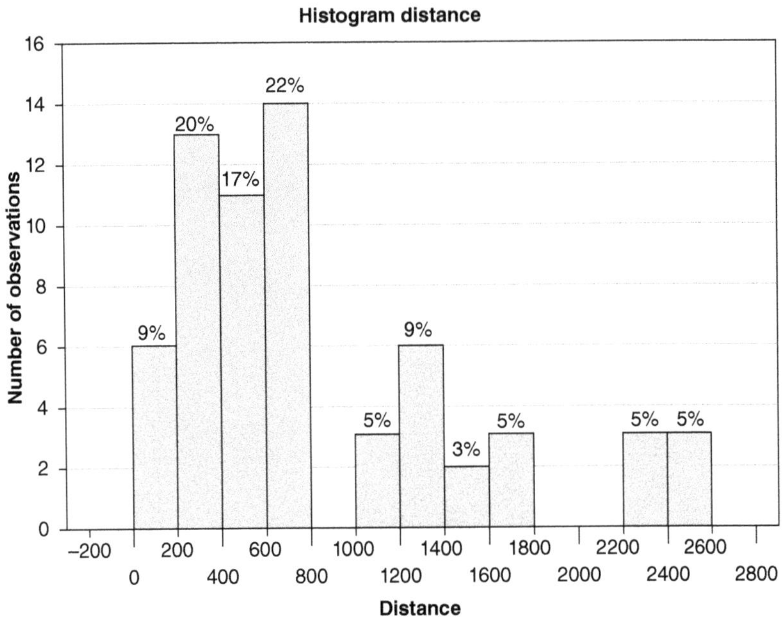

Chart 7.7 Third algorithm distances

Source: Own study.

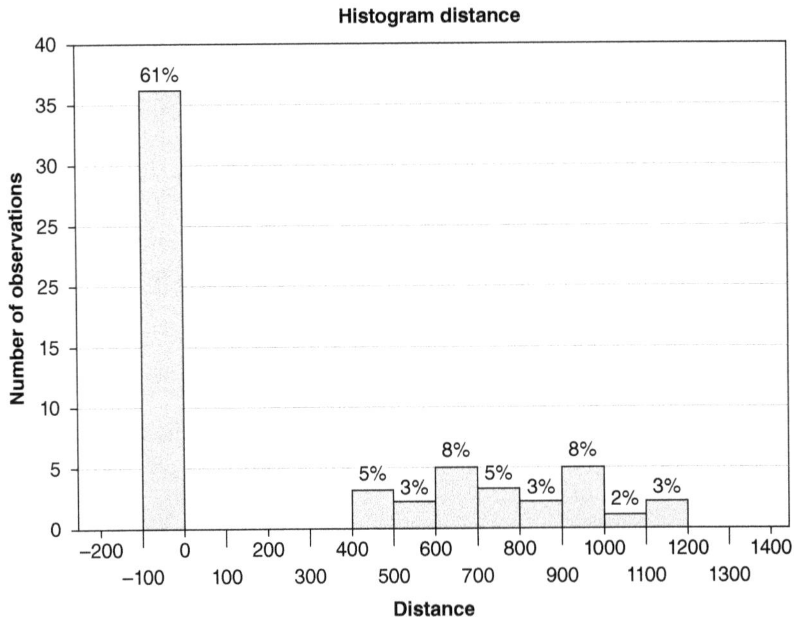

Chart 7.8 First algorithm collisions

Source: Own study.

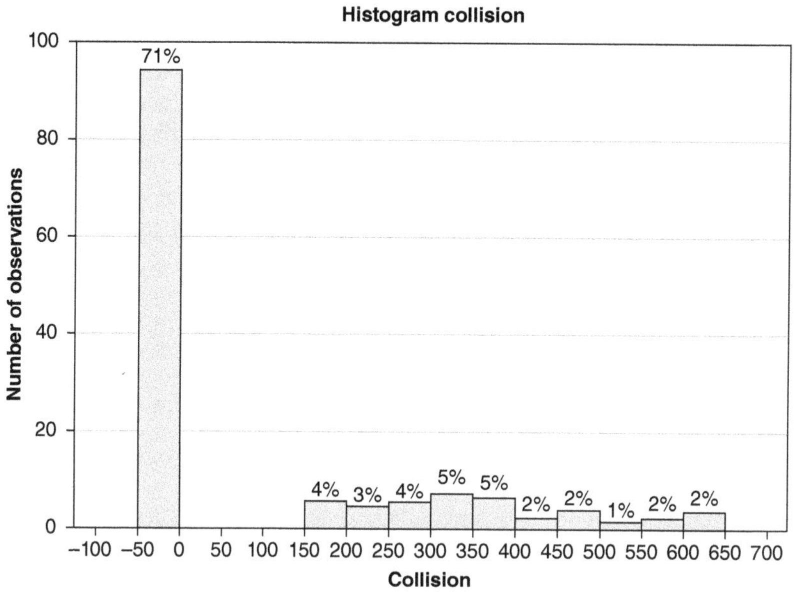

Chart 7.9 Second algorithm collisions

Source: Own study.

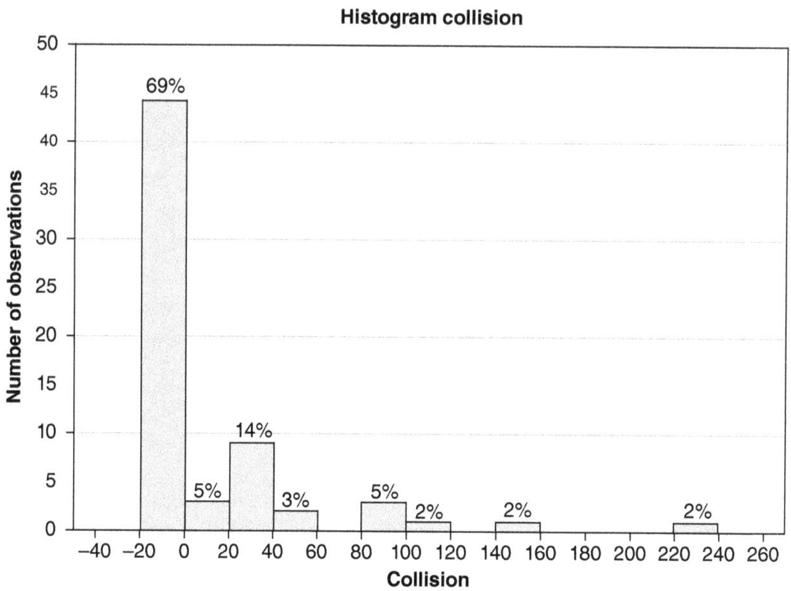

Chart 7.10 Third algorithm collisions

Source: Own study.

Neural modelling

Various tools can be used for data analysis, e.g. a transport cycle card (Głodowska, 2018), a computer simulation method (Brzeziński, Waśniewski, Kijek, 2015; Kozicki, 2018), the use of the ARIMA model (Grzelak, 2019) or neural networks (Jóźwiak, 2017; Kozicki, 2018). The research into the possibility and method of using artificial neural networks for road transport simulation modelling, the data was generated from a simulation model in the form of a database. To use neural networks, quantitative input and output signals were defined, and the following were classified as such:

- input signal:
    - v – vehicle speed in the model [m/s];
    - d – distance between the vehicles moving in the model, [m]
- output signal: n – number of collisions

Out of numerous types of neural networks and algorithms for their learning, further research employed the *Multilayer Perceptron* and learning algorithms: conjugate gradient method; steepest descent method, BFGS method (*Broyden – Fletcher – Goldfarb – Shanno*). The neural network that was used belongs to the groups:

- one-way networks, with one-way flow of information (from the input to the output of the neural network);
- the so-called supervised networks, where the learning process takes place under the supervision of the teacher (there is a reference signal among the outbound signals).

Using the Statistica 13.3 computer program, based on the generated data, the process of neural network training was carried out. Along with the indication of the input data, the sizes of the sets were defined. It was determined that:

- 80% of the data would be the training set used to modify the weights;
- 10% would be a test set intended for ongoing monitoring of the learning process;
- 10% would be a validation set for network quality assessment after completion of the learning process.

The basic parameters of the network were then specified, i.e.: type of network (multi-layer perceptron – MLP), minimum number of hidden neurons, maximum number of hidden neurons, number of training networks, number of retained networks, function of activating hidden and output neurons, weight reduction values for the hidden layer and the output layer.

After defining the data and parameters of the network, the neural network training process was carried out using the collected data. To obtain the best

Table 7.4 Examples of neural network designs

Network ID	*Network name*	*Quality (learning)*	*Quality (testing)*	*Quality (validation)*	*Learning algorithm*	*Activation (hidden)*	*Activation (output)*
12	MLP 2–3–1	0.940416	0.984310	0.994042	BFGS 16	Tanh	Linear
13	MLP 2–14–1	0.931625	0.986719	0.981549	BFGS 18	Sinus	Sinus
14	MLP 2–2–1	0.914518	0.987091	0.967558	BFGS 6	Logistic	Sinus
15	MLP 2–16–1	0.910349	0.969875	0.965915	BFGS 5	Sinus	Sinus
19	MLP 2–32–1	0.935561	0.996984	0.998224	BFGS 3	Linear	Logistic
21	MLP 2–6–1	0.936371	0.995529	0.994798	BFGS 24	Sinus	Logistic
22	MLP 2–12–1	0.913189	0.970385	0.971270	BFGS 8	Linear	Linear
24	MLP 2–4–1	0.962172	0.981749	0.996307	BFGS 24	Exponential	Tanh
25	MLP 2–33–1	0.970990	0.986942	0.996316	BFGS 27	Tanh	Tanh
32	MLP 2–8–1	0.910359	0.970411	0.966007	BFGS 5	Linear	Sinus

Source: Own study.

representative data, the outliers were discarded from this data for each parameter. The examples of the results of this process are presented in Table 7.4.

The structure of the best network assumed the form of MLP 2–4–1, which means 2 neurons in the input layer, 4 neurons in the hidden layer and 1 neuron in the output layer.

The columns "Quality learning", "Quality testing" and "Quality validation" show a very positive result of the learning process, where the values range from 94% to 98% probability of indicating the correct value at the neural network output. The neural network learning plot also (Jóźwiak, 2017) confirms the good quality of this network, which shows that the learning error was estimated at the level of 0.004 (Chart 7.11).

Chart 7.12 is shown by a scatterplot of the dependent variable and its prediction, which also confirms the high quality of the selected networks (Table 7.4).

The plot enables one to read to what extent the neural network output signals reflect the actual value of the output variable – the number of collisions.

Chart 7.13 also confirms the high quality of the selected network, as the input data (number of collisions) corresponds to the data obtained during the training of the neural network in over 90%. The obtained results point to the possibility of using neural networks, in this case a single-layer MLP network, to predict the number of collisions on the roads. Based on the collected historical data, the neural network allows for making decisions about the current or future process of moving vehicles on the roads with specific parameters.

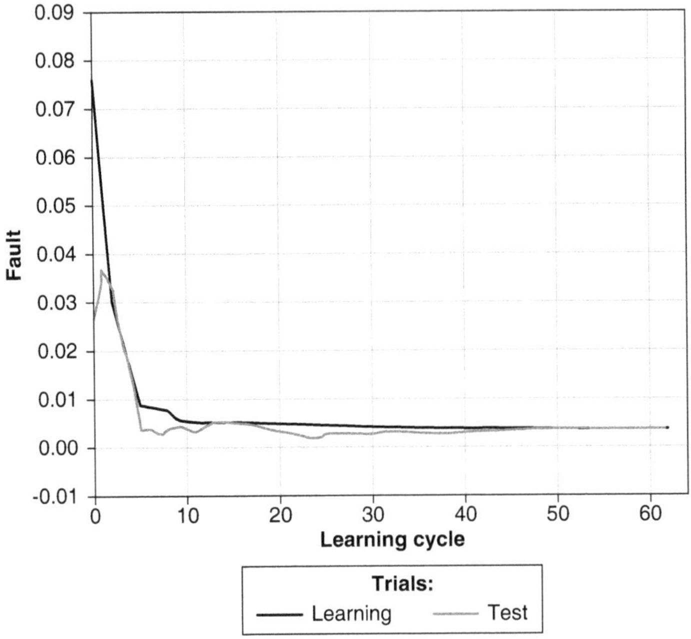

Chart 7.11 The learning diagram of the indicated MLP 2–4–1 neural network

Source: Own study.

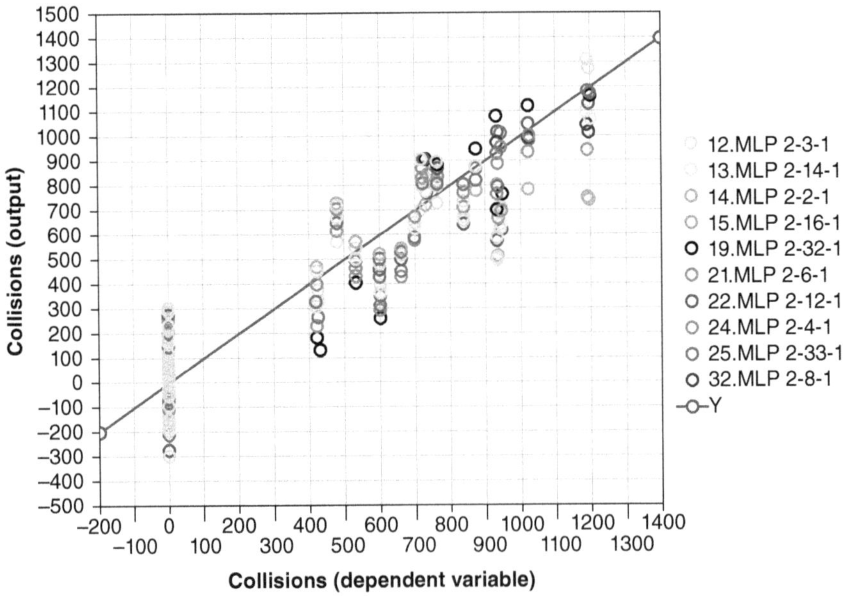

Chart 7.12 The scatterplot of the dependent variable of selected neural networks

Source: Own study.

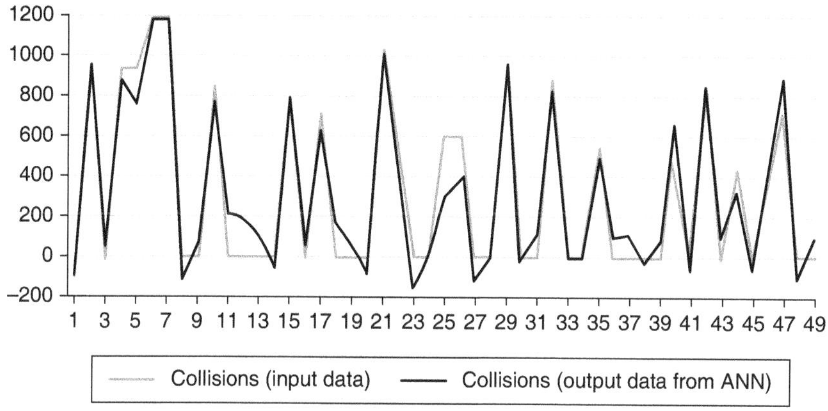

Chart 7.13 The plot of the dependent variable with reference to the output value

Source: Own study.

Conclusions

The simulation models presented in this work confirm that it is a good tool for modelling motor transport in various conditions. The presented example with the application of speed and distance parameters between vehicles reflects the number of collisions on the roads with pre-set restrictions.

The presented method of using neural networks shows that the data generated from simulation models provide the basis, in a way, a foundation for neural network designs, which, according to the analysis of the generated data, can predict future values of the output signals.

The presented approach to modelling motor transport with the use of simulation models and artificial neural networks is just a simple example illustrating the validity of employing these tools. Subsequent analyses and research should focus on other parameters and limitations of road transport, so that the designed models will reflect the actual road conditions as accurately as possible.

Notes

1 The lack of some data results from the fact that they are not available to EUROSTAT/N/ or confidential /PF/, and it does not concern some countries.

2 "Cabotage transport" is the case in which a transport company provides road transport services as part of its business activity, **while not having its headquarters in a given country**. For example, a Polish carrier provides cabotage through carrying out a transport order from Frankfurt to Munich.

3 "Inter-trade transport" refers to the transport of goods between enterprises engaged in goods distribution.

References

Brzeziński, M., Waśniewski, T. and Kijek, M. (2015). Modelowanie systemu organizacji przewozów w firmie transportowej. *Gospodarka Materiałowa i Logistyka*, 4.

Gandini, P., Studer, L. and Borghetti, F. (2015). *Assessment of areas exposed to damage by dangerous goods transportation: application of analytic hierarchy process method for land covers weighing*. IEEE 18th International Conference on Intelligent Transportation Systems, Gran Canaria.

Głodowska, K. (2018). Karta cykli transportowych jako narzędzie do analizy. *Systemy Logistyczne Wojsk*, 49.

Grzelak, M. (2019). Zastosowanie modelu ARIMA do prognozowania wielkości produkcji w przedsiębiorstwie. *Systemy Logistyczne Wojsk*, 50.

Hu, T. and Chen, L. (2012). Traffic signal optimization with greedy randomized tabu search algorithm. *Journal of Transportation Engineering*, 138(8), 1040–1050.

https://ec.europa.eu/eurostat/data/statistics-a-z/abc.

https://ec.europa.eu/eurostat/statistics-explained/index.php?oldid=409088.

https://ec.europa.eu/eurostat/web/covid-19/agriculture-energy-transport-tourism#vis.

https://ec.europa.eu/eurostat/web/covid-19/overview.

https://ec.europa.eu/eurostat/web/covid-19/visualisation.

https://ec.europa.eu/eurostat/web/products-eurostat-news.

https://ec.europa.eu/eurostat/web/structural-business-statistics/global-value-chains/international-sourcing access.

https://stat.gov.pl/files/gfx/portalinformacyjny/pl/defaultaktualnosci/5511/9/17/1/transport_wyniki_dzialalnosci_w_2017.pdf.

Jóźwiak, A. (2017). Application of Kohonen's network in logistics. *Gospodarka Materiałowa i Logistyka*, 5, 258–271.

Jóźwiak, A., Owczarek, P., Prochowski, L. and Świderski, A. (2020). Analysis of the impact of the use time of n1 motor vehicles on the economic efficiency of their maintenance. *Eksploatacja i Niezawodność – Maintenance and Reliability*, 22(1), 121–129.

Kozicki, B. (2018). Metoda prognozowania zysku w przedsiębiorstwie. *Systemy Logistyczne Wojsk*, 49.

Owczarek, P. and Jóźwiak, K. (2019). *Modelowanie neuronowe systemu eksploatacji pojazdów ciężarowych*. Warszawa: Prace Naukowe Politechniki Warszawskiej Transport.

Sedgewick, R. and Wayne, K. (2017). *Algorytmy*. Gliwice: Helion.

Siskos, Y., Grigoroudis, E. and Matsatsinis, N.F. (2005). *Multiple criteria decision analysis, state of the art surveys*. New York: Springer.

Świderski, A. (2009). Studies and quality assurance neural modelling of the technical transport means. *Archive of Transport*, 21(3–4).

Świderski, A., Jóźwiak, A. and Jachimowski, R. (2018). Operational quality measures of vehicles applied for the transport services evaluation using artificial neural networks. *Eksploatacja i Niezawodność – Maintenance and Reliability*, 20(2), 2920299.

8 Carriage of passengers by air transport in the context of the COVID-19 pandemic emergence

Bartosz Kozicki

Introduction

Transport is undoubtedly a key element in the provision of services in the field of moving material and human resources in the supply chain (Gołembska, Bentyn, Gołembski, 2017, p. 48). The purpose of this chapter is to conduct a multivariate comparative analysis of the data on air passenger transport in terms of economic security for the period 2000–2018. Over 120 countries, classified into seven regions of the world, were considered and analysed in terms of the number of air passengers. The research methods used include an analysis of the literature on air transport, as well as a multivariate comparative, and security analysis. The research tools include grouped line and bar charts and a fixed-base dynamics index. The study consists of an introduction, two substantive paragraphs, a summary and conclusions.

Analysis of the literature on the subject

In the literature on the subject, transport is considered as a system category, the purpose of which is the movement of passengers and cargo. It is defined by the type, number and features of the objects transported, as well as transportation routes and its quality parameters (Jacyna, 2009, p. 14). The literature describes various types of transport, the fastest of which is air transport. The chapter analyses air passenger transport in 124 countries around the world in terms of this dynamic. The market of passenger air transport services is driven by demand – in other words, it is shaped by the customers' willingness to move in time and space. At the same time, the demand must be balanced with the supply of services provided by airline operators in terms of passenger movement by air from the starting point to the destination. Its function depends on such factors as information, regulations on the conditions for concluding transactions, as well as movement of people and goods (Rucińska, Ruciński, Wyszomirski, 2004, p. 34). From 2000 to 2019, there was a growing trend in the number of air travellers. This was related to technological development, globalisation, economic growth of individual countries and generally available fast and cheap transport even to the farthest corners of the globe.

DOI: 10.4324/9781003285731-8

At the end of 2019, an infectious disease named COVID-19 was first reported in Wuhan, China (Tia et al., 2020; Zhu et al., 2020). Several months later, on March 11, 2020, the World Health Organisation declared COVID-19 a global pandemic (https://pulsmedycyny.pl/who-grozba-pandemii-koronawirusa-jest-realna-984550; Satomi et al., 2020).

To prevent the spread of the disease, individual countries imposed various restrictions and regulations, including wearing face masks, using hand and surface disinfectants, and measuring temperature in public spaces. Restrictions were imposed on international travels due to closed borders (Yan et al., 2020; Pike, Saini, 2020).

The pandemic has caused global economies to slow down (Luisetto, Fiazza, Latiyshev, 2020). COVID-19 has led to increased social distancing as well as a reduction in new purchases and sales transactions. In the United States, around 20.5 million people lost their jobs during this period, pushing the unemployment rate to 14.7% (CNN, 2020).

The pandemic has caused a significant decrease in the number of air passengers since March 2020. This, in turn, reduced the global demand on oil and its prices. Since March 2020, the price per barrel of crude oil has been the lowest in years (just below $40).

This chapter presents an attempt at a multivariate comparative analysis of passenger air transport in seven regions of the world in terms of the impact of COVID-19 on this sector of the economy and the economic security.

According to M. Łuniewska, a multivariate comparative analysis comprises a number of statistical methods in order to simultaneously analyse at least two variables describing each examined object (Łuniewska, 2006, p. 9). In other words, it involves arranging the homogeneous sets in question in such a way as to observe their similarities and differences. The collected data was grouped and then compiled on Chernoff's faces, as well as line and bar charts. It should be emphasised that interpretation of Chernoff's faces uses the innate human ability to recognise faces and the ability to sense the slightest variations in facial features (Morris, Ebert, 2000).

The purpose of the conducted multivariate analysis was to determine regular patterns and then to compare them to changes caused by the COVID-19 pandemic and to look at the number of global air passengers in terms of the broadly understood economic security.

The critical analysis of the literature on the subject shows that "security" is identified with inner trust, peace of mind and certainty in situations that may give rise to fear or anxiety (Kitler, 2011, p. 22). One of its subcategories is economic security, understood as a guarantee of the existence and development of the economic system of the state and international organisations and the preservation of an appropriate standard of living of the citizens (Nurzyńska, 2016, p. 22). In this chapter, economic security was analysed in terms of the sweeping changes caused by the COVID-19 pandemic in the sector of passenger air transport as compared to the trends in the industry observed for the period 2000–2018. These trends were described in the initial stages of the research through multivariate comparative analysis.

Multivariate analysis of the number of air passengers in various regions of the world

The first step was to present the data on the number of air passengers in 124 countries (divided into seven regions) during the years 2000–2018 and place them on a ranked bar chart (X2 axis). The data presented in Chart 8.1 indicates that the region with the highest number of air passengers in the years 2000–2018 was North America, comprising only two countries (14,904,964,547 passengers). North America was followed by the East Asia-Pacific region (containing 22 countries) with 13,362,738,589 passengers. The third region was Europe and Central Asia with a total number of 12,633,167,532 passengers between 2000 and 2018. As part of the analysed region, 39 countries were considered. Next in the ranking were the following regions: Middle East and North Africa (6,697,453,885 passengers – 16 countries), Latin America and the Caribbean (3,243,312,544 passengers – 18 countries), South Asia (1,463,042,099 passengers – 6 countries) and the last was Sub-Saharan Africa (602,071,420 passengers – 21 countries).

The subsequent part of the research involved a multivariate analysis of the data on the number of air passengers in the seven analysed regions in each year between 2000 and 2018. The Chernoff's faces method was adopted for this purpose. Each face was assigned one dependent variable in the form of a region. Individual facial features, in turn, were assigned explanatory variables in the form of the number of air passengers in individual regions in each year between 2000 and 2018. Individual explanatory variables were assigned to the facial features as

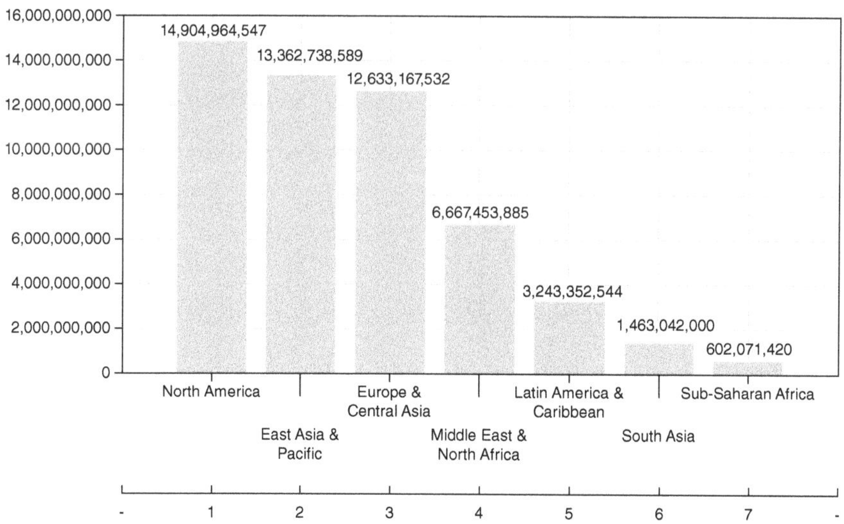

Chart 8.1 Grouped bar chart (X2 axis) of data on the number of air passengers in 124 countries in seven regions of the world, for the time period 2000–2018

Source*:* Own study based on data obtained from the website: https://databank.worldbank.org/ (02.11.2020).

follows: face width = 2000, ear height = 2001, half face height = 2002, upper face eccentricity = 2003, lower face eccentricity = 2004, nose length = 2005, position of the centre of the mouth = 2006, mouth curvature = 2007, mouth length = 2008, ear height = 2009, eye spacing = 2010, eye slant = 2011, eye eccentricity = 2012, eye length = 2013, pupil position = 2014, eyebrow height = 2015, eyebrow length = 2017, ear radius = 2018. The results are presented in Chart 8.2.

The data presented indicates that from 2000 to 2011 North America was the undisputed world leader in terms of the number of air passengers. The two faces that represent the regions of East Asia and the Pacific as well as Europe and Central Asia are similar, which means that the number of air passengers in both regions in the analysed time period was similar. The same was true for two

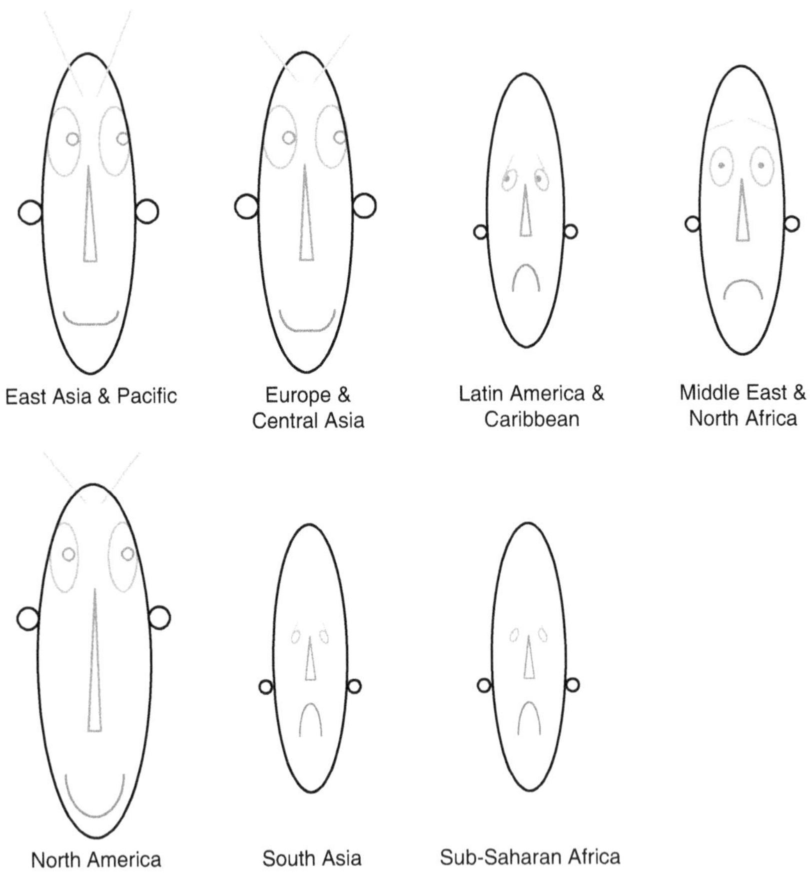

Chart 8.2 Chernoff's faces representing multivariate comparative analysis of data on the number of air passengers in 124 countries, in seven regions of the world, in the time period 2000–2018

Source: Own study based on data obtained from the website: https://databank.worldbank.org/ (02.11.2020).

other faces: South Asia and Sub-Saharan Africa. In 2011, North America recorded 796,874,012 passengers, followed by East Asia and Pacific with a slightly lower number of passengers (748,222,761). In Chart 8.2 this is reflected in the eccentric eyes of the faces. In 2012, East Asia and the Pacific overtook North America as the leader in passenger transport. In 2015, Europe and Central Asia moved up to second in the ranking, while North America fell to the third place. The greatest differences between the leaders in 2017 can be observed in the eyebrow length. The leader with the longest eyebrows is East Asia and the Pacific (1,265,092,208 passengers), followed by Europe and Central Asia (1,011,881,275 passengers). North America is third with 940,807,001 passengers. A similar trend is observed for the year 2018, reflected in the ear radius. The face representing East Asia and the Pacific has the largest ear radius (1,361,486,860 passengers). Europe and Central Asia ranks second with a slightly lower number compared to the previous year (1,079,186,342 passengers), while North America ranks third with 978,402,000 passengers. The lowest ranked regions are Sub-Saharan Africa and South Asia. Both regions are represented by the smallest faces with the shortest features (e.g. in terms of the length of the nose, height of the ears and others features described earlier).

The next stage of the research involved an analysis of the dynamics of changes in the number of air passengers in the seven regions in question in the time period from 2000 to 2018. Fixed-base dynamics indices were used for this purpose. The results of the analysis are shown in Chart 8.3.

The data presented in Chart 8.3 shows that among the examined regions, the greatest dynamic growth was observed for South Asia. From 2000 (26,357,717 passengers) to 2018 (186,355,608 passengers), there was an increase of 607.02%. South Asia was followed by East Asia and the Pacific, where from 2000 (337,534,748 passengers) to 2018 (1,361,486,860 passengers), there was an increase of 303.36%. The lowest-ranked region in terms of growth was North America, where from 2000 (707,095,388 passengers) to 2018 (978,402,000 passengers), only a slight increase of 38.37% was recorded.

The next stage of the analysis examined the overall trend in the number of air passengers for each of the seven analysed regions of the world in the time period 2000–2018. For this purpose, a grouped line chart was prepared for the data on the number of air passengers, as well as its median and arithmetic mean, for 124 countries in seven regions of the world for each year between 2000 and 2018 (data on the number of air passengers – left Y axis; arithmetic mean – 1st right Y axis; median – 2nd right Y axis) (Chart 8.4).

Analysis of Chart 8.4 allows one to conclude that there was a growing linear trend. A slight decrease in the number of air passengers was recorded from 2000 to 2002. Another point worth mentioning is a slowdown in growth between 2007 and 2009 during the global financial crisis. Between 2009 and 2010, there was a sharp increase in the number of passengers, which soared from 2,418,168,792 to 2,825,713,513 people. It should also be emphasised that in the analysed period of 2009–2010, the highest increase in the arithmetic mean of passengers was also recorded (from 1,996,982 to 2,968,514). In total, from 2000 to 2018, the number

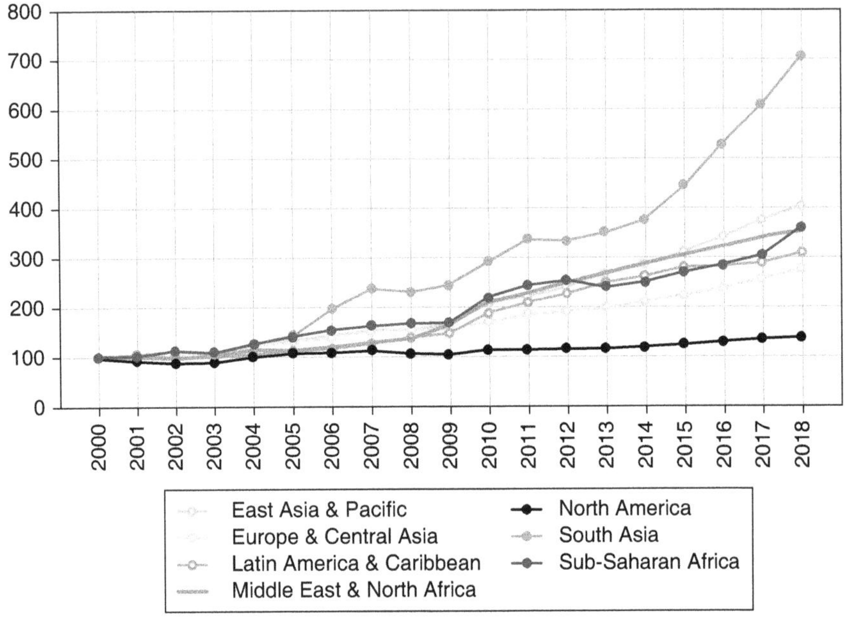

Chart 8.3 Grouped line chart of fixed-base dynamic indices for the number of air passengers in 124 countries in seven regions of the world for the time period 2000–2018 (the fixed base = the number of passengers in 2000 for each region)

Source*:* Own study based on data obtained from the website: https://databank.worldbank.org/ (02.11.2020).

of passengers increased from 1,751,311,746 to 4,580,770,130 (a difference of 2,829,458,384 people).

The next stage of the research involved ranking the total number of air passengers in 124 countries in the time period 2000–2018. For reference purposes, 15 leaders in this regard have been presented in Chart 8.5.

Considering the total number of air passengers, the United States remains the undisputed leader with 13,779,176,365 passengers, followed by China with 5,029,887,316 passengers and Kuwait with 2,892,058,241 passengers. Next in the ranking are the United Arab Emirates (2,172,433,103 passengers), Great Britain (2,039,424,866 passengers), Japan (2,019,154,664 passengers), Germany (1,828,571,646 passengers), Ireland (1,444,450,947 passengers), Brazil (1,267,623,981 passengers), India (1,210,699,116 passengers), France (1,127,264,977 passengers), Canada (1,125,788,182 passengers), Australia (1,048,741,290 passengers), Spain (1,012,062,812 passengers) and Indonesia (1,007,337,518 passengers).

The last stage of the research was an analysis of the impact of the COVID-19 pandemic on the number of air passengers for the global leader – the United States – from March 1 to November 3, 2020. The results are presented in Chart 8.6.

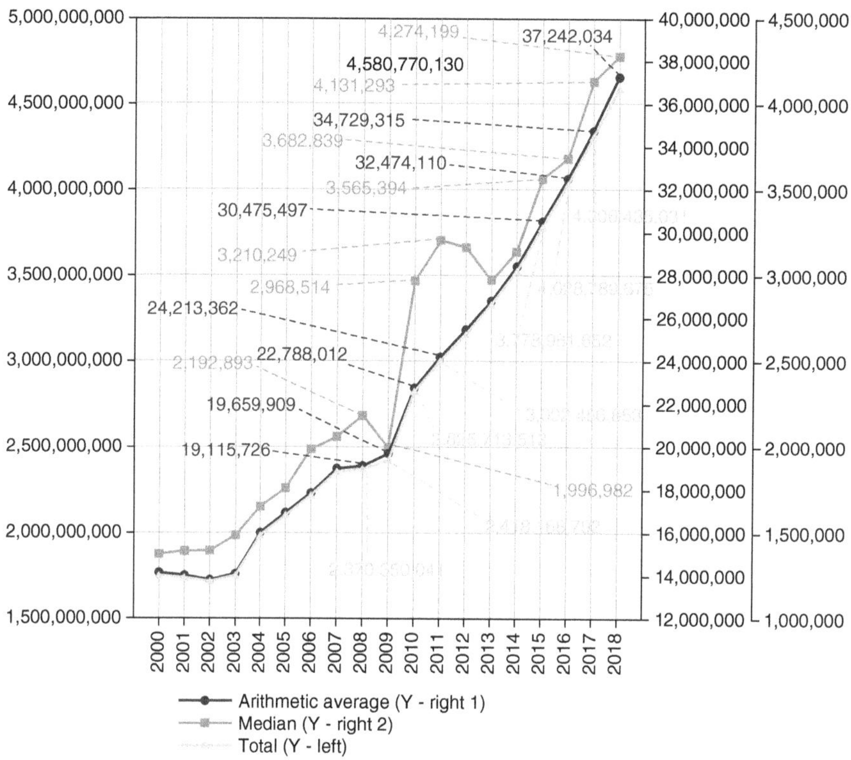

Chart 8.4 Grouped line chart of the data on the number of air passengers, its median and arithmetic mean, for 124 countries in seven regions of the world for each year between 2000 and 2018 (data on the number of air passengers – left Y axis; arithmetic mean – 1st right Y axis; median – 2nd right Y axis)

Source: Own study based on data obtained from the website: https://databank.worldbank.org/ (02.11.2020).

The data presented in Chart 8.6 clearly indicates that the growing trend in the number of air passengers in the United States observed between 2000 and 2019 has been affected by the COVID-19 pandemic, causing a significant decline. The median number of passengers in the United States in the period from March 1 to November 3, 2019, was 2,450,494, while for the same time period a year later it decreased to only 573,390 passengers. This shows a downturn in the air transport sector in the United States. The observation of the economic situation and the changes caused by the COVID-19 pandemic in other countries around the world allows one to conclude that passenger air travel has also been undergoing a deep crisis, and a sharp decrease in the number of passengers mirrors that observed for the global leader – the United States.

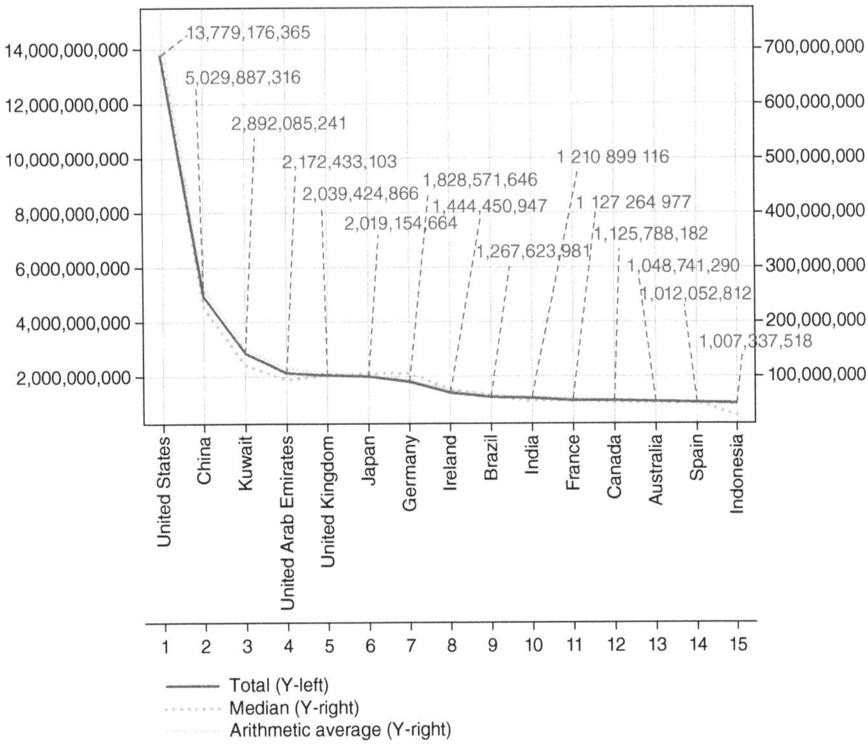

Chart 8.5 Grouped line chart showing the 15 highest-ranked countries with the largest total number of air passengers in the time period 2000–2018 (data on the number of passengers – left Y axis; arithmetic mean, median – 1st right Y axis)

Source: Own study based on data obtained from the website: https://databank.worldbank.org/ (02.11.2020).

Conclusions

The research shows that between 2000 and 2018, the largest number of air passengers (14,904,964,547 people) was recorded in North America (in this chapter the region comprised two countries). East Asia and the Pacific (with 22 countries) ranked second with 13,362,738,589 air passengers. The third-ranked region was Europe and Central Asia (comprising 39 countries) with a total number of 12,633,167,532 passengers. The following regions followed the top three in a decreasing order in terms of the number of passengers: Middle East and North Africa (6,697,453,885 passengers – 16 countries), Latin America and the Caribbean (3,243,312,544 passengers – 18 countries), South Asia (1,463,042,099 passengers – 6 countries). Sub-Saharan Africa (21 countries) was the lowest-ranked region with a total of 602,071,420 passengers.

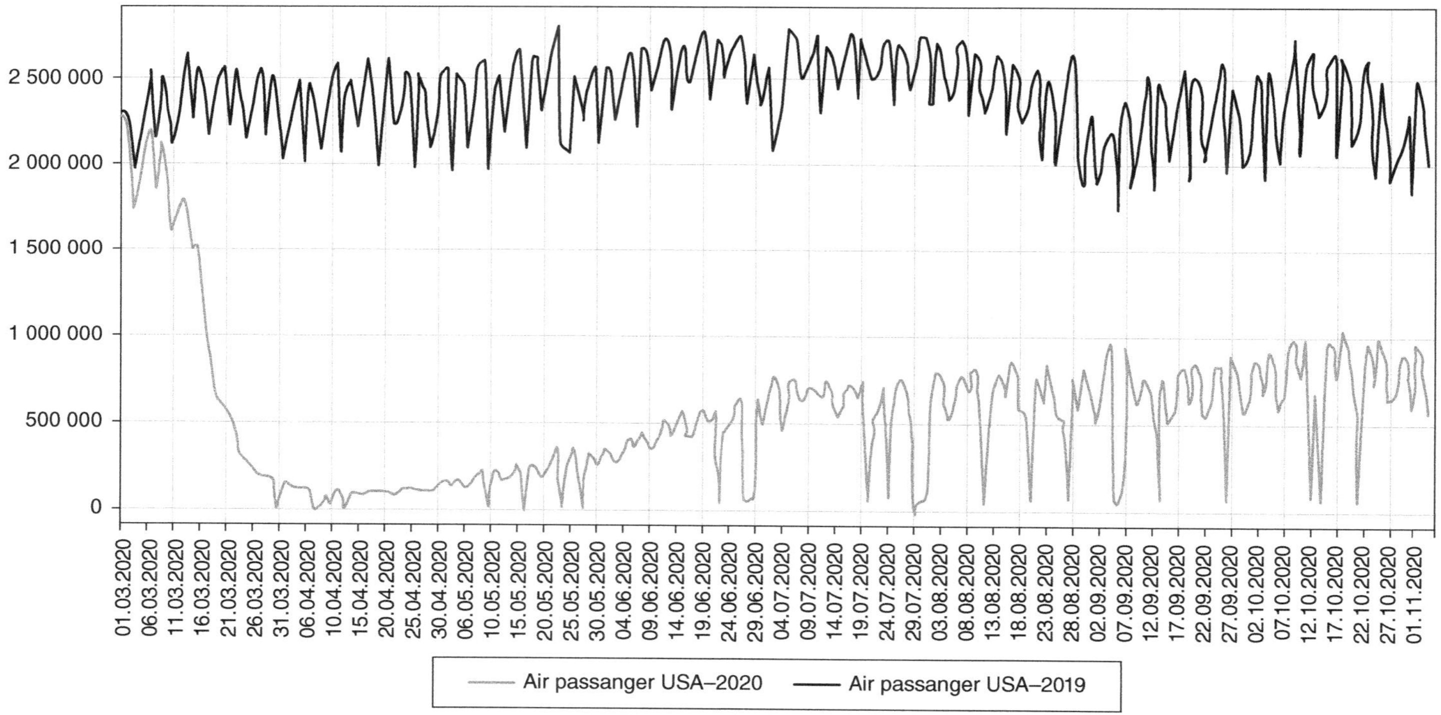

Chart 8.6 Grouped line chart of the time series showing the number of air passengers in the USA on a daily basis in the period from March 1 to November 3 in 2019 and the same period in 2020

Source: Own study based on data obtained from the website: www.tsa.gov (05.11.2020)

From 2000 to 2011, North America was the global leader in terms of the number of air passengers (Chart 8.2), but in 2012, it was overtaken by East Asia and the Pacific, only to drop to third thanks to Europe and Central Asia in 2015. In Chart 8.2, the most significant difference between the leading regions is observed changes in the eyebrow length representative of the year 2017. The leader with the longest eyebrows is East Asia and the Pacific (1,265,092,208 passengers), followed by Europe and Central Asia (1,011,881,275 passengers). North America is third with 940,807,001 passengers. A similar trend is observed for the year 2018, reflected by ear radius. The face representing East Asia and the Pacific has the largest ear radius (1,361,486,860 passengers). Europe and Central Asia ranks second with a slightly lower number compared to the previous year (1,079,186,342 passengers), while North America ranks third with 978,402,000 passengers. The lowest ranked regions are Sub-Saharan Africa and South Asia. Both regions are represented by the smallest faces with the shortest features (e.g. in terms of the length of the nose, height of the ears, and others features).

Among the examined regions, the greatest growth dynamics in terms of the number of air passengers was observed for South Asia (Chart 8.3). From 2000 (26,357,717 passengers) to 2018 (186,355,608 passengers), it recorded an increase of 607.02%. South Asia was followed by East Asia and the Pacific, where from 2000 (337,534,748 passengers) to 2018 (1,361,486,860 passengers) there was an increase of 303.36%. The lowest-ranked region in terms of growth dynamics for the number of air passengers was North America, where from 2000 (707,095,388 passengers) to 2018 (978,402,000 passengers) the region experienced only a slight 38.37% increase.

For all 124 examined countries, a growing linear trend in terms of the number of air passengers was observed for the time period 2000–2018 (Chart 8.4). A slight decrease in that number was recorded between 2000 and 2002. A slowdown in the growth rate was also observed between 2007 and 2009 during the global financial crisis. Between 2009 and 2010, there was a sharp increase in the number of passengers, which soared from 2,418,168,792 to 2,825,713,513. It should also be emphasised that the analysed period of 2009–2010 recorded the highest increase in the arithmetic mean of passengers (from 1,996,982 to 2,968,514). In total, from 2000 to 2018, the number of passengers increased from 1,751,311,746 to 4,580,770,130, an increase of 2,829,458,384 people.

In terms of the total number of air passengers, the United States remains the undisputed leader with 13,779,176,365 passengers (Chart 8.5), followed by China with 5,029,887,316 passengers and Kuwait with 2,892,058,241 passengers.

The growing trend in the number of air passengers in the United States observed between 2000 and 2019 has drastically declined because of the COVID-19 pandemic. The median number of passengers in the United States in the period from March 1 to November 3, 2019, was 2,450,494, while for the same time frame in 2020, it decreased to only 573,390 passengers.

The COVID-19 pandemic has had a great impact on various sectors of world economies. One of the most visible changes is the unprecedented decline in the number of air passengers. There is no doubt that the difficult situation will have a negative impact in many other sectors of the economy. An example is the decline in global oil prices caused by the reduction in the number of passengers, and consequently, the reduction in the global demand for crude oil. The countries whose economies are based on the sales of crude oil will certainly be negatively affected by the drastic changes. Such countries include Russia, the countries of the Middle East, and other economic powers. Recovery to pre-COVID-19 economic conditions will most likely take a long time and will depend on whether the spread of the disease is successfully stopped or successfully mitigated. It will also require coordinated international agreements on the organisation of transport and increasing the growth dynamics of other economic sectors affected by the pandemic.

References

CNN (2020). https://edition.cnn.com/2020/05/08/economy/april-jobs-report-2020-coronavirus/index.html.

https://databank.worldbank.org/.

Gołembska, E., Bentyn, Z. and Gołembski, M. (2017). *Logistyka usług*. Warszawa: PWN.

Jacyna, M. (2009). *Wybrane zagadnienia modelowania systemów transportowych*. Warszawa: Oficyna Wydawnicza Politechniki Warszawskiej.

Kitler, W. (2011). *Bezpieczeństwo narodowe RP: podstawowe kategorie. Uwarunkowania. System*. Warszawa: AON.

Luisetto, M., Fiazza, C. and Latiyshev, O.Y. (2020). COVID-19 pandemia and the management strategy for business and economy #COVID-19 #coronavirus #management #economy #emergency #infectious disease #virologist. *Management and Business Administration IMA Academy Lab*, 1. https://lupinepublishers.com/clinical-community-medicine/fulltext/covid-19-pandemic-and-the-management-strategy-for-business-and-economy.ID.000129.php ISSN: 2690-5760.

Łuniewska, M. (2006). *Metody wielowymiarowej analizy porównawczej na rynku kapitałowym*. Warszawa: PWN.

Morris, C.J. and Ebert, D.P. (2000). An experimental analysis of the effectiveness of features in Chernoff faces. *Proceedings of SPIE – The International Society for Optical Engineering*, 28. https://engineering.purdue.edu/~ebertd/papers/Chernoff_990402.PDF.

Nurzyńska, A. (2016). *Bezpieczeństwo usług w międzynarodowym transporcie lotniczym przewozów pasażerskich*. Katowice: SOPHIA.

Pike, T.W. and Saini, V. (2020). An international comparison of the second derivative of COVID-19 deaths after implementation of social distancing measures. *BMJ*, https://doi.org/10.1101/2020.03.25.20041475.

Rucińska, D., Ruciński, A. and Wyszomirski, O. (2004). *Zarządzanie marketingowe na rynku usług transportowych*. Gdańsk: Wydawnictwo Uniwersytetu Gdańskiego.

Satomi, E. et al. (2020). Alocação justa de recuros de saúde escassos diante da pandemia de COVID-19. *Considerações éticas*, 18(2), 1–5.

Tia, H. et al. (2020). *An investigation of transmission control measures during the first 50 days of the COVID-19 epidemic in China*. Washington: Science.

www.tsa.gov.

Yan, Y. et al. (2020). The first 75 days of novel coronavirus (SARS-CoV-2) outbreak: recent advances, prevention, and treatment. *International Journal of Environmental Research and Public Health*, 17(7).

Zhu, N. et al. (2020). A novel coronavirus from patients with pneumonia in China. *New England Journal of Medicine*, 382, 727–733.

9 The analysis of the number of passengers departing from Great Britain before and during the COVID-19 pandemic

Mieczysław Pawlisiak and Bartosz Kozicki

Introduction

The development of transport affects economic development, and this clearly translates into an increase in national revenue (Nurzyńska, 2016, p. 110). Until 2019, a growing trend in the number of carried passengers has been observed in the world, especially in air passenger transport. Its growth was recorded globally each year. It should be emphasised that the pace of its growth depends on the economic situation and vice versa.

The aim of this study was to carry out a multivariate comparative analysis of the number of passengers departing from Great Britain in two groups: the total number and the British, before the pandemic and during the COVID-19 pandemic in terms of security. The subject of the research is Great Britain, and the object of the research is the number of passengers carried by air transport in Great Britain in 2010–2019, as well as the number of passengers departing from Great Britain in the homonymous time frame in 2019–2020.

This chapter uses research methods in the form of literature analysis related to air transport, multivariate comparative analysis and economic security. The following tools were used in the research: categorised line charts, categorised bar charts and constant base dynamics indicators.

The study consists of an introduction, three content-related sections, a summary and conclusions.

Analysis of the literature on the subject of the research

Air transport is a branch of the economy that showed a fast pace of development until the end of 2019. Thus, it guaranteed jobs for people, for example in airports and travel agencies.

According to the literature, transport is a concept that describes activities related to the movement of resources in the supply chain (Gołembska, Bentyn, Gołembski, 2017, p. 48). One of the fastest modes of transport is air transport. The study covers passenger air transport. It is considered as an activity of the movement of persons through the airspace. One of the leaders of this industry in Europe is Great Britain, where the highest number of passengers is transported, and their

DOI: 10.4324/9781003285731-9

number has been systematically increasing (www.pasazer.com/news/29996/przybywa,pasazerow,w,wielkiej,brytanii.html) till the end of 2019. Undoubtedly, enormous changes in the entire world of transport were recorded in 2020 with the emergence of the rapidly spreading disease called COVID-19.

This disease was first recorded in the Chinese city of Wuhan in December 2019 (Tia et al., 2020; Zhu et al., 2020). This disease was declared a pandemic on March 11, 2020 (https://pulsmedycyny.pl/who-grozba-pandemii-koronawirusa-jest-realna-984550; Satomi et al., 2020).

The disease has resulted in many common restrictions in countries around the world: the use of masks and disinfectants, and restrictions in movement and group meetings (Yan et al., 2020; Pike, Saini, 2020).

The greatest limitations were experienced by air passenger transport, where huge long-term declines in the number of people traveling by this means of transport were recorded. These limitations and a large reduction in the number of people traveling by air transport slowed down the development of world economies (Luisetto, Fiazza, Latiyshev, 2020).

Further changes triggered by the pandemic concern the reduction of global oil demand. This, in turn, caused significant drops in its prices. Unemployment began to appear in economic powers such as the United States. Such strong dynamics of its growth has not yet been recorded in the history of this country. From February to April 2020, the unemployment rate increased by approximately 11.2 percentage points. Even during the Great Depression in the United States, such strong dynamics was not recorded (www.bls.gov/charts/employment-situation/civilian-unemployment-rate.htm; https://fred.stlouisfed.org/series/M0892AUSM156SNBR). Increases in unemployment could also be watched in other countries of the world, including European ones.

The study attempts to investigate the impact of the COVID-19 pandemic on the number of passengers carried by air in the industry leader in Europe, i.e. the United Kingdom. The multivariate comparative analyses were used for the research.

The multivariate comparative analysis allows one to explain the structure of connections between the observed characteristics of objects (Panek, Zwierzchowski, 2013, p. 15). These analyses may concern the units of space or time variables that make up the dependent variables. The explanatory variables are the other elements of the analysis describing the dependent variables.

In the study, as part of multivariate comparative analyses, the primary data was grouped and untangled to emphasise changes in the number of passengers carried by air in Great Britain in terms of economic security.

The analysis of the literature shows that the term *security* is multifaceted, and it is difficult to interpret unequivocally in such dynamically changing times. According to the *Dictionary of the Polish Language*, security is a state of non-threat, peace and certainty (Szymczak, 1981, p. 147). Other authors believe that security is a state of stability, non-threatening, a sense of certainty that guarantees its preservation and should be considered in three dimensions: state, process and the main need (Wiśniewski, 2013, p. 37). One type of security is economic security. It is characterised by a large spread. It is interpreted as a state of reality that

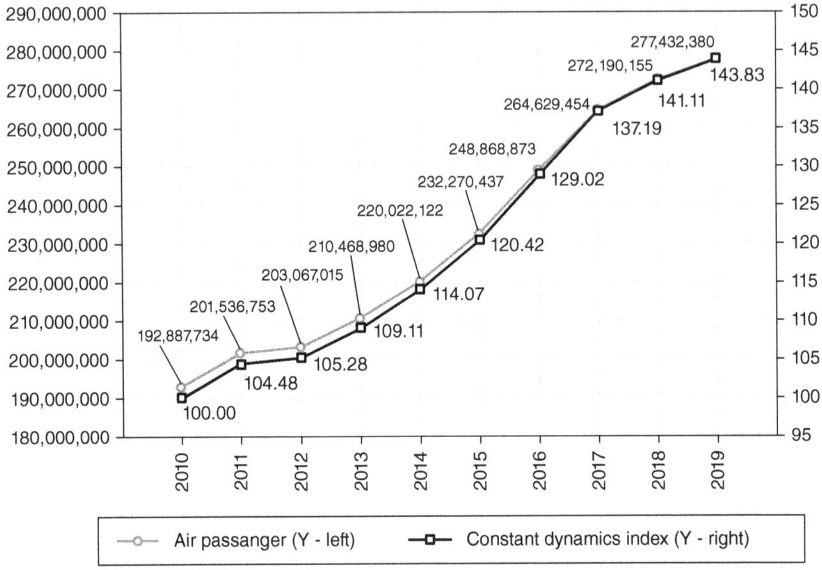

Chart 9.1 The categorised line chart of data on the number and the constant basis dynamics indexes (constant – the number of passengers transported by air in Great Britain in 2010) of passengers carried by air in Great Britain in 2010–2019 (left Y axis – number of passengers; right Y axis – the constant basis dynamics indexes)

Source: Own study based on data obtained from the website: https://ec.europa.eu (10.11.2020).

allows for the development of the economy and for ensuring a proper standard of living for citizens through continuous access to raw materials, capital, technology or information (Szubrycht, 2006, pp. 87–98).

In the study, economic security was considered from a perspective of large changes in the number of passengers carried by air in Great Britain, changes caused by the spreading infectious disease in 2020. The research highlights the differences observed before the pandemic and during the COVID-19 pandemic in terms of the number of people carried by air in the analysed subject of the research.

The first content-related point was focused on a multivariate comparative analysis of the number of people carried by air in Great Britain in the past, i.e. in the years 2000–2019, in terms of observing such a regularity as the trend and its characteristics.

The multivariate analysis of the number of passengers carried by air in Great Britain in 2000–2019

The research began with the implementation of a categorised line chart of data on the number and the constant basis dynamics indexes of passengers carried by air in Great Britain in 2010–2019.

The data presented in Chart 9.1 shows that the number of passengers carried by air in Great Britain in 2010–2019 shows an increasing trend. In 2010, 192,887,734 passengers were carried by air in Great Britain. In 2019, the number of passengers increased to 277,432,380. From 2010 to 2019, an increase in the number of passengers carried by air in Great Britain, by 84,544,646 i.e. by 43.83 percentage points, was observed. In the time frame from 2010 to 2019, the strongest growth dynamics was recorded in 2016–2017. In the indicated time period, the increase was by 8.88 percentage points, i.e. by 15,760,581 passengers.

In March 2020, the COVID-19 pandemic was proclaimed worldwide. It resulted in the introduction by individual countries of many restrictions in various sectors of the national economies. It has also caused a huge drop in the number of passengers traveling by air. The study set out to investigate the impact of the COVID-19 pandemic on the number of passengers departing from Great Britain before and after this proclamation.

The multivariate comparative analysis of the number of passengers departing from Great Britain before and during the COVID-19 pandemic

The first stage of the study was the preparation of a categorised line chart of data on the total number of passengers and British departing from Great Britain in the homonymous time frame from January 1 to July 31 in 2019–2020.

The data presented in Chart 9.2 shows that the COVID-19 pandemic resulted in large drops in the number of passengers carried by air. On March 11, 2020, the total number of passengers departing from Great Britain was 175,700, and on April 1, 2020, it dropped to 4,400. Similar declines were observed among the British group, where 88,600 passengers departed from Great Britain on March 11, 2020, and only 2,200 on April 1. The huge declines continued until the end of the time frame under consideration, i.e. until July 31, 2020, with a slight upward trend.

The next stage of the research was the calculation of dynamics indexes based on a constant total number of passengers and British people departing from Great Britain in the homonymous time period from January 1 to July 31 in 2019–2020 and their delineation, shown in Chart 9.3.

The observation of the data presented in Chart 9.3 allows for the conclusion that since March 2020 the constant base dynamics indexes have decreased. From April 1 to the end of June 2020, the median in the group of the fixed-base dynamics indexes of passengers departing from Great Britain is 1.90 percentage points, while in the group of British the median is 1.99 percentage points. In July 2020, the median increases to 16.51 percentage points in the total number of passengers, and to 18.91 percentage points in the British group. It should be emphasised that the median in 2019 from January to July was 123.1 percentage points in the group of the total number of passengers, while in the group of Britons it was 141.68 percentage points.

The further stage of the research was to group the considered primary data in the group of dependent variables of the total number of passengers in the

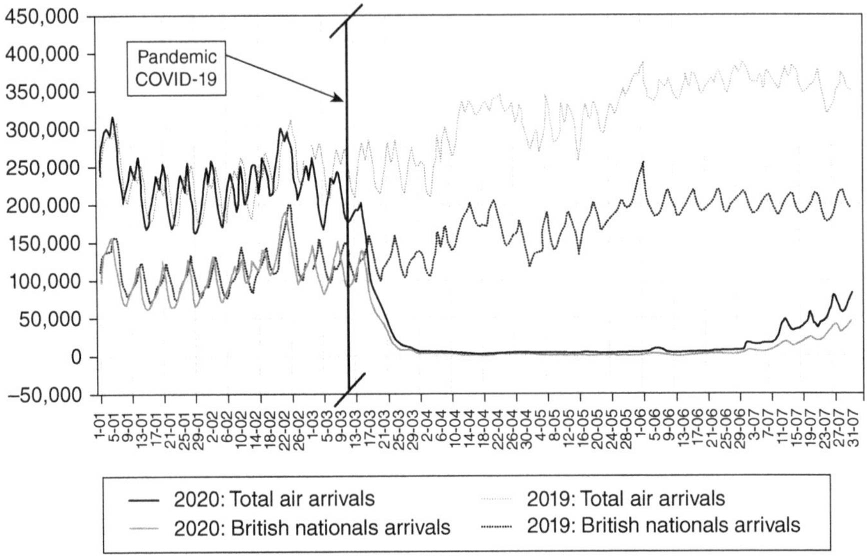

Chart 9.2 The categorised line chart of data on the total number of passengers and British departing Great Britain in the homonymous time frame from January 1 to July 31, 2019–2020

Source: Own study based on data obtained from the website www.google.com/url?sa=t&rct=j&q=&esrc=s&source=web&cd=&cad=rja&uact=8&ved=2ahUKEwjTz9bGtffs AhWKl4sKHfx_DeoQFjACegQIBhAC&url=https%3A%2F%2 Fassets.publishing.service.gov.uk%2Fgovernment%2 Fuploads%2 Fsystem%2Fuploads%2Fattachment_data%2Ffile% 2F910893 (10.11.2020).

homonymous months in the years 2019–2020 and to perform a comparative analysis, shown in Chart 9.4.

Chart 9.4 shows that from March 2020, large drops in the total number of passengers carried in the homonymous time frames under consideration (January–July) can be seen. In March 2019, 7,816,900 passengers were transported, while in the homonymous month in 2020, 3,815,100. Even higher declines were recorded in the following months, when 9,120,600 people left Great Britain in April 2019, and 112,500 in the same period in 2020. In May 2019, 9,754,200 passengers departed from the United Kingdom, and in the homonymous month in 2020, 139,300 passengers. Slight increases were recorded in June, where 10,770,900 passengers departed from Great Britain in 2019, and 194,800 in 2020. In July 2020, the number of passengers transported increased to 1,160,500. This is still much less than in the homonymous month in 2019, when records show that 11,130,100 passengers departed from Great Britain.

For illustrative purposes, the categorised bar chart of the difference in the total number of passengers departing from Great Britain between the homonymous months in 2020 and 2019 is outlined in Chart 9.5.

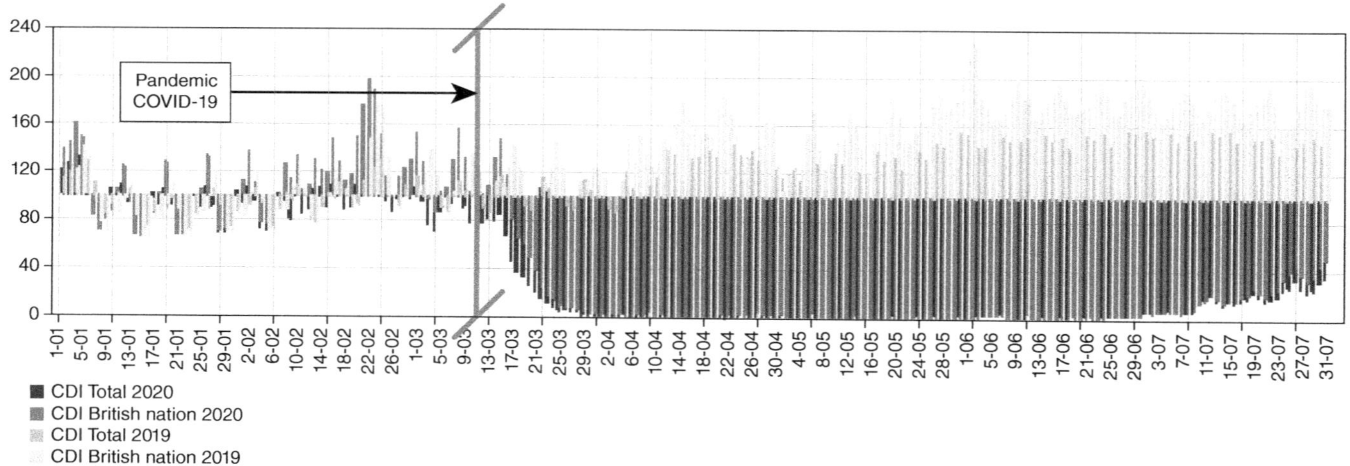

Chart 9.3 The categorised line chart of the fixed-base dynamics indexes (the constant – total number of passengers and British departing from the Great Britain on January 1, 2019) of the total number of passengers and British departing from Great Britain in the homonymous time frame from January 1 to July 31 in 2019–2020

Source*:* Own study based on data obtained from the website www.google.com/url?sa=t&rct=j&q=&esrc=s&source=web&cd=&cad=rja&uact=8&ved= 2ahUKEwjTz9bGtffsAh WKl4sKHfx_ DeoQFjACegQIBhAC&url= https%3A%2F%2Fassets. publishing.service.gov. uk%2Fgovernment%2Fuploads%2F system% 2Fuploads%2Fattachment_data% 2Ffile%2F910893 (10.11.2020).

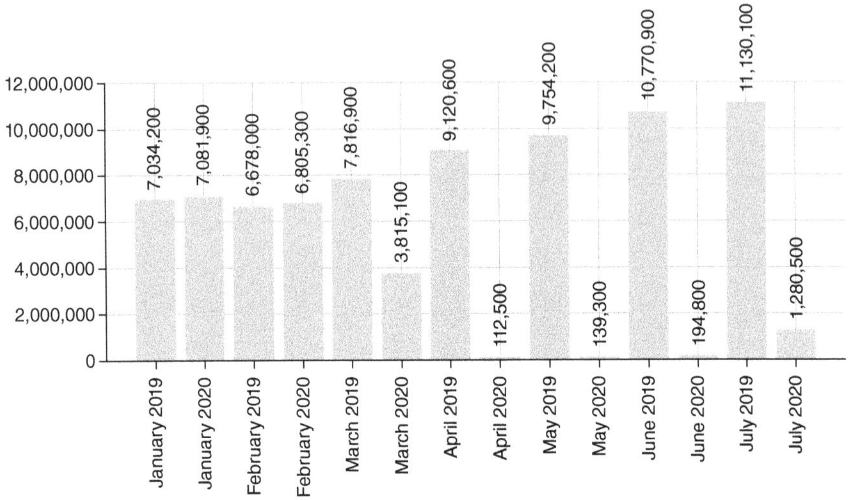

Chart 9.4 The categorised bar chart of the comparative analysis of the total number of passengers departing Great Britain in homonymous months for 2019–2020

Source: Own study based on data obtained from the website www.google.com/url?sa=t&rct=j&q=&esrc=s&source=web&cd=&cad=rja&uact=8&ved=2ahUKEwjTz9bGtffs AhWKl4sKHfx_DeoQ FjACegQIBhAC&url=https% 3A%2F%2Fassets.publishing.service.gov.uk%2Fgovernment% 2Fuploads%2Fsystem%2Fuploads%2Fattachment_data%2Ffile% 2F910893 (10.11.2020).

The data presented in Chart 9.5 shows that the largest difference in the number of passengers departing from the United Kingdom between the homonymous months in 2019–2020 was in June (– 10,576,100) then in July (– 9,869,600). In third place was May (– 9,614,900). The next places in the ranking are April (– 9,008,100), March (– 4,001,800), February (127,300) and January (47,700). It should be emphasised that in January and February 2020 only, there was an increase compared to the homonymous months in 2019. In the remaining months, the differences were negative.

Then the second dependent variable in the form of British departing from the United Kingdom in the homonymous months January–July in 2019–2020 was analysed. The results are outlined in Chart 9.6.

Declines similar to those observed for the total number of passengers departing from Great Britain, outlined in Chart 9.4, can also be seen in Chart 9.6. In March 2019, 3,897,500 British departed from Great Britain airports, while only 2,195,700 departed from airports in 2020 during the same time frame. Higher declines were recorded in the subsequent months. In April, a decrease from 4,853,700 (2019) to 63,200 (2020), in May from 5,322,800 (2019) to 50,600 (2020), in June from 6,119,800 (2019) to 65,400 (2020) and in July from 6,152,100 (2019) to 621,200 (2020).

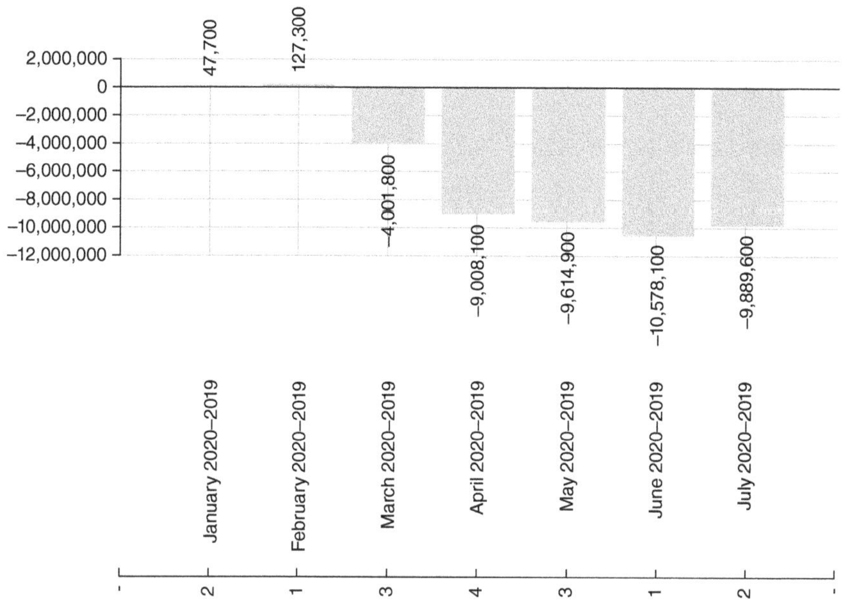

Chart 9.5 The categorised bar chart of the difference in total number of passengers departing Great Britain between homonymous months in 2020 and 2019 (X2 axis – ranking the data)

Source: Own study based on data obtained from the website www.google.com/url?sa=t&rct=j&q=&esrc=s&source=web&cd=&cad=rja&uact=8&ved=2ahUKEwjTz9bGtffs AhWKl4sKHfx_DeoQFjACegQIBhAC&url=https%3A%2F%2 Fassets.publishing.service.gov.uk%2Fgovernment%2Fuploads%2 Fsystem%2Fuploads%2Fattachment_data%2Ffile% 2F910893 (10.11.2020).

The categorised bar chart of the difference in the number of British departing Great Britain between the homonymous months in 2020 and 2019 is outlined in Chart 9.7.

The data presented in Chart 9.7 shows that the largest declines in the homonymous months in 2019–2020 in the group of British departing from Great Britain were recorded in June (– 6,054,400), July (– 5,530,900), May (– 5,272,200), April (– 4,790,500), March (– 1,701,800), January (– 298,300) and February (83,500). It should be emphasised that the difference between the number of British people departing from Great Britain in homonymous months in 2020 and 2019 was positive in February only. In other cases it was negative.

The next stage of the research was to outline the categorised bar chart of the comparative analysis of the total number of passengers and British departing from Great Britain in the homonymous time frames from January to July in 2019–2020.

In the considered homonymous time frame, from January to July 2019, 62,304,900 passengers departed from airports in Great Britain in 2019. In

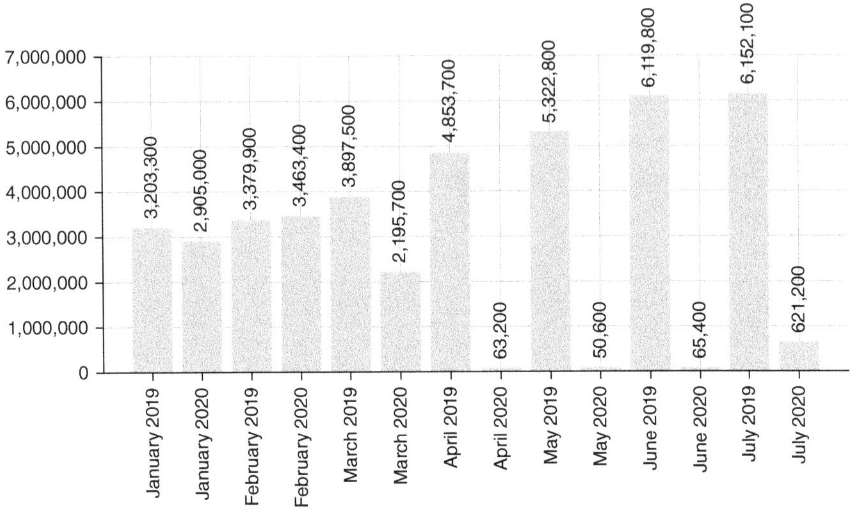

Chart 9.6 The categorised bar chart of the comparative analysis of British departing Great Britain in homonymous months for 2019–2020

Source: Own study based on data obtained from the website www.google.com/url?sa=t&rct=j&q=&esrc=s&source=web&cd=&cad=rja&uact=8&ved=2ahUKEwjTz9bGtffs AhWKl4sKHfx_DeoQFjACegQIBhAC&url=https%3A%2F%2 Fassets.publishing.service.gov.uk%2Fgovernment% 2Fuploads%2Fsystem%2Fuploads%2Fattachment_data%2 Ffile%2F910893 (10.11.2020).

2020, the number of passengers dropped to 19,409,400. Thus, the decline was 42,895,500 passengers. Considering the dependent variable of British passengers in the homonymous time frame, it was found that in 2019 32,929,100 passengers departed from Great Britain, while in 2020 only 9,364,500 passengers. The decrease in British passenger numbers was 23,564,600.

Conclusions

The research shows that the number of passengers carried by air in Great Britain in 2010–2019 shows an increasing trend (Chart 9.1). From 2010 to 2019, there was an increase in the number of passengers carried by air in Great Britain by 84,544,646, i.e. by 43.83 percentage points. The strongest growth dynamics was recorded in 2016–2017. In the indicated time period, the increase was by 8.88 percentage points, i.e. by 15,760,581 passengers.

Since 2020, the number of passengers carried by air transport worldwide has fallen sharply due to the COVID-19 pandemic. From March 11 to April 1, 2020, the total number of passengers departing from Great Britain dropped from 175,700 to 4,400 (Chart 9.2). Similar declines were observed among the British group departing from Great Britain in the homonymous time frame, from 88,600

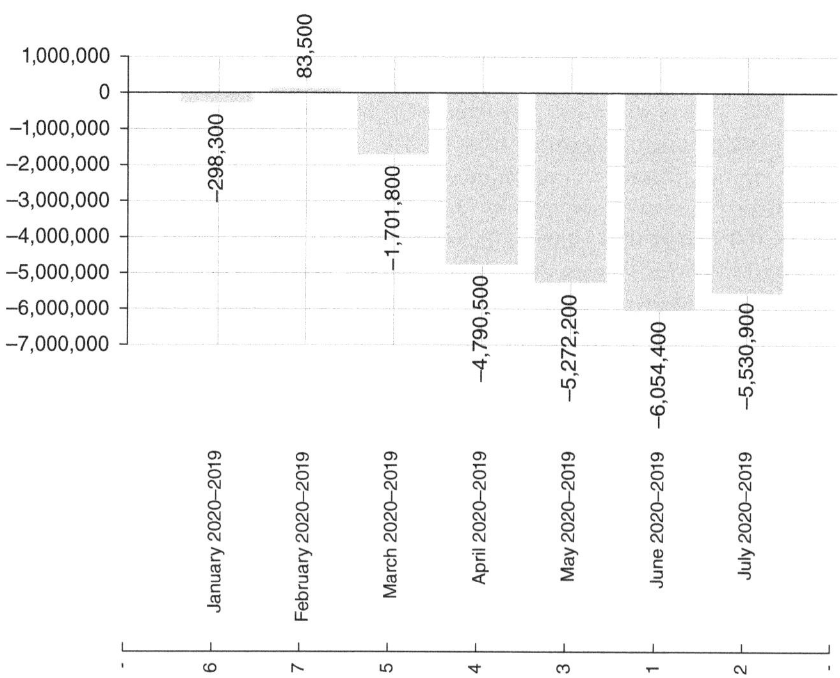

Chart 9.7 The categorised bar chart of the difference in total number of British departing Great Britain between homonymous months in 2020 and 2019 (X2 axis – ranking the data)

Source: Own study based on data obtained from the website www.google.com/url?sa=t&rct=j&q=&esrc=s&source=web&cd=&cad=rja&uact=8&ved=2ahUKEwjTz9bGtffs AhWKl4sKHfx_ DeoQFjACegQIBhAC&url=https%3A%2F%2Fassets. publishing.service.gov.uk%2Fgovernment%2Fuploads%2Fsystem%2Fuploads%2Fattachment_data%2Ffile%2F910893 (10.11.2020).

passengers to just 2,200. The huge declines continued until the end of the time frame under consideration, i.e. until July 31, 2020, with a slight upward trend.

The median of the fixed-basis dynamics indexes for passengers departing from the Great Britain in 2019 from January to July was 123.1 percentage points, while in the British group it was 141.68 percentage points. The COVID-19 pandemic led to the situation that from April 1 to the end of June 2020, the median in the total group of the fixed basis dynamics indexes for passengers departing from Great Britain was 1.90 percentage points, while in the group of the British the median was 1.99 percentage points. In the group of passengers in total, in July 2020 the median increased to 16.51 percentage points, and in the group of Britons, to 18.91 percentage points.

In March 2019, 7,816,900 passengers departed from Great Britain, while in the homonymous month in 2020, 3,815,100 (Chart 9.4). In April, in 2019, 9,120,600 passengers departed from Great Britain, and in the homonymous time frame in

2020, 112,500. In May 2019, 9,754,200 passengers departed from Great Britain, and 139,300 in the homonymous month in 2020. Slight increases were recorded in June, where 10,770,900 passengers departed from Great Britain in 2019, and 194,800 in 2020. In July 2020, the number of passengers transported increased to 1,160,500. This is still much less than in the homonymous month in 2019, when 11,130,100 passengers departed from the UK.

The largest difference in the number of passengers departing from Great Britain between homonymous months (January–July) in 2019–2020 was in June: – 10,576,100 (Chart 9.5). July came second with 9,869,600. May came in third with 9,614,900 passengers departing. The next places in the ranking are April (– 9,008,100), March (– 4,001,800), February (– 127,300) and January (– 47,700). It should be emphasised that in January and February 2020 only, there was an increase compared to the homonymous months in 2019. In the remaining months, the differences were negative.

In March 2019, 3,897,500 British departed from Great Britain airports, while only 2,195,700 departed from airports in 2020 (Chart 9.6). Higher declines were recorded in the subsequent months. In April, a decrease from 4,853,700 (2019) to 63,200 (2020), in May from 5,322,800 (2019) to 50,600 (2020), in June from 6,119,800 (2019) to 65,400 (2020) and in July from 6,152,100 (2019) to 621,200 (2020).

The largest declines in the homonymous months (January–July) in 2019–2020 in the group of British departing from Great Britain were recorded in June (– 6,054,400), July (– 5,530,900), May (– 5,272,200), April (– 4,790,500), March (– 1,701,800), January (– 298,300) and February (83,500) (Chart 9.7). It should be emphasised that the difference between the number of British people departing from Great Britain in the homonymous months in 2020 and 2019 was positive in February only. In other cases it was negative.

In the time frame from January to July 2019, 62,304,900 passengers in total departed from airports in Great Britain. However, in 2020, in the same time frame, the number of passengers dropped to 19,409,400 (Chart 9.8). There was a decrease by 42,895,500 passengers between the time frames under consideration. Considering the dependent variable in the form of British passengers in the same time frame, it was found that 32,929,100 departed Great Britain in 2019 from January to July, while only 9,364,500 in 2020. The drop in British passengers was 23,564,600.

The COVID-19 pandemic has resulted in major changes around the world, especially in the passenger air transport sector in terms of economic security. From March 2020, huge drops in the number of passengers have been observed. This, in turn, translated into low oil prices due to the global decline in demand for oil. Since April, such economic powers as the United States have seen a huge increase in unemployment rates to the level of 14.7 percentage points. In other countries, the impact of the pandemic is also visible, resulting in closed workplaces and factories, spikes in the prices of certain products and numerous restrictions on people movement. A return to the pre-pandemic situation, especially in

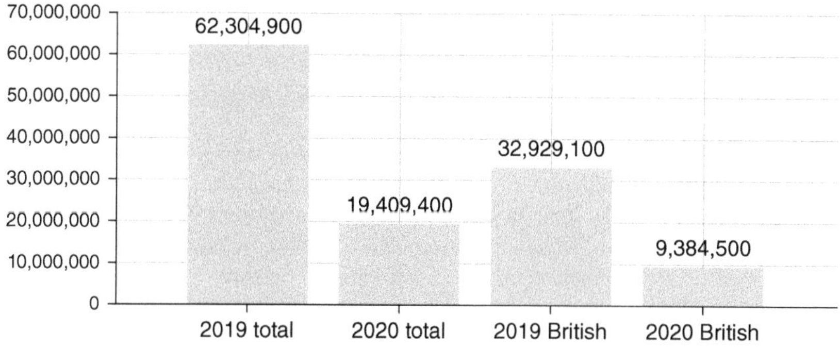

Chart 9.8 The categorised bar chart of the comparative analysis of the total number of passengers and British departing from Great Britain in homonymous time frames from January to July for 2019–2020

Source: Own study based on data obtained from the website www.google.com/url?sa=t&rct=j&q=&esrc=s&source=web&cd=&cad=rja&uact=8&ved=2ahUKEwjTz9bGtffs AhWKl4sKHfx_DeoQFjACegQIBhAC&url=https%3A%2F%2Fassets. publishing.service.gov.uk%2Fgovernment%2Fuploads%2Fsystem%2Fuploads%2 Fattachment_data%2Ffile%2F910893 (10.11.2020).

the passenger air transport sector, requires the signing of well-thought-out and coordinated international agreements on rules to determine the number of passengers and the manner of their movement.

References

www.bls.gov/charts/employment-situation/civilian-unemployment-rate.htm.

https://ec.europa.eu/.

https://fred.stlouisfed.org/series/M0892AUSM156SNBR.

Gołembska, E., Bentyn, Z. and Gołembski, M. (2017). *Logistyka usług*. Warszawa: Wydawnictwo Naukowe PWN.

www.google.com/url?sa=t&rct=j&q=&esrc=s&source=web&cd=&cad=rja&uact=8&ved=2ahUKEwjTz9bGtffsAhWKl4sKHfx_DeoQFjACegQIBhAC&url=https%3A%2F%2Fassets.publishing.service.gov.uk%2Fgovernment%2Fuploads%2Fsystem%2Fuploads%2Fattachment_data%2Ffile%2F910893.

Luisetto, M., Fiazza, C. and Latiyshev, O.Y. (2020). COVID-19 pandemia and the management strategy for business and economy #covid-19 #coronavirus #management #economy #emergency #infectious disease #virologist. *Management and Business Administration IMA Academy Lab*, 1. https://lupinepublishers.com/clinical-community-medicine/fulltext/covid-19-pandemic-and-the-management-strategy-for-business-and-economy.ID.000129.php ISSN: 2690-5760.

Nurzyńska, A. (2016). *Bezpieczeństwo usług w międzynarodowym transporcie lotniczym przewozów pasażerskich*. Katowice: SOPHIA.

Panek, T. and Zwierzchowski, J. (2013). *Statystyczne metody wielowymiarowej analizy porównawczej. Teoria i zastosowania*. Warszawa: Oficyna Wydawnicza Szkoły Głównej Handlowej.

www.pasazer.com/news/29996/przybywa,pasazerow,w,wielkiej,brytanii.html.

Pike, T.W. and Saini, V. (2020). An international comparison of the second derivative of COVID-19 deaths after implementation of social distancing measures. *BMJ*, https://doi.org/10.1101/2020.03.25.20041475.

Satomi, E. et al. (2020). Alocação justa de recuros de saúde escassos diante da pandemia de COVID-19. *Considerações éticas*, 18(2), 1–5.

Szubrycht, T. (2006). Współczesne aspekty bezpieczeństwa. *Zeszyty Naukowe Marynarki Wojennej*, 4(167), 87–98.

Szymczak, M. (Ed.) (1981). *Słownik języka polskiego*. Warszawa: PWN.

Tia, H. et al. (2020). *An investigation of transmission control measures during the first 50 days of the COVID-19 epidemic in China*. Washington: Science.

Wiśniewski, B. (2013). *System bezpieczeństwa państwa. Konteksty teoretyczne i praktyczne*. Szczytno: Wyższa Szkoła Policji.

Yan, Y. et al. (2020). The first 75 days of novel coronavirus (SARS-CoV-2) outbreak: recent advances, prevention, and treatment. *International Journal of Environmental Research and Public Health*, 17(7).

Zhu, N. et al. (2020). A novel coronavirus from patients with pneumonia in China. *New England Journal of Medicine*, 382, 727–733.

10 The analysis of the number of passengers landing in Germany and the changes caused by the COVID-19 pandemic

Mieczysław Pawlisiak and Bartosz Kozicki

Introduction

Transport is characterised by the complexity of technical, operational, organisational and legal connections as well as the diversity of movement of people and cargo in time and space (Wojewódzka-Król, Załoga, 2016, p. 9). One of the fastest modes of transport is air transport.

The aim of this study was to conduct a multivariate comparative analysis of the sum of the number of passengers landing in Germany by five continents of their travel destinations in the years 2000–2019 and the changes caused by the COVID-19 pandemic in terms of economic security. The subject of the research is five world regions and 26 European countries, and the object of the study is the number of passengers landing in Germany by the destination continent and the number of passengers transported by air in the first and second quarter in 26 European countries in 2019–2020.

The chapter uses research methods in the form of a literature analysis concerning air passenger transport, multivariate comparative analyses and security. The following tools were used in the research: categorised line charts and bar charts, Chernoff's faces and dynamics indexes with a constant basis.

The study consists of an introduction, three content-related sections, a summary and conclusions.

Analysis of the literature on the subject of the research

In the literature on the subject, the concept of transport is interpreted differently. It is usually considered in a systemic perspective with the following components: roads, means of transport, engineering structures (Jacyna, 2009, p. 15). The study examined air passenger transport, passengers transported at different times and the changes in the transport caused by the COVID-19 pandemic at one of the leaders in the number of people transported by air in this industry in Europe: Germany.

The infectious disease COVID-19 is assumed to be first diagnosed in Wuhan, China, in December 2019 (Tia et al., 2020; Zhu et al., 2020). In the press, you can find unconfirmed reports that COVID-19 appeared much earlier in various other places around the world (www.medonet.pl/koronawirus/

DOI: 10.4324/9781003285731-10

koronawirus-na-swiecie,kiedy-naprawde-pojawil-sie-koronawirus – moze-byc-posrod-nas-dluzej-niz-sadzilismy,artykul,15673280.html). The World Health Organisation identified COVID-19 as a pandemic on March 11, 2020 (https://pulsmedycyny.pl/who-grozba-pandemii-koronawirusa-jest-realna-984550; Satomi et al., 2020).

The emergence of the COVID-19 pandemic resulted in the fact that the authorities of individual countries began to introduce restrictions in the form of orders to wear masks, measure temperature in strictly defined places and prohibitions to travel, especially by passenger air transport (Yan et al., 2020).

This, in turn, affected the functioning of many world economies and caused them to slow down (Luisetto, Fiazza, Latiyshev, 2020). The consequence of this was an increase in unemployment rates in such economic powers as the United States, where in April 2020 the unemployment rate measure reached the level of 14.7 percentage points, unprecedented since the Great Depression of 1929–1933 (https://edition.cnn.com/2020/05/08/economy/april-jobs-report-2020-coronavirus/index.html).

Another consequence of the drastic reduction in passenger air transport was a lower global demand for crude oil, which resulted in a huge drop in its price, remaining below the level of $ 40 a barrel.

The study attempts to investigate the impact of the COVID-19 pandemic on the number of passengers transported by air passenger transport. The research began by observing existing trends in the past in terms of the number of passengers traveling by air and landing in Germany by their destination (five continents). For this purpose, a multivariate comparative analysis was used.

This analysis consists in ordering a relatively homogeneous pattern of an object (or feature) to make decisions about the choice of an object (or feature) according to a predetermined criterion. On the other hand, Pluta believes that multivariate comparative analysis is a set of various methods for detecting regularities in statistical communities (Pluta, 1977, p. 8). In the study, a multivariate comparative analysis was used to compare objects in the form of continents to indicate their differences and similarities, considering the explanatory variables in the form of the number of passengers landing in Germany by five target continents in the years 2000–2019. Researchers also wanted to observe regularities in the considered mass phenomena and to examine the changes caused by the COVID-19 pandemic in terms of economic security. One of the research tools used were the Chernoff's faces (Morris, Ebert, 2000; Cooksey, 2014), which were used to study the similarities and differences between the analysed objects.

In literature, economic security is considered to be a state of development of the national economic system, which (a state) ensures functioning through the use of internal development factors, as well as the ability to effectively resist external pressures that may lead to development disorders (Stachowiak, 1994, p. 189). Undoubtedly, the infectious disease COVID-19 in 2020 had an impact on economic security in various sectors of the economies, especially in air passenger transport.

The study attempts to examine the changes caused by the COVID-19 pandemic in terms of economic security, preceded by a multivariate comparative analysis of primary data on the number of passengers landing in Germany according to the continent of their destination.

The next content-related chapter will be focused on conducting a multivariate comparative analysis of the number of passengers landing in Germany by destination (continent) in the years 2000–2019.

A multi-dimensional analysis of the number of passengers landing in Germany by five destination continents

The study began with a categorised ranking bar chart (X2 axis) of data on the sum of the number of passengers landing in Germany by five destination continents in 2000–2019.

The data presented in Chart 10.1 shows that the largest number of passengers landing in Germany were people ultimately destined for European countries: in the years 2000–2019 there were 1,112,156,717 passengers. This represents approximately 77.3 percentage points of the total number of passengers landing in Germany by five destination continents in the years 2000–2019. The second place in the ranking is America with the result of 137,008,886, which is approximately 9.52 percentage points of the total data considered. The third place, with a result similar to America's, was taken by Asia: 131,373,437, which is about 9.13 percentage points of the total number of passengers. Africa is in fourth place with a result of 57,645,732, and the last one is Australia; 548,875 passengers have been registered, who will ultimately reach this continent and land in Germany.

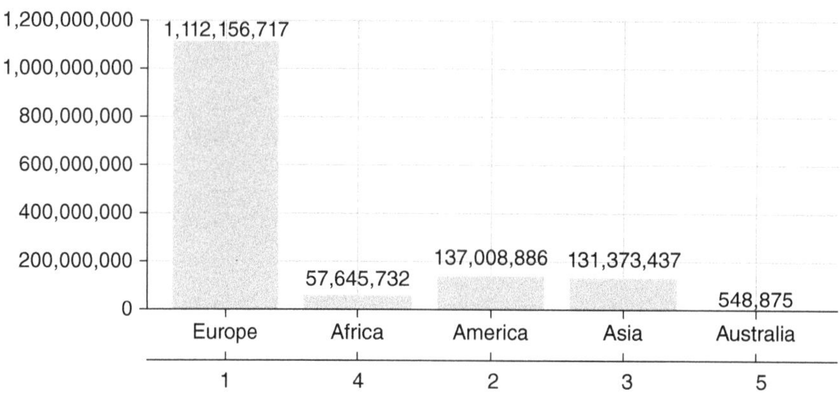

Chart 10.1 The categorised bar chart of the ranking (X2 axis) of data on the sum of the number of passengers landing in Germany by five destination continents, 2000–2019

Source*:* Own study based on data obtained from the website: www.destatis.de/EN/ (06.11.2020).

The next stage of the research was to perform a multivariate analysis of data on the number of passengers landing in Germany by five target continents in the years 2000–2019. Chernoff's faces were used in the research. Each face was marked with one dependent variable in the form of continents. Individual facial features were assigned explanatory variables in the form of the number of passengers landing in Germany by five destination continents in the years 2000–2019: face width = 2019, ear level = 2018, half face height = 2017, upper face eccentricity = 2016, lower face eccentricity = 2015, nose length = 2014, position of the centre of the mouth = 2013, lip curvature = 2012, mouth length = 2011, eye line height = 2010, eye gap = 2009, eye slope = 2008, eye eccentricity = 2007, half eye length = 2006, eye pupil position = 2005, eyebrow height = 2004, eyebrow angle = 2003, eyebrow length = 2002, radius of ears = 2001, nose width = 2000.

The study with the use of Chernoff's faces was carried out on four similar continents in terms of the size of the variables explaining primary data: America, Asia, Australia and Africa. It should be emphasised that the data on the size of the variables explaining Europe was considered extremely different from the arithmetic average of all the variables explaining the five continents under consideration. This became the premise to carry out the research for the four continents only. The research results are shown in Chart 10.2.

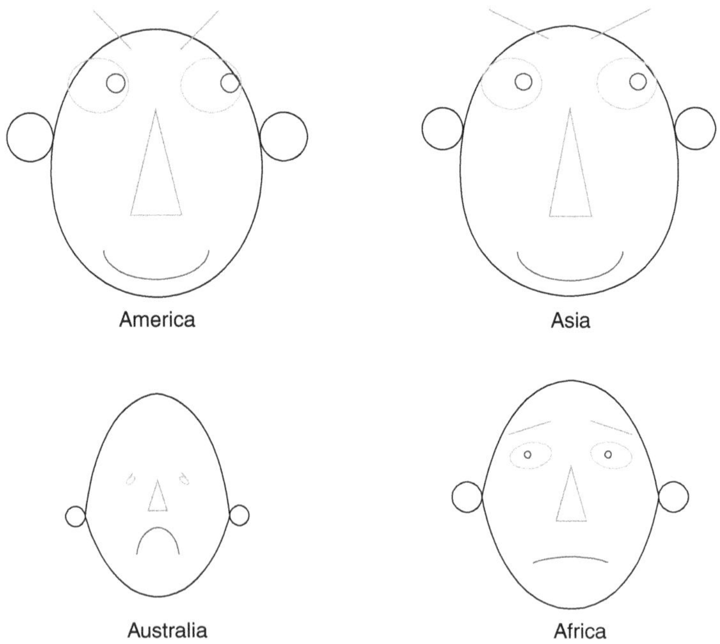

Chart 10.2 Chernoff's faces. The multivariate comparative analysis of data on the number of passengers landing in Germany by five destination continents in the years 2000–2019

Source: Own study based on data obtained from the website: www.destatis.de/EN/ (06.11.2020).

The research shows that from 2000 to 2010, America was the obvious leader in terms of people who landed in Germany by the destination continents (Europe was not included in the research). Since 2011, Asia has gradually become the leader. A clear difference can be seen in the explanatory variables in the form of face width – 2019; ear level – 2018; half the height of the face – 2017. Africa ranks third. The face assigned to Africa is smaller than the faces of the two considered leaders, and all its outlined features are smaller. This proves that in the years 2000–2019 fewer passengers were in Africa than in America and Asia. Australia is at the lowest position in the ranking. Australia's face is smaller than all the other faces tested.

The next stage of the research was to analyse the changes in the number of people landing in Germany by the five destination continents in the years 2000–2019. The first step was to outline, as shown in Chart 10.3, the categorised line graph of data on the number of passengers landing in Germany by destination continents in the years 2000–2019. Due to the large disproportion in the analysed data of the variables explaining the dependent variables, the data was grouped and assigned to separate scales, which are described in the title of Chart 10.3.

The observation shows that between 2000 and 2019 there was a growing trend in the number of people landing in Germany by the five continents under consideration (blue line – scale, left Y axis). Worldwide declines were visible in 2001–2002 only, and during the Great Depression in 2009. The leader of the ranking in terms of people landing in Germany by destination continent in the years 2000–2019 is Europe (red colour – scale left-hand axis), where the median was 54,161,618 passengers and the arithmetic average was 55,607,836 passengers. Until 2010, America was second in the ranking, and Asia has been second since 2011 (scale – right, 1st Y axis). The fourth place in the ranking is taken by Africa (scale – right 1st Y axis), and the fifth place by Australia (scale – right 2nd Y axis).

Then constant-base dynamics indexes were used to study changes in the number of people landing in Germany by the five destination continents in 2000–2019. The number in 2000 was constant. The research results are outlined in Chart 10.4.

For illustrative purposes, to outline the trends in individual dependent variables under consideration more clearly, the variable *Africa* was assigned the separate scale of the right axis Y. Chart 10.4 shows that the highest dynamics of increases and decreases in the data on the number of passengers landing in Germany by continent was visible in Australia. The highest dynamics index could be noticed in 2008, and it amounted to 1140 percentage points; the lowest index was 0 percentage points in 2018 and 2019. The largest upward trend in dynamics indexes in the years 2000–2019 was recorded in Asia, where from 2010 to 2019 there was an increase in dynamics indexes by 139 percentage points. Europe was second, with an increase of 116 percentage points in the analysed time frame. Africa ranks third, with an increase of 54 percentage points in 2000–2019. The fourth place is occupied by America, with an increase in the analysed time frame of 43 percentage points. Australia is in last place, with a decline of 100 percentage points.

The growing trend was recorded for the whole world; from 2000 to 2019 an increase was recorded by 105 percentage points. Since 2020, there have been

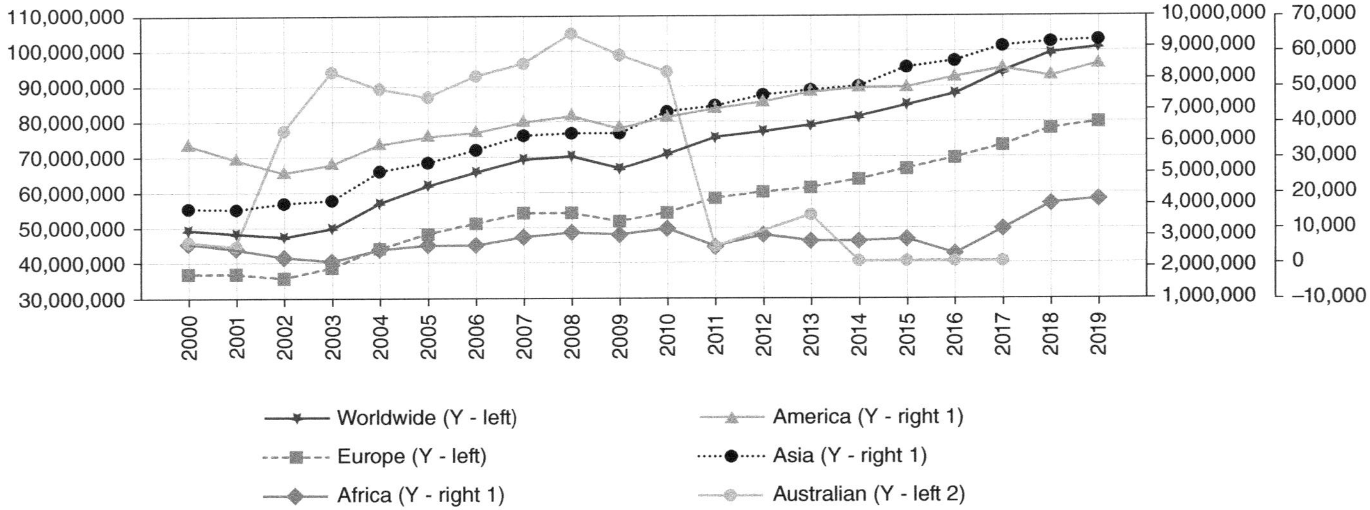

Chart 10.3 Categorised line chart of data on the number of passengers landing in Germany by continent of destination from 2000 to 2019 (whole world – left Y axis; Europe – left Y axis; Africa – 1. right Y axis; America – 1. right Y axis; Asia – 1. right Y axis; Australia – 2. right Y axis)

Source: Own study based on data obtained from the website: www.destatis.de/EN/ (06.11.2020).

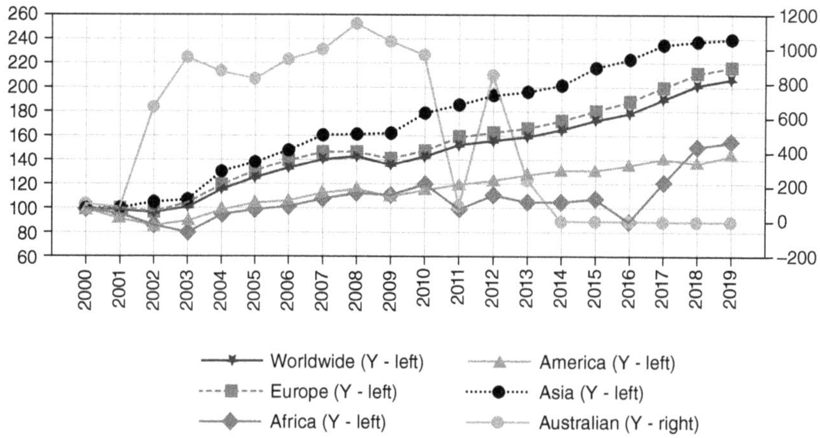

Chart 10.4 Categorised line chart of dynamics indexes with constant data on the number of passengers landing in Germany by destination continents in 2000–2019 (Australia – right Y axis)

Source: Own study based on data obtained from the website: www.destatis.de/EN/ (06.11.2020).

large worldwide declines in the number of passengers traveling by air due to the COVID-19 pandemic.

In the further part of the study, the declines in passenger numbers in 26 European countries in two homonymous quarters (the first and the second) in 2019–2020 were examined.

The multivariate comparative analysis of the number of passengers carried by air before and during the COVID-19 pandemic in Europe

The first stage of the research was to outline a bar chart of a comparative analysis of changes in the number of passengers carried by air in a total of 26 European countries in homonymous quarters in 2019–2020.

The data presented in Chart 10.5 shows that in the first and second quarter of 2020, compared to the homonymous time frames in 2019, there were drops in the number of passengers carried in 26 analysed European countries. In the first quarter of 2020, there was a decrease by 65,670,887 passengers compared to the first quarter of 2019. This represents a reduction in the number of passengers carried by air of 20.23 percentage points. However, in the second quarter of 2020, the number was reduced by 399,817,320 compared to the homonymous quarter in 2019. This is a decrease of 97.30 percentage points.

The next stage of the research was to draw the categorised bar chart (Chart 10.6) of a comparative analysis of changes in the number of passengers carried by air in 26 European countries in the homonymous first quarter in 2019–2020.

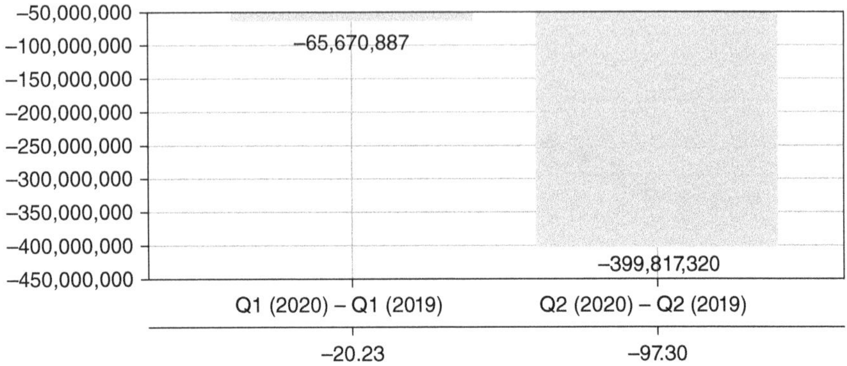

Chart 10.5 A bar chart of a comparative analysis of changes in the number of passengers carried by air in a total of 26 European countries in homonymous quarters in 2019–2020 (axis 2. X – medians of changes in the number of passengers carried by air in homonymous quarters in 26 European countries in total)

Source*:* Own study based on data obtained from the website: https://ec.europa.eu/ (06.11.2020).

The data presented in Chart 10.6 shows that in the first quarter of 2020, compared to the homonymous time frame in 2019, only one in 26 analysed countries saw an increase in the number of passengers carried by air. An increase of 4.49 percentage points was recorded in Bulgaria. The lowest drops in the number of passengers carried by air in the first quarter in 2020 compared to the homonymous quarter in 2019 were recorded in Slovenia (44 pp), Iceland (38.97 pp), Italy (31.79 pp), Germany (24.49 pp), Croatia (23.84 pp). The arithmetic average of decreases in the first quarter in 2020 compared to the homonymous time frame in 2019 is 20.07 percentage points in the 26 analysed European countries.

For illustrative purposes, the categorised bar chart (Chart 10.7) of the difference between the number of passengers transported by air in 26 European countries in the homonymous first quarter between 2019 and 2020 was outlined.

The information presented in Chart 10.7 shows that in Bulgaria in the first quarter of 2020 compared to the homonymous quarter in 2019, there was an increase in the number of passengers carried by air of 77,455. In the remaining 25 countries, decreases were recorded. The largest decreases occurred in the following countries: Great Britain (11,378,657), Germany (11,101,838), Italy (9,781,385), Spain (9,084,962), France (6,731,203), the Netherlands (3,472,641), Switzerland (2,824,234). In each of the remaining 16 countries considered, there was a decrease of fewer than 2,000,000 passengers in the homonymous time frame in 2019–2020.

Then an analysis of the decline in the number of passengers transported by air in the 26 European countries under consideration in the second quarter of 2019–2020 was carried out. The first stage of the analysis was the preparation of a categorised bar chart (Chart 10.8) of changes in the number of passengers carried

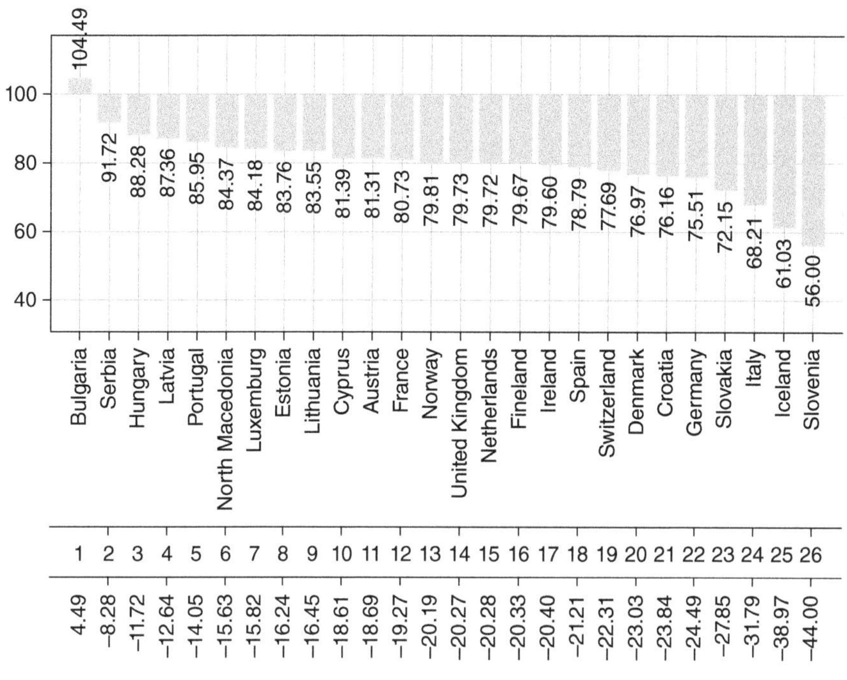

Chart 10.6 The categorised bar chart of a comparative analysis of changes in the number of passengers carried by air in 26 European countries in the homonymous first quarter in 2019–2020 (axis 2.Y – ranking the change in the number of passengers carried by air from the smallest change to the largest change; axis 3.Y – percentage points of the change in the number of passengers carried by air between the homonymous 1st quarter of 2019 and 2020)

Source: Own study based on data obtained from the website: https://ec.europa.eu/ (06.11.2020).

by air transport in 26 European countries in the homonymous second quarter in 2019–2020.

Chart 10.8 shows that in the second quarter of 2020, compared to the homonymous quarter in 2019, there was a decrease in the number of passengers transported by air in 26 analysed European countries of 96.94 percentage points on average. The largest declines were recorded in North Macedonia (99.55 pp), Slovakia (99.30 pp), Slovenia (98.98 pp) and Spain (98.53 pp).

For illustrative purposes, Chart 10.9 presents a categorised bar chart of the difference between the numbers of passengers carried by air in 26 European countries in the homonymous second quarter between 2019 and 2020.

Chart 10.9 shows that the largest drops in the number of passengers carried by air in the second quarter of 2020 compared to 2019 were recorded in the following countries: United Kingdom (73,589,932), Spain (61,573,414), Germany (59,051,956), France (44,176,740), Italy (42,625,270), Netherlands (20,918,229),

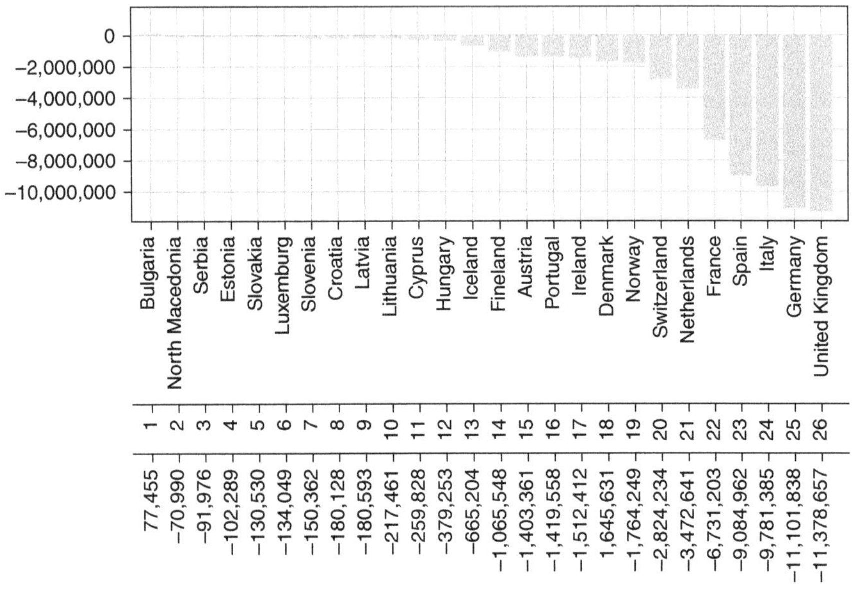

Chart 10.7 The categorised bar chart of the difference between the numbers of passengers carried by air in 26 European countries in the homonymous first quarter between 2019 and 2020 (axis 2. Y – ranking the difference between the numbers of passengers carried by air in 26 European countries in the homonymous 1st quarter between 2019 and 2020 from the smallest difference to the largest difference; axis 3. Y – the difference between the numbers of passengers carried by air in 26 European countries in the homonymous 1st quarter between 2019 and 2020)

Source*:* Own study based on data obtained from the website: https://ec.europa.eu/ (06.11.2020).

Portugal (14,975,117), Switzerland (14,599,781), Ireland (10,287,589). In each of the remaining 17 countries, the drop over the time frame considered was less than 10,000,000 passengers. The arithmetic average of the drop in the number of passengers in the second quarter between 2019 and 2020 in the 26 analysed European countries is 15,377,589.

Conclusions

The research shows that the largest number of passengers landing in Germany in the years 2000–2019 (1,112,156,717) was ultimately to be delivered to European countries (Chart 10.1). This is about 77.3 percentage points of all passengers landing in Germany in the years 2000–2019. The second place in the ranking is America, with the result of 137,008,886, which is approximately 9.52 percentage points of the total data considered. Asia came in third with 131,373,437, which is

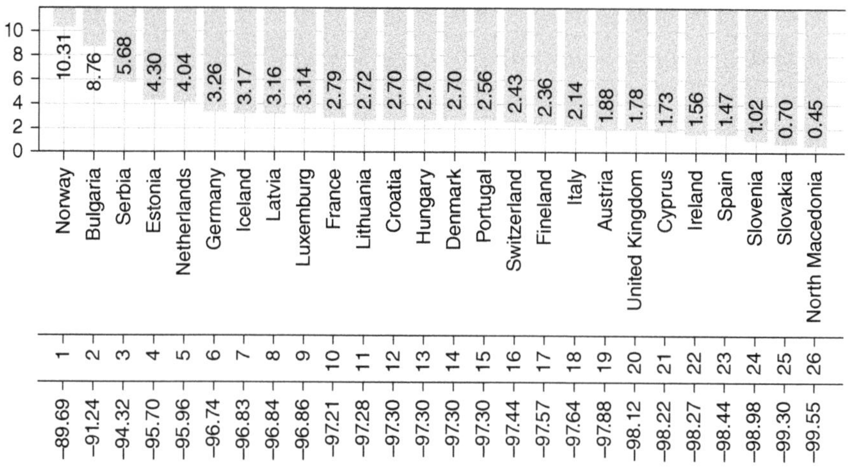

Chart 10.8 The categorised bar chart of a comparative analysis of changes in the number of passengers carried by air in 26 European countries in the homonymous second quarter in 2019–2020 (axis 2. Y – ranking the change in the number of passengers carried by air from the lowest change to the highest change; axis 3. Y – percentage points of the changes in the number of passengers transported between the homonymous second quarter of 2019 and 2020)

Source: Own study based on data obtained from the website: https://ec.europa.eu/ (06.11.2020).

about 9.13 percentage points of the total number of passengers. Africa was fourth with 57,645,732, and Australia was last with 548,875 passengers.

America was the leader in terms of people who landed in Germany by destination continents (Chart 10.2). It should be emphasised that the analyses omitted Europe, which was considered an extreme outlier compared to the others, making it impossible to highlight the regularities ruling the phenomenon under consideration. Since 2011, Asia has gradually become a minor leader. A clear difference can be seen in the explanatory variables in the form of face width – 2019; ear level – 2018; half the height of the face – 2017. Africa ranks third. The face assigned to Africa is smaller than the faces of the two considered leaders, as all its outlined features are smaller (Chart 10.2). This proves that in the years 2000–2019 fewer passengers were in Africa than in America and Asia. Australia is at the lowest position in the ranking. Australia's face is smaller than all the other faces tested.

In the years 2000–2019, a growing trend in the number of people landing in Germany by five continents under consideration was observed (Chart 10.3). Worldwide declines were visible only in 2001–2002 and during the Great Depression in 2009. The leader of the ranking in terms of people landing in Germany by destination continent in 2000–2019 is Europe, where the median was 54,161,618 passengers and the arithmetic average was 55,607,836 passengers. The second

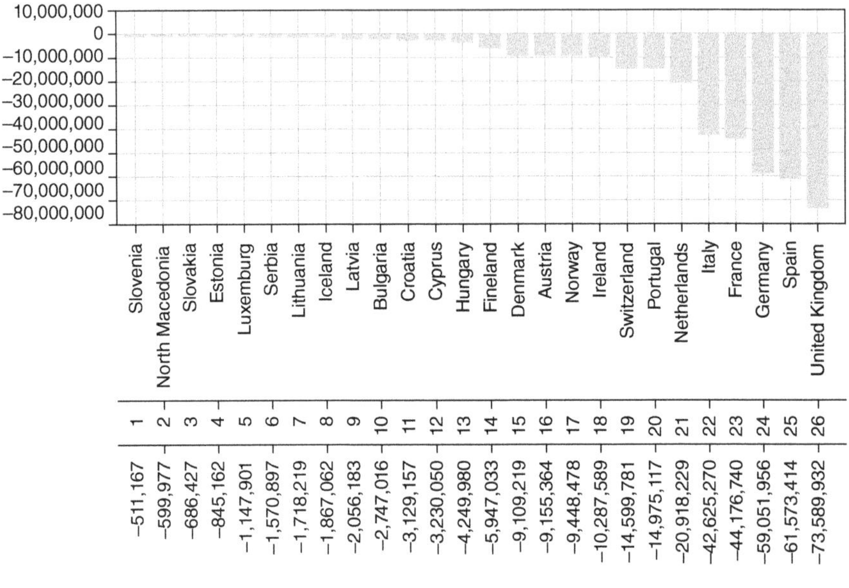

Chart 10.9 The categorised bar chart of the difference between the numbers of passengers carried by air in 26 European countries in the homonymous second quarter between 2019 and 2020 (axis 2. Y – ranking the difference between the numbers of passengers carried by air in 26 European countries in the homonymous 2nd quarter between 2019 and 2020 from the smallest difference to the largest difference; axis 3. Y – difference between the numbers of passengers transported by air in 26 European countries in the homonymous 2nd quarter between 2019 and 2020)

Source: Own study based on data obtained from the website: https://ec.europa.eu/ (06.11.2020).

place in the ranking was taken by America until 2010, and in 2011 by Asia. Africa is fourth in the ranking under consideration, and Australia is fifth.

The highest dynamics of increases and decreases in the data on the number of passengers landing in Germany by continent was visible in Australia (Chart 10.4). The largest increase in the dynamics indexes on a constant basis in the analysed continents was visible in Asia, where from 2010 to 2019 there was an increase by 139 percentage points. Europe was second, with an increase of 116 percentage points in the analysed time frame. Africa ranks third in the ranking with an increase of 54 percentage points in 2000–2019. The next places are occupied by America, with an increase in the analysed time frame by 43 percentage points, and Australia, with a decrease by 100 percentage points.

The observed growing trends in the number of passengers carried by air in the world have changed due to the COVID-19 infectious disease. The research was carried out based on 26 European countries, where homonymous time frames for the number of carried passengers were compared in terms of dynamics. The research shows that the COVID-19 pandemic resulted in a decrease in the number of passengers carried by air in 26 analysed European countries (Chart 10.5). In the first quarter of 2020, there was a decrease of 65,670,887 passengers compared to the first quarter of 2019. This represents a reduction in the number of passengers carried by air of 20.23 percentage points. However, in the second quarter of 2020 the number was reduced by 399,817,320 compared to the homonymous quarter in 2019. This is a decrease of 97.30 percentage points.

When untangling the primary variables, it was observed that in the first quarter of 2020, compared to the homonymous time frame in 2019, only one in 26 analysed countries saw an increase in the number of passengers. An increase was observed in Bulgaria by 4.49 percentage points (Chart 10.6). The lowest drops in the number of passengers in the first quarter in 2020 compared to the homonymous quarter in 2019 were recorded in Slovenia (44 pp), Iceland (38.97 pp), Italy (31.79 pp), Germany (24.49 pp), Croatia (23.84 pp). The arithmetic average of decreases in the first quarter in 2020 compared to the homonymous time frame in 2019 is 20.07 percentage points.

Only in Bulgaria, out of the 26 analysed countries, in the first quarter of 2020, compared to the homonymous quarter in 2019, there was an increase in the number of passengers carried by air of 77,455 (Chart 10.7). The largest decreases were recorded in the following countries: Great Britain (11,378,657), Germany (11,101,838), Italy (9,781,385), Spain (9,084,962), France (6,731,203), the Netherlands (3,472,641), Switzerland (2 824 234). In each of the remaining 16 countries considered, there was a decrease of fewer than 2,000,000 passengers in the homonymous time frame in 2019–2020.

On the other hand, in the second quarter of 2020, compared to the homonymous quarter in 2019, the number of passengers carried by air in 26 analysed European countries decreased on average by 96.94 percentage points (Chart 10.8). The largest declines were recorded in North Macedonia (99.55 pp), Slovakia (99.30 pp), Slovenia (98.98 pp) and Spain (98.53 pp).

The raw data shows that the largest decreases in the number of passengers carried by air transport in the second quarter of 2020 compared to 2019 were recorded in the following countries: United Kingdom (73,589,932), Spain (61,573,414), Germany (59,051,956), France (44,176,740), Italy (42,625,270), Netherlands (20,918,229), Portugal (14,975,117), Switzerland (14,599,781), Ireland (10,287,589). In each of the remaining 17 countries, the decrease over the period considered was less than 10,000,000 passengers. The arithmetic average of the drop in the number of passengers in the second quarter between 2019 and 2020 in the 26 analysed European countries is 15,377,589.

The COVID-19 pandemic has slowed many sectors of global economies, and one of the most affected is the passenger air transport sector. Since the proclamation of the global pandemic, national borders have been closed, flights have been cancelled, and many unprecedented restrictions have been introduced which have contributed to reducing global oil demand. This, in turn, led to low world oil prices, the production of which is unprofitable for many world leaders in this industry. Countries whose main income was the sale of this raw material have been reporting huge financial losses for several months. Russia, for example, is one of these countries. It should also be emphasised that the enormous and long-term reduction in air passenger transport was reflected in an increase in unemployment in the economies of various countries, including the United States, where in April 2020 unemployment at the level of 11.7 percentage points was recorded (www.statista.com/statistics/273909/seasonally-adjusted-monthly-unemployment-rate-in-the-us/). Recovery from the pre-pandemic state may turn out to be lengthy, and it will certainly require the introduction of many international coordinated agreements that must be accepted and implemented by key industry leaders to re-increase the dynamics of all sectors of the economy and return to the track observed before the current global crisis in terms of ensuring economic security.

References

Cooksey, R.W. (2014). *Illustrating statistical procedures: finding meaning in quantitative data*. Singapore: Springer Nature.

https://ec.europa.eu/.

https://edition.cnn.com/2020/05/08/economy/april-jobs-report-2020-coronavirus/index.html.

www.destatis.de/EN/.

Grabiński, T. et al. (1989). *Metody taksonomii numerycznej w modelowaniu zjawisk społeczno-gospodarczych*. Warszawa: PWN.

Jacyna, M. (2009). *Wybrane zagadnienia modelowania systemów transportowych*. Warszawa: Oficyna Wydawnicza Politechniki Warszawskiej.

Luisetto, M., Fiazza, C. and Latiyshev, O.Y. (2020). COVID-19 pandemia and the management strategy for business and economy #COVID-19 #coronavirus #management #economy #emergency #infectious disease #virologist. *Management and Business Administration IMA Academy Lab*, 1. https://lupinepublishers.com/clinical-community-medicine/fulltext/covid-19-pandemic-and-the-management-strategy-for-business-and-economy.ID.000129.php ISSN: 2690-5760.

www.medonet.pl/koronawirus/koronawirus-na-swiecie,kiedy-naprawde-pojawil-sie-koronawirus-moze-byc-posrod-nas-dluzej-niz-sadzilismy,artykul,15673280.html.

Morris, C.J. and Ebert, D.S. (2000). An experimental analysis of the effectiveness of features in Chernoff faces. *Proceedings of SPIE – The International Society for Optical Engineering*, 28. https://engineering.purdue.edu/~ebertd/papers/Chernoff_990402.PDF.

Pluta, W. (1977). *Wielowymiarowa analiza porównawcza w badaniach ekonomicznych*. Warszawa: PWE.

Satomi, E. et al. (2020). Alocação justa de recuros de saúde escassos diante da pandemia de COVID-19. *Considerações éticas*, 18(2), 1–5.

Stachowiak, E. (1994). *Bezpieczeństwo ekonomiczne*. Warszawa: AON.

www.statista.com/.

Tia, H. et al. (2020). *An investigation of transmission control measures during the first 50 days of the COVID-19 epidemic in China*. Washington: Science.

Wojewódzka-Król, K. and Załoga, E. (Eds.) (2016). *Transport. Nowe wyzwania*. Warszawa: PWN.

Yan, Y. et al. (2020). The first 75 days of novel coronavirus (SARS-CoV-2) outbreak: recent advances, prevention, and treatment. *International Journal of Environmental Research and Public Health*, 17(7).

Zhu, N. et al. (2020). A novel coronavirus from patients with pneumonia in China. *New England Journal of Medicine*, 382, 727–733.

11 Online shopping processes

Perspective of purchase transactions in the COVID-19 era

Jacek Woźniak, Wioletta Sylwia Wereda and Paweł Wereda

Introduction

The modern world is changing rapidly, affecting people's behaviour, including purchasing processes. The systematic increase in the potential of information and communication technologies (ICTs) gives consumers the opportunity to make changes in the way purchasing processes are carried out. The modern customer does not think of a shopping process as a visit to a stationary store, but rather as online shopping (von Leipzig, 2017). For many years, the e-commerce market has been developing both globally and nationally (E-Commerce Industry, 2020; Statista, 2020), which can be seen as a kind of human progress and the streamlining of one key area of people's lives. Nevertheless, the development of ICTs has various consequences (both negative and positive). A particularly important example is the evolving phenomenon of digital risk. For today's consumers, this type of risk should be extremely important. It is worth remembering that digital risk can be a source of both risks and benefits for customers who shop online. Actual research is focused primarily on the issues of the identification of factors that may affect the complexity of digital risk (Curran, 2020; Buckner, 2016; Zaki, 2020), as well as the degree of its perception by customers (Drenten, Zayer, 2018). Attention is also drawn to the propensity of customers to use ICTs in purchasing processes and the benefits of this (McLean, Wilson, 2019) – but the relationship between the phenomenon of digital risk and the use of ICTs in purchasing processes has not been tested yet. This chapter attempts to fill in this cognitive gap.

Literature review and theoretical foundation

According to the standard and generally accepted definition, *digital risk* covers various situations in which certain entities are exposed to potential losses, e.g. as a result of the use of electronic equipment (e.g. computers) and the processing of information resources in virtual reality (Śliwiński, 2018). Digital risk may be linked e.g. to the online activity of people, as well as the storage of data (including personal data) (Olsen, 2013). It is worth stressing that today digital risk – as a kind of socio-economic and technological phenomenon – covers basically every area of people's lives, including the implementation of purchasing processes.

DOI: 10.4324/9781003285731-11

Digital-natured risks, in the context of e-shopping, i.a. include (Clark, 2019; Research and Markets, 2020; Zaki, 2020; Marriott, Williams, Dwivedi, 2017; Bornschein, Schmidt, Maier, 2020):

- identity theft because of a security breach;
- interruption of the trading portal by a hacker;
- costs related to data corruption;
- theft of valuable digital assets, including customer lists and trade secrets;
- introduction of malware;
- human error leading to the inadvertent disclosure of confidential information.

At this point, however, it should be noted that digital risk, especially in the context of shaping and analysing consumer behaviour, should not be viewed solely through the lens of threats. An important "face" of the development of digital risk is to support innovative processes and exploit the potential of people/consumers, to reduce the cost of sales processes (Kazachek et al., 2020), as well as to increase the amount of information consumers can obtain about the seller or the entire sales process (Varadarajan, 2020) and to support environmental analysis (e.g. of the market) (Akter et al., 2020). In addition, digital risk (and in general the use of ICTs in purchasing processes) determines the specificity of a commercial company's relationship with different groups of stakeholders, mainly customers (Sun et al., 2020), suppliers (Intalar, Jeenanunta, 2019) and even sponsors (Scheinbaum, 2016). Digital risk can be a simultaneous source of opportunities and threats for both the company (the seller) and the consumer (Christensen, 2020). However, customers should not depreciate the role and importance of threats associated with digital risk – especially in the context of the loss of personal data (or even online identity) (Singtel, 2018). It is worth noting here that threats associated with digital risk are operational-natured (and often are immediate) and have mainly a financial face. On the other hand, opportunities within the digital risk phenomenon generally relate to intangible benefits (e.g. access to information, innovation, relationship building, etc.) and materialise rather in the long term (Stanimir, 2016). In order to benefit from the development of digital risk, it is appropriate to address threats in the first step (and take preventive or elimination actions) (Şerbănescu, 2011). This is necessary because the number and complexity of factors determining the scale of the digital risk (in the global scale) is getting higher and higher (Dunkel, 2020; Raschke, Mann, 2017).

Digital risk management, aimed at reducing the scale of threats – from the perspective of both sellers and customers – is primarily related to increasing the so-called digital competences of users (including skills and propensity to use ICTs) (van Tonder et al., 2018; Jen-Hui Wang, 2020). As research by Samson, Mehta, Chandani (2014) and Eigenraam et al. (2018) show, consumers' propensity to use new ICTs in purchasing processes is relatively high. Consumers use social media in a large scale (Müller et al., 2018), online forums, as well as mobile phone apps – which make the shopping process much easier. Today's new generation of customers ("the Customers 4.0") (Dash, Kiefer, Paul, 2021) is not able to function in the goods and services markets at all without strong ICT support. The trust of this generation of customers in ICTs is very high (Wereda, Woźniak, 2019). Therefore, as researches by Sjödin et al. (2020) and Sutherland et al. (2020) show, the propensity of modern consumers to use ICTs in purchasing processes, as well as the complexity of activities related to the use of ICTs in such processes, are at relatively high level. New generations of customers are somewhat "immersed" in digital risk and "tamed" by it (Wereda, Woźniak, 2019). This results in a situation in which customers can identify and counteract basic threats' classes and become aware of the potential negative consequences of the digital risk. Clark (2019) notes that these actions are often unconscious and intuitive, so that do not always have to correspond to the real digital threat. Therefore, as the research by Eigenraam et al. (2018) shows, despite the awareness of occurrence and the complexity of the digital risk in the opinion of modern consumers, they do not give a sufficiently high level of importance to digital risk, e.g. in purchasing processes. Van Tonder et al. (2018) also point out that digital risk is an immanent feature of modern purchasing processes, and therefore consumers do not see it, treating it as a kind of "natural phenomenon".

At this point, it is worth noting that the increase in the digitisation of people's lives, which also increases the phenomenon of the digital risk, also determines the scale and complexity of the use of ICTs – including purchasing processes. This is confirmed by the results of the study by Birch-Jensen, Gremyr, Halldórsson (2020), which indicate that the complexity of using ICTs in purchasing processes is relatively high, and IT technologies offer consumers various benefits during the implementation of purchasing processes (e.g. shortening time, savings, more efficient communication with the seller or higher awareness of the commercial offer). It is worth noting, however, that customers, expecting certain benefits from the use of ICTs in purchasing processes, expose themselves to materialising the threats associated with the digital risk.

Research model and hypothesis development

Four hypotheses were evaluated to achieve the goal of the study:

- Hypothesis No. 1: There is a strong positive correlation between (Figure 11.1):
  a. the digital risk complexity and the digital risk importance;
  b. the digital risk complexity and the consumers' use of ICTs complexity;
  c. the digital risk importance and the consumers' use of ICTs complexity.
- Hypothesis No. 2: There is a strong positive correlation between (Figure 11.2):
  a. the number of IT devices used in purchasing transactions and the digital risk complexity;
  b. the number of IT devices used in purchasing transactions and the digital risk importance;
  c. the number of IT devices used in purchasing transactions and the consumers' use of ICTs complexity.

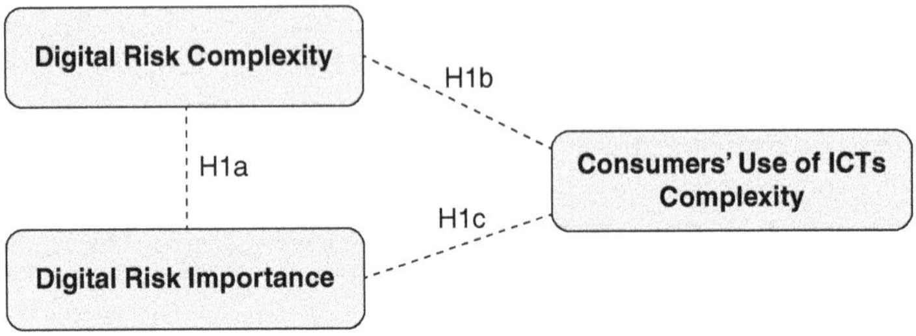

Figure 11.1 Theoretical correlations between digital risk and consumers' use of ICTs

Source: Own study.

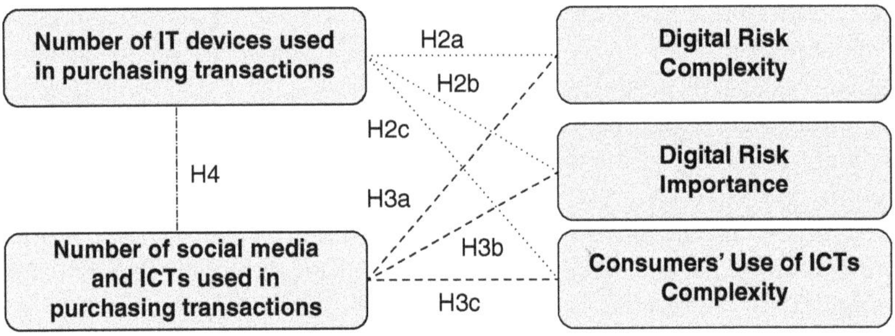

Figure 11.2 Theoretical correlations between the number of IT devices, the number of social media and ICTs used in purchasing transactions, as well as the digital risk and consumers' use of ICTs

Source: Own study.

- Hypothesis No. 3: There is a strong positive correlation between (Figure 11.2):
  a. the number of social media and ICTs used in purchasing transactions and the digital risk complexity;
  b. the number of social media and ICTs used in purchasing transactions and the digital risk importance;
  c. the number of social media and ICTs used in purchasing transactions and the consumers' use of ICTs complexity.
- Hypothesis No. 4: There is a strong positive correlation between the number of IT devices used in purchasing transactions and the number of social media and ICTs used in purchasing transactions (Figure 11.2).

To verify Hypotheses No. 1, 2, 3 and 4, three composite indexes were constructed – i.e. the Digital Risk Complexity Index – DRCI, the Digital Risk Importance Index – DRII, as well as the Consumers' Use of ICTs Complexity

Index – CUICI. The Pearson's parametric correlation (for Hypothesis No. 1) and Rho Spearman correlation (for Hypotheses No. 2, 3, and 4) were also used.

Methodology

This study will present selected results of the survey of factors determining the digital risk phenomenon in the opinion of Polish customers making regular electronic purchases. The study is also intended to demonstrate factors that have the greatest impact on the complexity of digital risk as well as factors that respondents believe reflect the importance of digital risk in purchasing processes. In addition, the study addresses the scale and complexity of the use of ICTs by Polish customers in purchasing processes – in conditions of development of the phenomenon of digital risk. The aim of the study is to bring together two main issues: (1) the peculiarity of the phenomenon of digital risk; and (2) the use of ICT in purchasing processes. In other words, the primary aim of the study is to identify and assess the correlation between the complexity and importance of digital risk in the opinion of Polish customers and the complexity of the use of ICTs in purchasing processes. The research problem is: What is the relationship between the complexity and importance of digital risk in customers' opinions, as well as the complexity of the use of ICTs in purchasing processes?

Sample and data collection procedures

The subject of the study is specificity of the use of ICTs in purchasing processes in the conditions of development of the phenomenon of digital risk in the opinion of Polish consumers. Respondents' opinions were used to assess the level of complexity and importance of digital risk, as well as the complexity of consumers' use of ICTs in purchasing processes.

The empirical study was conducted using the Computer Assisted Telephone-Interviewing (CATI) form on a sample of 320 Polish customers who regularly make online purchases (at least five purchases in electronic form in the last six months). The empirical study was conducted between March 2020 and April 2020. The research covered customers operating throughout Poland (16 *voivodships*). The study was carried out by the *Instytut Badawczy IPC Sp. z o.o.*, located in Wrocław (Poland). The study used a random systematic selection (considering the voivodship/administrative region in which the consumer resides) in layers (determined by the age of respondents, which reflects the structure in the age of Polish consumers making electronic purchases). Specification of the research sample is presented in Table 11.1.

The main research tool was the CATI questionnaire. The data analyses were supported by the IBM SPSS Statistics version 25. The questionnaire applied a screening question to determine whether customers had successfully made at least five electronic purchases in the last six months. During the CATI interview, respondents assessed specific factors (Table 11.2) on a 5-point scale. If the respondent assessed the factor at "1", this meant that there was a lack of implementation

Table 11.1 Structure of the research sample – CATI study (N=320)

Basic criteria for specification of the research sample	*N**	*%***
Sex		
Female	168	52.5
Male	152	47.5
Education		
Primary education	13	4.1
Secondary education	188	58.8
Higher education – bachelor's degree	42	13.1
Higher education – master's degree	15	4.7
Higher education – Ph.D.	10	3.1
National Vocational Qualification	52	16.3
Age (years)		
18–20	16	5.0
21–39	104	32.5
40–49	53	16.6
50–74	118	36.9
75 and more	29	9.1
Family/matrimonial status		
Divorced	3	1
Single	138	43.1
Married	179	55.9
Net revenues per month (EUR)		
0–500	142	44.4
501–750	102	31.9
751–1000	44	13.8
1001–1500	17	5.3
1501 and more	15	4.7
Number of IT devices used in purchasing transactions		
Small – up to 2 devices	103	32.2
Large – at least 3 different devices	217	67.8
Number of social media and ICTs used in purchasing transactions		
Small – up to 5 media and ICTs	206	64.4
Large – at least 6 media and ICTs	114	35.6
Level of satisfaction with the use of the internet connection		
Very satisfied	134	41.9
Moderately satisfied	154	48.1
Not satisfied	32	10
Total	**320**	**100.0**

Source: Own study.

* *Number of customers in the research sample.*
** *Percentage share of the number of customers in the research sample.*

of the factor (or its importance was very low); and if it was assessed at "5", the factor was fully implemented (or its importance was very high). In the following parts of this work, the results of the study of the use of ICTs in the development of the digital risk phenomenon – using the analysis of basic descriptive statistics

Table 11.2 Main specific factors in areas of determining the complexity and importance of digital risk, as well as determining the complexity of customers' use of ICTs (N=320)

Specific factors	*Mean*	*Median*	*Dominant*	*Standard deviation*	*Variance*	*Skew*	*Coefficient of variation*
GROUP I: Factors determining the complexity of digital risk in customers' opinion							
f1: Ability to share data, including personal data and other sensitive data	3.20	3.00	3	1.412	1.993	–0.257	44%
f2: No direct communication with the seller/contractor	2.79	3.00	3	1.293	1.673	0.148	46%
f3: Virtual money circulation (card, wire transfer, online consumer credit, etc.)	3.98	4.00	5	1.261	1.589	–1.093	32%
f4: Lack of detailed and important information in the purchasing process (hiding information by the seller and creating a so-called information asymmetry between customer and seller)	2.49	2.00	2	1.203	1.448	0.285	48%
f5: Lack of reliability of the seller	2.25	2.00	2	1.111	1.235	0.652	49%
f6: Hard-to-estimate time of order fulfilment	2.56	2.50	1	1.258	1.582	0.281	49%
f7: Poor quality of order fulfilment (lack of completeness of the package, destruction of goods, etc.)	2.11	2.00	1	1.188	1.411	0.843	56%
f8: Hidden costs of the purchase transaction (courier fee, insurance, duty, etc.)	2.08	1.00	1	1.307	1.709	0.829	63%
f9: Difficult complaint process	2.53	3.00	1	1.242	1.541	0.205	49%
f10: Make purchases and look at the entire store offer on one website	3.42	4.00	4	1.252	1.568	–0.424	37%

(*Continued*)

Table 11.2 (Continued)

Specific factors	*Mean*	*Median*	*Dominant*	*Standard deviation*	*Variance*	*Skew*	*Coefficient of variation*
f11: Ability to check online reviews about the seller and increase in consumer awareness	3.62	4.00	4	1.221	1.490	–0.723	34%
f12: Ability to influence the seller's rating and image	3.57	4.00	5	1.242	1.543	–0.526	35%
f13: Ability to contact other consumers and exchange information	2.88	3.00	4	1.321	1.745	–0.163	46%
f14: Ability to influence the seller's commercial offer and the quality of commercial transactions	2.84	3.00	3	1.203	1.447	0.001	42%
GROUP II: Factors determining the importance of digital risk phenomenon for customers							
f1: Ability to share data, including personal data and other sensitive data	3.14	3.00	3	1.419	2.012	–0.165	45%
f2: No direct communication with the seller/contractor	3.16	3.00	3	1.253	1.570	–0.083	40%
f3: Virtual money circulation (card, wire transfer, online consumer credit, etc.)	3.59	4.00	5	1.327	1.760	–0.603	37%
f4: Lack of detailed and important information in the purchasing process (hiding information by the seller and creating a so-called information asymmetry between customer and seller)	3.25	3.00	4	1.367	1.870	–0.236	42%
f5: Lack of reliability of the seller	3.18	3.00	3	1.370	1.877	–0.097	43%
f6: Hard-to-estimate time of order fulfilment	3.21	3.00	3	1.229	1.510	–0.167	38%

Specific factors	*Mean*	*Median*	*Dominant*	*Standard deviation*	*Variance*	*Skew*	*Coefficient of variation*
f7: Poor quality of order fulfilment (lack of completeness of the package, destruction of goods, etc.)	3.24	3.00	5	1.437	2.066	–0.173	44%
f8: Hidden costs of the purchase transaction (courier fee, insurance, duty, etc.)	3.25	3.00	5	1.438	2.069	–0.254	44%
f9: Difficult complaint process	3.25	3.00	3	1.244	1.547	–0.212	38%
f10: Make purchases and look at the entire store offer on one website	3.24	3.00	3	1.306	1.705	–0.175	40%
f11: Ability to check online reviews about the seller and increase in consumer awareness	3.80	4.00	5	1.236	1.527	–0.858	33%
f12: Ability to influence the seller's rating and image	2.98	3.00	4	1.333	1.777	–0.048	45%
f13: Ability to contact other consumers and exchange information	3.30	3.00	3	1.260	1.589	–0.338	38%
f14: Ability to influence the seller's commercial offer and the quality of commercial transactions	3.23	3.00	4	1.245	1.550	–0.254	39%
GROUP III: Factors determining the complexity of customers' use of ICTs in the electronic purchasing process							
f1: Financial benefits and value for consumers	3.57	4.00	5	1.337	1.788	–0.623	37%
f2: Digital risk resistance	3.52	4.00	3	1.158	1.341	–0.521	33%
f3: Ethics and control of access to data and their use only by online stores	3.81	4.00	5	1.109	1.229	–0.583	29%

(*Continued*)

Table 11.2 (Continued)

Specific factors	*Mean*	*Median*	*Dominant*	*Standard deviation*	*Variance*	*Skew*	*Coefficient of variation*
f4: Integration with the store and the ability to re-make a purchase by creating a customer account	3.58	4.00	4	1.155	1.335	–0.674	32%
f5: Integrity of ordering, payment and shipment process	3.70	4.00	4	1.194	1.426	–0.777	32%
f6: Quick online interaction	3.72	4.00	5	1.328	1.763	–0.716	36%
f7: Trust in a given ICT's brand	3.75	4.00	4	1.171	1.371	–0.841	31%
f8: Protection of personal data by shops	3.88	4.00	5	1.184	1.401	–0.863	31%
f9: No direct contact with the seller	3.09	3.00	3	1.116	1.246	–0.133	36%
f10: Risk of data theft	3.26	3.00	4	1.472	2.168	–0.254	45%
f11: Control and security of data determined by stores	3.56	4.00	4	1.194	1.426	–0.660	34%
f12: Ability to leave store ratings on social media	3.34	4.00	4	1.244	1.548	–0.472	37%
f13: Liability systems in the form of regulations of online stores	3.28	3.00	4	1.140	1.299	–0.421	35%
f14: Accuracy of data recorded by a given IT system	3.27	3.00	3	1.134	1.287	–0.394	35%
f15: Store performance (service speed, resource consumption, product availability)	3.54	4.00	4	1.236	1.528	–0.525	35%
f16: Usability (human factors, aesthetics, consistency, documentation, responsiveness) and business continuity (availability, predictability, accuracy)	3.63	4.00	4	1.129	1.275	–0.598	31%

Source: Own study.

and correlations, as well as factor analysis (i.e. Principal Components Analysis method – PCA) – are described.

Measures

The empirical study considered 30 specific factors that could have a potential impact either on the complexity and importance of digital risk or on the complexity of using ICTs in purchasing processes (Table 11.2). These factors were detailed on the basis of the studies conducted by Banyt, Vitkauskait, Milašius (2008), Rudnicki (2017), Idzikowski, Cieśliński (2014), Lee, Trimi, Yang (2014), Polo Peña, Frías Jamilena, Rodríguez Molina (2013), Rasool, Shah, Islam (2020), Fernández-Rovira et al. (2021), Matarazzo et al. (2021), Curran (2018), Bamberger (2010) and Donning (2019). Specific factors are included in three groups: (1) factors determining the complexity of digital risk in customers' opinion; (2) factors determining the importance of digital risk phenomenon for customers; as well as (3) factors determining the complexity of customers' use of ICTs in the electronic purchasing process. The first two groups of factors refer to the same 14 factors – assessed by respondents in terms of their prevalence in shaping both the complexity and importance of digital risk. This approach is determined by the desire to meet the basic principles of the systemic analysis (Zaskórski, 2012) and to identify those factors that can most strongly determine complexity and importance of digital risk, as well as the complexity of using ICTs in purchasing processes.

Based on respondents' assessment of the degree of implementation/importance of the various factors related to shaping the complexity and importance of digital risk, as well as the complexity of using ICTs in purchasing processes on a 5-point scale, the dominant factors were specified (Table 11.2). For Group I this is "virtual money circulation (card, wire transfer, online consumer credit, etc.)" (mean at the 3.98 level). For Group II this is "ability to check online reviews about the seller and increase in the consumer awareness" (mean at the 3.80 level). In Group III, ensuring "protection of personal data by shops" is the dominating factor (mean at the 3.88 level).

Overall, it can be noted that all 14 factors dedicated to shaping the complexity and importance of digital risk have been evaluated by respondents at relatively low or moderate levels (the average score is between 2.08 and 3.98 for factors determining the complexity of digital risk, as well between 2.98 to 3.80 for factors determining the importance of digital risk phenomenon). In turn, 16 factors dedicated to shaping the complexity of customers' use of ICTs in the electronic purchasing process were assessed at a slightly higher level, but this level is rather moderate than high (from 3.09 to 3.88 in a 5-point scale).

As already explained noted, to verify all hypotheses, three composite indexes were constructed:

- the Digital Risk Complexity Index (DRCI);
- the Digital Risk Importance Index (DRII);
- the Consumers' Use of ICTs Complexity Index (CUICI).

The digital risk complexity should be defined as the number of actions (factors) that respondents consider as important in shaping the scale and complexity of the digital risk phenomenon. In this case, respondents assessed 14 factors (Table 11.2) in the context of frequency of contact with a given factor. The more customers/respondents encounter a given factor, the greater its contribution to shaping the complexity of the digital risk phenomenon.

The digital risk importance should be seen as the importance of digital risk in consumers' opinion for the implementation of purchasing processes. Respondents assessed the importance of 14 factors in their purchasing activities. The higher the assessment of a factor, the more it raises the importance of digital risk.

The consumers' use of ICTs complexity reflects the scale and propensity of customers to use ICTs in purchasing processes. Respondents assessed 16 factors (Table 11.2) in terms of the extent to which the factors encouraged them to use digital technology in the electronic purchasing process. The higher customers/respondents rated a factor, the more important it is in shaping consumers' use of ICTs complexity.

The methodology of constructing the DRCI, DRII and CUICI indexes, referring to specific factors (Table 11.2), will be presented. The composite indexes were used in the study because (Nardo et al., 2005):

- they offer the opportunity to include a large number of factors that can potentially be treated as part of shaping the complexity and importance of digital risk, as well as the complexity of using ICTs in purchasing processes;
- they provide the basis for reliable quantification and assessment of factors important in shaping the complexity and importance of digital risk, as well as the complexity of using ICTs in purchasing processes;
- they enable the reduction of the dimensions of the analysis of the level of complexity and importance of digital risk, as well as the level of complexity of using ICTs in purchasing processes.

Factors included in the study were measured on a 5-point scale. The reliability of the scale was analysed using Cronbach's alpha coefficient to verify the quality of the data (Tables 11.3, 11.4, 11.5). For a full list of 14 factors for the DRCI, the value of the coefficient was 0.635. This value may have been raised (to the level of 0.645) – factor no. 3 has been removed for this purpose: "virtual money circulation (card, wire transfer, online consumer credit, etc.)". For the DRII, the value of Cronbach's alpha coefficient was 0.679. For a full list of 16 factors for the CUICI, the value of the coefficient was 0.854. In this case too, one of the specific factors (factor no. 10: "risk of data theft") could be removed when the value of the coefficient increased to 0.867. Taking into account the methodological recommendations, the obtained values can be considered sufficient.

For construction of the DRCI, DRII and CUICI, methodological recommendations for the development of composite indexes, developed by OECD (2008),

Table 11.3 Alfa Cronbach factor for constructing DRCI (N=320)

Alfa Cronbach	*Number of specific factors*
0.635	14
0.645	13

Source: Own study.

Removal – factor no. 3: "virtual money circulation (card, wire transfer, online consumer credit, etc.)"

Table 11.4 Alfa Cronbach factor for constructing DRII (N=320)

Alfa Cronbach	*Number of specific factors*
0.679	14

Source: Own study.

Table 11.5 Alfa Cronbach factor for constructing CUICI (N=320)

Alfa Cronbach	*Number of specific factors*
0.854	16
0.867	15

Source: Own study.

Removal – factor no. 10: "risk of data theft"

were used. The adopted DRCI, DRII and CUICI construction methodology included the following stages (Nardo et al., 2005):

1 determining the scope of measurement and the legitimacy of using the composite index;
2 selection of partial factors;
3 evaluation of the quality of empirical data;
4 assessment of the relationship between partial factors;
5 giving weight to the partial factors and their aggregation to the composite index.

The results of the implementation of the first three stages are included in Tables 11.2, 11.3, 11.4, 11.5. In the assessment of the relationship between partial factors and their aggregation to the DRCI, DRII and CUICI composite indexes, the factor analysis method was used (by means of the principal component analysis – PCA) (Hudrliková, 2013). The Kaiser-Mayer-Olkin coefficient and the Bartlett sphericity test were used to verify the correctness of the PCA analysis. The limit value of the KMO coefficient is commonly adopted at the level of 0.5 to 0.7 (Williams, Brown, Onsman, 2012). In the analysed cases of the DRCI, DRII and CUICI indexes, the KMO coefficient assumed values of 0.726 for DRCI, 0.732 for DRII and 0.912 for CUICI. Bartlett's sphericity test showed that the hypothesis of uncorrelated coefficients can be rejected – the statistic of the test is 403.575 for DRCI, 455.362 for DRII and 1418.635 for CUICI – with a significance level of less than 0.001. Further PCA analyses are justified and methodically correct (Tables 11.6, 11.7, 11.8).

In the further analysis, the method of distinguishing main component factors with Varimax rotation was applied. However, the selection of components was based on the Kaiser criterion, which assumes that the eigenvalues of factors will be greater than one. For the DRCI, the factor analysis (matrix of rotated components) offered the basis for qualifying 13 factors to 4 components. The sum of squares of charges after rotation was approximately 49% (Table 11.9). For the DRII, the factor analysis offered the basis for qualifying 14 factors to 4 components. In this case the sum of squares of charges after rotation was approximately

Table 11.6 KMO sample adequacy and Bartlett test for constructing DRCI (N=320)

KMO sample adequacy		*0.726*
Bartlett test	**Approximate chi-square**	403.575
	df	78
	p	0.000

Source: Own study.

Table 11.7 KMO sample adequacy and Bartlett test for constructing DRII (N=320)

KMO sample adequacy		*0.732*
Bartlett test	**Approximate chi-square**	455.362
	df	91
	p	0.000

Source: Own study.

Table 11.8 KMO sample adequacy and Bartlett test for constructing CUICI (N=320)

KMO sample adequacy		*0.912*
Bartlett test	**Approximate chi-square**	1418.635
	df	105
	p	0.000

Source: Own study.

Table 11.9 Four main components of the DRCI (N=320)

Component	*Name of component*	*Defined % of variance after rotation*	*Cumulated % of variance after rotation*	*Weight for DRCI*
C1	Purchasing relationships with the manufacturer	16.644	16.644	0.34
C2	Obtaining information by a customer about the offer	12.323	28.967	0.25
C3	Information flow in the purchasing process	10.553	39.520	0.22
C4	Impact of a consumer on the offer	9.395	48.915	0.19

Source: Own study.

Method of extracting factors – principal components. Rotation method – Varimax with Kaiser's normalisation.
Rotation reached convergence in 5 iterations.

Table 11.10 Four main components of the DRII (N=320)

Component	*Name of component*	*Defined % of variance after rotation*	*Cumulated % of variance after rotation*	*Weight for DRII*
C1	Purchase transaction information	14.622	14.622	0.32
C2	Commercial offer	11.327	25.949	0.24
C3	Sales process	11.145	37.094	0.24
C4	Relationships with the seller	9.292	46.386	0.20

Source: Own study.

Method of extracting factors – principal components. Rotation method – Varimax with Kaiser's normalisation.
Rotation reached convergence in 7 iterations.

46% (Table 11.10). For the CUICI, the factor analysis offered the basis for qualifying 15 factors to 3 components. In this case the sum of squares of charges after rotation was approximately 51% (Table 11.10).

Assigning individual factors to the components made it possible to name all components of the DRCI, DRII and CUICI, and to assign component weights (Tables: 11.9, 11.10, 11.11). The weights were normalised by the sums of the squares of charges that correspond to the part of the variance explained by the given component. The developed composite indexes adopted the formulas as follows:

$$\text{DRCI} = 0.34(f5+f6+f7+f8+f9)/5 + 0.25(f10+f11+f12)/3 + \\ + 0.22(f1+f2+f4)/3 + 0.19(f13+f14)/2. \tag{11.1}$$

$$\text{DRII} = 0.32(f4+f5+f6+f7+f8)/5 + 0.24(f1+f9+f14)/3 + \\ + 0.24(f10+f11+f12+f13)/4 + 0.20(f2+f3)/2. \tag{11.2}$$

$$\text{CUICI} = 0.53(f1+f2+f4+f5+f6+f7+f8+f15+f16)/9 + \\ + 0.27(f9+f12+f13+f14)/4 + 0.21(f3+f11)/2. \tag{11.3}$$

Table 11.11 Three main components of the CUICI (N=320)

Component	*Name of component*	*Defined % of variance after rotation*	*Cumulated % of variance after rotation*	*Weight for CUICI*
C1	Value creation for a customer	26.908	26.908	0.53
C2	Relationships with the seller	13.650	40.558	0.27
C3	Data security	10.486	51.043	0.21

Source: Own study.

Method of extracting factors – principal components. Rotation method – Varimax with Kaiser's normalisation.
Rotation reached convergence in 6 iterations.

Based on the specified formulas, it was possible to estimate the average level of the DRCI, DRII and CUICI in the research sample and, therefore, to attempt to verify hypotheses.

Data analysis and results

To verify Hypothesis No. 1, the Pearson's parametric correlation was used (Table 11.12):

a. between the digital risk complexity and the digital risk importance, there is a moderate positive correlation ($p < 0.01$);
b. between the digital risk complexity and the consumers' use of ICTs complexity, there is a quite weak positive correlation ($p < 0.01$);
c. between the digital risk importance and the consumers' use of ICTs complexity, there is a moderate positive correlation ($p < 0.01$).

Based on the these statistics, Hypothesis No. 1, which states that there is a strong positive correlation between:

a. the digital risk complexity and the digital risk importance;
b. the digital risk complexity and the consumers' use of ICTs complexity;
c. the digital risk importance and the consumers' use of ICTs complexity, can be partially verified positively (i.e. confirmed).

To verify Hypotheses No. 2, 3 and 4, the Rho Spearman Correlation was used. For Hypothesis No. 2, it can be noted that (Table 11.13):

a. between the number of IT devices used in purchasing transactions and the digital risk complexity, there is a very weak positive correlation ($p < 0.05$);
b. between the number of IT devices used in purchasing transactions and the digital risk importance, there is a very weak positive correlation ($p < 0.05$);
c. between the number of IT devices used in purchasing transactions and the consumers' use of ICTs complexity, there is a very weak positive correlation ($p < 0.01$).

Table 11.12 Pearson's Correlation between digital risk complexity, digital risk importance and consumers' use of ICTs complexity (N=320)

		Digital risk importance (DRII)	*Consumers' use of ICTs complexity (CUICI)*
Digital risk complexity (DRCI)	Pearson's correlation	0.428**	0.369**
	p	0.000	0.000
Digital risk importance (DRII)	Pearson's correlation		0.452**
	p		0.000

Source: Own study.

** $p < 0.01$.

Table 11.13 Rho Spearman Correlation between the number of IT devices and the number of social media and ICTs used in purchasing transactions, as well as CUICI, DRCI, and DRII (N=320)

		Consumers' use of ICTs complexity (CUICI)	*Digital risk complexity (DRCI)*	*Digital risk importance (DRII)*
Number of IT devices used in purchasing transactions	Rho Spearman Correlation Coefficient	0.184**	0.120*	0.133*
	p	.001	.031	.017
Number of social media and ICTs used in purchasing transactions	Rho Spearman Correlation Coefficient	–0.074***	–0.028***	0.020***
	p	0.184	0.618	0.725

Source: Own study.

* $p < 0.05$.
** $p < 0.01$.
*** $p > 0.05$.

Based on the these statistics, Hypothesis No. 2, which states that there is a strong positive correlation between:

a. the number of IT devices used in purchasing transactions and the digital risk complexity;
b. the number of IT devices used in purchasing transactions and the digital risk importance;
c. the number of IT devices used in purchasing transactions and the consumers' use of ICTs complexity, can be verified negatively (i.e. falsified).

For Hypothesis No. 3, it can be noted that (Table 11.13):

a. between the number of social media and ICTs used in purchasing transactions and the digital risk complexity, there is no statistically important correlation ($p > 0.05$);

b. between the number of social media and ICTs used in purchasing transactions and the digital risk importance, there is no statistically important correlation ($p > 0.05$);
c. between the number of social media and ICTs used in purchasing transactions and the consumers' use of ICTs complexity, there is no statistically important correlation ($p > 0.05$).

Based on the these statistics, Hypothesis No. 3, which states that there is a strong positive correlation between:

a. the number of social media and ICTs used in purchasing transactions and the digital risk complexity;
b. the number of social media and ICTs used in purchasing transactions and the digital risk importance;
c. the number of social media and ICTs used in purchasing transactions and the consumers' use of ICTs complexity, can be verified negatively (i.e. falsified).

For Hypothesis No. 4 (Table 11.14), it can be noted that there is a weak positive correlation between the number of IT devices used in purchasing transactions and the number of social media and ICTs used in purchasing transactions ($p < 0.01$).

Based on the these statistics, Hypothesis No. 4, which states that there is a strong positive correlation between the number of IT devices used in purchasing transactions and the number of social media and ICTs used in purchasing transactions, can be verified negatively (i.e. falsified).

Conclusions

Purchasing processes, especially in a virtual form, are an important component of people's lives today. The overall digitalisation of life, e.g. improving the purchasing processes, also leads to the development of digital risk. Therefore, it is important how people (and consumers, in particular) assess digital risk (its complexity and importance in purchasing processes). It is also important which ICTs are used

Table 11.14 Rho Spearman Correlation between the number of IT devices and the number of social media and ICTs used in purchasing transactions (N=320)

		Number of social media and ICTs used in purchasing transactions
Number of IT devices used in purchasing transactions	Rho Spearman Correlation Coefficient	0.219**
	p	0.000

Source: Own study.

** $p < 0.01$.

by consumers and what is the complexity of using ICTs in purchasing processes. The propensity to use ICTs, as well as the level of competences of their skilful use, determine the level of digital risk. To explore this issue, empirical studies were carried out with the aim to identify and assess the correlation between the complexity and importance of digital risk in the opinion of Polish customers and the complexity of the use of ICTs in purchasing processes.

The study showed that there is a moderate positive correlation between the digital risk complexity, the digital risk importance, and the consumers' use of ICTs complexity. The research by Jen-Hui Wang (2020) and Samson, Mehta, Chandani (2014) indicate a similar trend, i.e. the theoretical relationship between the use of ICTs in purchasing processes and the digital security of these activities. It is interesting to note that, between the number of social media and ICTs used in purchasing transactions, and the digital risk complexity, the digital risk importance, as well as the consumers' use of ICTs complexity, there are no statistically important correlations. To some extent, this kind of result may come as a surprise, as it may seem that more IT technologies (social networks, etc.) used in purchasing processes result in a higher level of the digital risk (mainly in the form of threats). Nevertheless, it is worth noting here that basically each IT technology in purchasing processes focuses on a relatively "closed" set of threats, e.g. identity theft, theft of valuable digital assets, as well as introduction of malware (Clark, 2019).

The study gave rise to identify and assess the correlation between the complexity and importance of digital risk in the opinion of customers and the complexity of the use of ICTs in purchasing processes, as well as to assess the complexity and importance of digital risk in customers' opinions and the complexity of the use of ICTs in purchasing processes – using the example of Polish consumers. The empirical study increased the scale of considerations for identifying the peculiarities of the digital risk in the conditions of purchasing processes. Today's conditions – the global COVID-19 pandemic – increase the scale of online shopping, which may in turn determine the increasing level of digital risk. The study clearly indicated that there is no strong correlation between the complexity and importance of digital risk and the complexity and propensity to use ICTs in purchasing processes – so the development of digital risk (in the opinion of customers) does not have to mean e.g. an increase in the complexity of using ICTs in purchasing processes (and the other way around). In addition, the study notes that, in fact, the complexity and importance of digital risk in customers' opinions is not at a high level, which may come as a surprise regarding e.g. an increase in the scale of online crime in recent years.

The research limitations of the following study are also presented. First of all, the sample is relatively small, and the surveyed customers lived only in Poland – so this study can be regarded as a pilot study and merely a substantive and methodological basis for further studies. Therefore, the results obtained cannot be extended to the whole population, and neither can they constitute a basis for constructing recommendations in shaping the expected level of the complexity and importance of digital risk in customers' opinions, as well as the complexity of the use of ICTs in purchasing processes. It is also worth remembering that Polish customers are a diverse (e.g. spatially) set of people. Furthermore, only customers' opinions were examined, which may have had an impact on distorting the actual state of the situation. The study also focused solely on selected aspects of shaping the digital risk phenomenon, as well as the complexity of the use of ICTs in purchasing processes, and the correlation between them, mainly due to research costs. Thus, the results' analysis may seem selective and substantively narrow.

At this place, an attempt can be made to outline further research recommendations in shaping the scale and complexity of the use of ICTs by customers in purchasing processes – in conditions of development of the phenomenon of digital risk. The leading direction of research should be identifying and analysing the basic opportunities and barriers associated with reaching an expected level of the complexity and importance of digital risk, as well as the complexity of the use of ICTs in purchasing processes. An important research issue could also include an advanced identification of cause-and-effect relationships between specific factors determining the digital risk phenomenon.

This study provides the basis for developing and implementing actions aimed at increasing security in online shopping processes from the perspective of customers. The survey indicates what actions customers think are most important in terms of shaping digital risk complexity. This is a direct indication of what to do to increase the level of security of e-shopping processes. In this case, it is worth focusing e.g. on the virtual money circulation (card, wire transfer, online consumer credit, etc.), ability to check online reviews about the seller and increase in the consumer awareness, as well as the ability to share data, including personal data and other sensitive data. Furthermore, the study indicates that sellers do not have to target their offer today solely to customers who use ICTs on a large scale. The propensity to use ICTs in purchasing processes is not at a very high level. Furthermore, the lack of strong customer awareness of security aspects may result in them not recognising the role and importance of digital risk and becoming victims of e.g. cyber criminals. Therefore, it is necessary to take measures to raise customers' awareness of the complexity and importance of digital risk in today's online purchasing processes.

References

Akter, S. et al. (2020). Building dynamic service analytics capabilities for the digital marketplace. *Journal of Business Research*, 118, 177–188.

Bamberger, K.A. (2010). Technologies of compliance: risk and regulation in a digital age. *Texas Law Review*, 88(4), 669–739.

Banyt, J., Vitkauskait, E. and Milašius, L. (2008). Impact of ICT on the buying behaviour of lithuanian construction companies. *Economics & Management*, 3, 239–246.

Birch-Jensen, A., Gremyr, I. and Halldórsson, Á. (2020). Digitally connected services: improvements through customer-initiated feedback. *European Management Journal*, 38(5), 814–825.

Bornschein, R., Schmidt, L. and Maier, E. (2020). The effect of consumers' perceived power and risk in digital information privacy: the example of cookie notices. *Journal of Public Policy & Marketing*, 39(2), 135–154.

Buckner, B. (2016). Physical security risk in a digital age. *RMA Journal*, 98(10), 40–43.
Christensen, B. (2020). Adapting to the dynamic risk environment: internal audit needs to move beyond analog processes to assess risks in a digital world. *Internal Auditor*, 77(5), 22–23.
Clark, C.Y. (2019). Focusing on risk oversight in the digital age. *NACD Directorship*, 2.
Curran, D. (2018). Risk, innovation, and democracy in the digital economy. *European Journal of Social Theory*, 21(2), 207–26.
Curran, D. (2020). Connecting risk: systemic risk from finance to the digital. *Economy & Society*, 49(2), 239–64.
Dash, G., Kiefer, K. and Paul, J. (2021). Marketing-to-millennials: marketing 4.0, customer satisfaction and purchase intention. *Journal of Business Research*, 122, 608–620.
Donning, H., Eriksson, M., Martikainen, M. and Lehner, O.M. (2019). Prevention and detection for risk and fraud in the digital age – the current situation. *ACRN Oxford Journal of Finance & Risk Perspectives*, 8, 86–97.
Drenten, J. and Zayer, L.T. (2018). The role of digital virtual consumption in navigating risk-laden life events. *Journal of the Association for Consumer Research*, 3(1), 46–62.
Dunkel, D. (2020). Trends in 2020: converged "digital" risk elevates the security executive. *Security: Solutions for Enterprise Security Leaders*, 57(2), 35–37.
E-commerce industry (2020). www.reportlinker.com/market-report/.
Eigenraam, A.W., Eelen, J., van Lin, A. and Verlegh, P.W.J. (2018). A consumer-based taxonomy of digital customer engagement practices. *Journal of Interactive Marketing*, 44, 102–121.
Fernández-Rovira, C., Valdés, J.A., Molleví, G. and Nicolas-Sans, R. (2021). The digital transformation of business: towards the datafication of the relationship with customers. *Technological Forecasting and Social Change*, 162, 120339.
Hudrliková, L. (2013). Composite indicators as a useful tool for international comparison: the Europe 2020 example. *Prague Economic Papers*, 4, 459–473.
Idzikowski, W. and Cieśliński, W.B. (2014). The designing of customer management strategies using ICT tools in pure jatomi. *Business Informatics*, 4(34), 85–93.
Intalar, N. and Jeenanunta, C. (2019). Effects of customer's investment in ICT on partners' decisions through the supply chain: an empirical study of the manufacturing industry in Thailand. *Asian Journal of Technology Innovation*, 27(2), 239–256.
Jen-Hui Wang, R. (2020). Branded mobile application adoption and customer engagement behavior. *Computers in Human Behavior*, 106, 106245.
Kazachek, N.A. et al. (2020). The risks of digital economy development in Russia. *Talent Development & Excellence*, 12, 531–541.
Lee, S.-G., Trimi, S. and Yang, C.-G. (2014). ICT service providers strategies and customer migration. *Industrial Management & Data Systems*, 114(7), 1036–1049.
Marriott, H.R., Williams, M.D. and Dwivedi, Y.K. (2017). Risk, privacy and security concerns in digital retail. *Marketing Review*, 17(3), 337–365.
Matarazzo, M., Penco, L., Profumo, G. and Quaglia, R. (2021). Digital transformation and customer value creation in made in Italy SMEs: a dynamic capabilities perspective. *Journal of Business Research*, 123, 642–656.
McLean, G. and Wilson, A. (2019). Shopping in the digital world: examining customer engagement through augmented reality mobile applications. *Computers in Human Behavior*, 101, 210–224.
Müller, J.M., Pommeranz, B., Weisser, J. and Voigt, K.-I. (2018). Digital, social media, and mobile marketing in industrial buying: still in need of customer segmentation? Empirical evidence from Poland and Germany. *Industrial Marketing Management*, 73, 70–83.

Nardo, M., Saisana, M., Saltelli, A. and Tarantola, S. (2005). *Tools for composite indicators*. Brussels: European Commission.

OECD (2008). *Handbook on constructing composite indicators: methodology and user guide*. Brussels: OECD.

Olsen, T. (2013). *Insurance cyber risk*. New York: Willis.

Polo Peña, A.I., Frías Jamilena, D.M. and Rodríguez Molina, M.Á. (2013). Impact of customer orientation and ICT use on the perceived performance of rural tourism enterprises. *Journal of Travel & Tourism Marketing*, 30(3), 272–289.

Raschke, R.L. and Mann, A. (2017). Enterprise content risk management: a conceptual framework for digital asset risk management. *Journal of Emerging Technologies in Accounting*, 14(1), 57–62.

Rasool, A., Shah, F.A. and Islam, J.U. (2020). Customer engagement in the digital age: a review and research agenda. *Current Opinion in Psychology*, 36, 96–100.

Research and Markets (2020). European digital risk protection (DRP) market report 2020 – researchandmarkets.com. *Business Wire* (English).

Rudnicki, M. (2017). Importance of group buying websites like groupon among other information and communication technology (ICT) in the making-decision process of a tourist. *Research Papers of the Wroclaw University of Economics*, 473, 476–88.

Samson, R., Mehta, M. and Chandani, A. (2014). Impact of online digital communication on customer buying decision. *Procedia Economics and Finance*, 11, 872–880.

Scheinbaum, A.C. (2016). Digital engagement: opportunities and risks for sponsors. *Journal of Advertising Research*, 56(4), 341–5.

Şerbănescu, L. (2011). Risk management in the digital age. *Agricultural Management*, 13(2), 295–302.

Singtel (2018). Digital transformation without security creates greater risks. *NetworkWorld Asia*, 16(1), 22.

Sjödin, D., Parida, V., Kohtamäki, M. and Wincent, J. (2020). An agile co-creation process for digital servitization: a micro-service innovation approach. *Journal of Business Research*, 112, 478–491.

Stanimir, A. (2016). Measurement of the digital divide – risks for generation Y. *Research Papers of the Wroclaw University of Economics*, 426, 194–205.

Statista (2020). *eCommerce report 2020*, www.statista.com/study/42335/ecommerce-report/.

Sun, Y., Yang, Ch., Shen, X.-L. and Wang, N. (2020). When digitalized customers meet digitalized services: a digitalized social cognitive perspective of omnichannel service usage. *International Journal of Information Management*, 54, 102200.

Sutherland, K., Freberg, K., Driver, C. and Khattab, U. (2020). Public relations and customer service: employer perspectives of social media proficiency. *Public Relations Review*, 46(4), 101954.

Śliwiński, A. (2018). Digital risk as an insurance sector challenge. *Research Papers of the Wroclaw University of Economics*, 541, 268–282.

van Tonder, E., Saunders, S.G., Lisita, I.T. and de Beer, L.T. (2018). The importance of customer citizenship behaviour in the modern retail environment: introducing and testing a social exchange model. *Journal of Retailing and Consumer Services*, 45, 92–102.

Varadarajan, R. (2020). Customer information resources advantage, marketing strategy and business performance: a market resources based view. *Industrial Marketing Management*, 89, 89–97.

von Leipzig, T. et al. (2017). Initialising customer-orientated digital transformation in enterprises. *Procedia Manufacturing*, 8, 517–524.

Wereda, W. and Woźniak, J. (2019). Building relationships with customer 4.0 in the era of marketing 4.0: the case study of innovative enterprises in Poland. *Social Sciences*, 8(6), 177.

Williams, B., Brown, T. and Onsman, A. (2012). Exploratory factor analysis: a five-step guide for novices. *Australian Journal of Paramedicine*, 8(3), 1–13.

Zaki, A. (2020). Emerging risks from the digital realm. *Asia Insurance Review*, 60–61.

Zaskórski, P. (2012). *Informational asymmetry in process management*. Warsaw: Military University of Technology.

Index

Page locators in **bold** indicate a table
Page locators in *italics* indicate a figure
Page locators in **<u>bold underline</u>** indicate a chart

For Product Safety Concerns and Information please contact our EU
representative GPSR@taylorandfrancis.com
Taylor & Francis Verlag GmbH, Kaufingerstraße 24, 80331 München, Germany

www.ingramcontent.com/pod-product-compliance
Ingram Content Group UK Ltd.
Pitfield, Milton Keynes, MK11 3LW, UK
UKHW020006200926
475702UK00015B/2499
9781032259352